TEN ADVENTUROUS

WALKS IN

WEST SUSSEX

Raymond Hugh

Illustrations by
Jackie Hei

ISBN 1 874476 01 2

Published by Morning Mist Publications 1992
PO Box 108, Reigate, Surrey RH2 9YP
©Raymond Hugh & Jackie Hei 1992

Designed and Printed by
Advanced Data Graphics, Sevenoaks

Every effort is taken in the accuracy of this book. However the author and the publisher cannot accept responsibility for any accidents resulting from the use of this guide.

INDEX

INTRODUCTION

THE ADVENTURE

The adventure must be yours, it is the thrill of exploration, the pleasure of experiencing something new and the surprise of the unexpected. You could do the same walk several times and each time it will be different. You may see a herd of deer bounding through the wood, a kingfisher dart above tranquil waters. On another occasion, a weasel could scamper across your path, a squirrel leap above it. On a summer's day, the Downs are alive with butterflies and birds, the chalkland flowers a distraction to the glorious views. In winter storm winds can lash the rain against your face, reducing the visibility to only a few feet. The weather cannot only change the appearance of a walk, it can also change the feel. The adventure is discovering the secrets of the route on the day.

THE REWARD

The reward is the sense of achievement and the knowledge that not only have you completed a respectable distance, you will have learned and experienced something of West Sussex which before was a mystery. There is no greater satisfaction than to discover the county as our ancestors did.

WHEN TO GO

Many walkers make the mistake of only walking in fine weather, leaving the hills at the slightest sign of rain. In wet and windy weather the countryside is untamed and with the majority of the population safe in their houses, one can really get a feeling of remoteness and a better idea of what West Sussex was like several hundred years ago. My suggestion is that you try and do the walks in all seasons and all weathers. At the end if you don't hate me, you will really begin to feel an affinity with the West Sussex countryside and the satisfaction of knowing West Sussex well. As for the time of day, I recommend that you try and time your walk to include either dawn or dusk. These to me are the best part of the day, unfortunately often missed by the majority.

PREPARATION

Planning the walk is as important and as enjoyable as doing the walk itself. Firstly consider whether you want to make a weekend of it. If you do, then I suggest that you book local accommodation. This not only cuts down on travelling on the day, but creates a seemingly longer weekend and allows you to remain familiar with the area at night.

There is nothing better in my mind than to finish a long walk and retire to local accommodation for a hot bath before a well earned visit to the local village pub, without having to worry about driving home. A selection of recommended accommodation is listed at the end of each walk.

Once you have decided on your walk, familiarise yourself with it. Read the walk through, following it on the map, to ensure you understand where it is you are going. The route descriptions contain points of interest and you may want to take time to stop and visit these. If you do, it might be worth borrowing a book from the Library to read up before your visit. When you have made up your mind on the points of interest to visit, try and estimate the length of your walk. The timings given on each walk are meant as a rough guide only and are based on a person being reasonably fit. If you are unsure, then I suggest you allow for approximately two miles per hour. Timing is important as you could find yourself stumbling back to the start in the dark.

Finally, make sure you are fit. The walks in this book are longer than the average walking book and can be hard work if you are unprepared. To help identify the gradients, a cross section is included at the start of each walk.

WHAT TO TAKE

A good map is essential. I recommend you use the Ordnance Survey Landranger maps and the start of each walk details the map(s) required. You can also use the Ordnance Survey Pathfinder maps which have far more detail such as field boundaries, but they can be harder to find and can ultimately be more expensive.

Once armed with your map, make sure you have sensible clothing. This means clothes which are loose and comfortable. Tight jeans and high heels are not recommended! No matter how good the weather is at the start of the day, always pack some waterproofs. Being caught out in the rain without the necessary protection is not an experience I would recommend. There is a wide range of waterproof clothing now available. The two recommendations I would make are:-

(1)   Make sure you are completely covered, that is buy trousers and a jacket.

(2)   Buy clothing made from one of the breathable materials - your local stockist will advise you on these.

Keeping warm helps avoid tiredness. Most importantly, make sure you have a good pair of shoes. If you can afford it, then buy a pair of walking boots. If not, then make sure your shoes are strong, comfortable and have soles with a good grip. Equally important are good socks. If you have boots then two pairs are advisable. Do not think that the socks you wear in the office will do!

Sensibly clothed, you can now think about other equipment you may need. A camera and a pair of binoculars are always useful and can enhance your day out. I always carry a pocket book on birds, you could do the same or add to this with a book on local flora or history. You will find the walk all the more enjoyable for a little bit of knowledge. Do not, though, get over enthusiastic and take a library or you may find yourself requiring a book on first aid!

A basic first aid kit though is always advisable. The West Sussex countryside may appear tame and so it is, compared to the Himalayas, but must still be treated with respect. The book and the map should be enough to find the route without difficulty, however a compass is always useful for finding your way when paths are undefined.

Refreshments are always an important consideration. There are places where you can get a bite to eat on every walk but even if you wish to use their facilities it is important to carry some basic snacks, especially in cold weather. You should always carry water and a thermos flask with hot soup or drink can also be very welcome. To carry all this one should have a comfortable day sack or small rucksack. These are now available from a wide assortment of shops, but before you purchase one, make sure it's strong and more importantly ensure it's comfortable.

Finally take your five senses with you - these are essential if you are to fully appreciate the walk and most importantly, **ENSURE YOU TAKE THIS BOOK!**

GETTING THERE

Most people will be mobile, i.e. a car or bicycle. Where practical I have listed railway stations, however buses are far more difficult as their routes and timetables tend to change with the wind. For those people relying on a bus to reach the start, I have listed the main bus companies serving the area below:-

Brighton & Hove Bus and Coach Co. (Tel: 0273 206666)
Coastline Express - Chichester (Tel: 0243 783251)
Hants & Sussex (Tel: 0243 376886)
Rider (Tel: 0273 482123)
Southdown (Tel: 0243 783251)

Sussex Bus (Tel: 0243 784492)

ROUTE FINDING

The route descriptions are instructional rather than poetic and should be followed without difficulty. To assist you a series of symbols in the left hand margin enable you to identify specific points on the walk at a glance. A good map is essential and should be used in conjunction with the route description. Please remember that like everything else, the countryside changes with time, a fenced path can become unfenced and vice versa.

Before setting out, make sure you have identified the route on the map. To pinpoint a starting point or place of interest I have used grid references. These are six figured numbers which identify a particular point on the map. Every Ordnance Survey map is covered by a national grid. The grid's lines are identified by numbers printed on the map's surround. To find a grid reference, take the first three numbers which refer to the vertical lines on your map and locate them on the top or bottom (north or south) of the map. The third number is an imaginary line in the square following the first two numbers. To find this line, divide the square into ten equal parts. Then take the latter three numbers, which refer to the horizontal lines and locate them on the left or right (east or west) of your map and follow the line of this reference until it meets the line of the first reference. Their meeting point is the grid reference point itself. Do not rely on the maps in this book, these are not to scale and are meant as a rough guide only.

It is important that you recognise the various types of footpath signs. Most are fairly obvious, i.e. wooden post with a sign marked "footpath" or "public bridleway", pointing in the direction of the right of way. Some will have the name of a specific route, for example, "The South Downs Way".

Over recent years many County Councils have standardised their signs to follow national guidelines. Footpaths are now shown with a yellow arrow and bridleways with a blue one. This form of route marking is still rare in West Sussex, but it could change in the future. Like the old wooden signs the arrows will point in the direction of the right of way. On top of all this, you will often find custom built signs. These can mark an official route but more often than not,

iv

are the work of local farmers guiding the walker across their land. An example of the former is "The South Downs Way", which, on occasion, is highlighted by a white acorn on a black background.

An important rule on route finding is to take your time, follow the map and read the route description thoroughly. If you do this then you will return to base without mishap.

LONG DISTANCE WALKS
Many of the routes meet long distance linear walks which run through West Sussex. In case you want to try any I have listed their names, with distances, below, along with the publisher who produces a description of the walk.

Downs Link - 30 miles (West Sussex County Council)
Lipchis Way - 26 miles (D & M Clark)
South Downs Way - 80 miles (HMSO)
Sussex Border Path - 150 miles (Ben Perkins)
Wey South Path - 36 miles (Aeneas Mackintosh)

AUTHOR'S NOTE
Every effort has been made to ensure that the route descriptions are accurate. Time changes things however and can alter the description of the route. If you have any difficulty in finding any part of a route, please write with details, giving a grid reference, to enable me to re-examine the route. A free copy of the next publication will be forwarded for any suggestions used in the next edition. Enjoy your walks.

IN ROMAN FOOTSTEPS

Distance: 10 miles (16 km)
Time: Allow approximately 5 hours
Map: Ordnance Survey Landranger Map 197

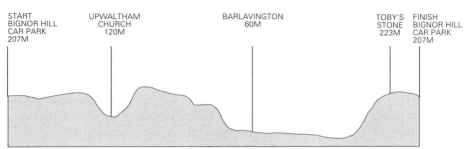

START	UPWALTHAM	BARLAVINGTON	TOBY'S	FINISH
BIGNOR HILL	CHURCH	60M	STONE	BIGNOR HILL
CAR PARK	120M		223M	CAR PARK
207M				207M

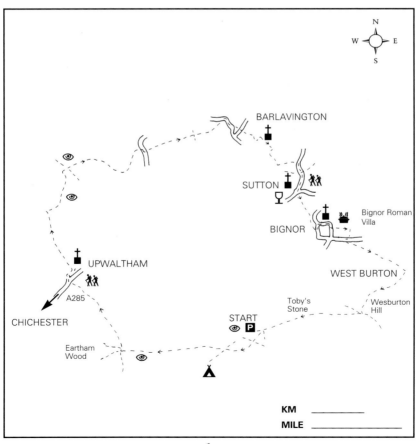

1

Walk Summary

As the description suggests, this walk explores an area in Sussex well known for its Roman connections. Not only does it follow some of the ancient Roman routes, but it also visits one of the best preserved Roman villas in the country. The historic connections, the beautiful countryside and the unspoilt villages through which you pass, makes this a walk you will almost certainly want to repeat. The going is fairly easy though there are some steep climbs, especially towards the end which can be tiring if you are not prepared.

Start - OS. 973129 Map 197

The walk starts from a National Trust car park at the top of Bignor Hill. To get there take the A29 between Pulborough and the coastal road, the A27. Almost half way between the two, take a minor road west signposted to West Burton, Bignor and Bignor Roman Villa. This is almost opposite the turning for Bury village. Follow the lane and signs to pass the villa. Shortly after the road bends right signposted to Sutton and Duncton. Ignore this to turn left instead between a barn and an old farmhouse and follow a narrow road to the top of Bignor Hill and the car park. N.B. In winter this road can be quite difficult and if you are unsure about your car or your capability as a driver, then I recommend you use an alternative start. There are two alternative starts, the first is the village of Upwaltham on the A285 (OS. 943138 Map 197), the second is Sutton village (OS. 979151 Map 197). Both villages have limited parking so please park considerately.

The nearest railway station is at Amberley. From there it is two and a half miles to the nearest point on the walk.

IN ROMAN FOOTSTEPS

You may have found the drive up Bignor hill enough adventure for one day, particularly if you are doing this walk in winter. However, the fresh air and fine views soon reassure you that it was worth it.

Bignor Hill (OS. 973129 Map 197). *The car park at the top of the hill is at a junction of tracks which are of Roman origin. The most famous of these is Stane Street, which was one of the most important roads from Londinium (London) to Regnum or Noviomagus Regnensium (Chichester). The Romans knew Bignor and its hill as Ad Decimum. The hill itself it 225m high and immediately offers panoramic views. Today it is part of the huge Slindon estate, run by the National Trust. The estate has always been run from "Slindon House" which is several miles south of Bignor Hill and built on the site of a former palace, the 13th century residence of the Archbishop of Canterbury. Archbishop*

Stephan Langton often visited the palace and eventually died here. This extraordinary man was responsible for some major changes in early British history and was one of those who persuaded King John to sign the Magna Carta. He is better remembered in Surrey where he was born. "The Leith Hill Limp", one of the "10 Adventurous Walks in Surrey", takes you through his birth place.

To start our walk take the public bridleway signposted to "Noviomagus" (Chichester), ignoring the signs for the South Downs Way. The bridleway soon joins a wider track and bends round to the right where you should ignore a track which forks off to the left. Continue along the bridleway bearing right and after a short distance, pass straight over a crossing track to run between scrub and woodland. The track descends to meet a junction of tracks. Turn right at the junction to meet a crossing path, Stane Street, after approximately thirty paces. (If you turn left here the path will take you to "Gumber Farm" and accommodation run by the National Trust). Go over this to continue straight on passing a post marked "Black Jack". As a guide you should now have woods to your left and open fields to your right with the aerial masts of Bignor Hill beyond.

Where the field on your right ends the path joins a track to continue straight on. There is now woodland to your right and open fields to the left. The magnificent view on your left covers most of the Chichester basin, dominated by Chichester cathedral. In the valley below you can see the National Trust owned "Gumber Farm". After some distance, ignore a bridleway on your right and carry straight on between fields heading for Eartham Wood. On reaching the wood ignore all other tracks to enter Eartham Wood itself. Continue straight on through the wood, which on a sunny summers day is an amazing assortment of green, until you see a signposted bridleway on your right just before a Forestry Commission sign for Eartham Wood. Turn right on to the bridleway and immediately after, take a left hand fork to continue ahead and ignore another bridleway shortly after on your left. You will now pass through more mixed woodland to meet a metal gate.

Pass through the gate and go straight on following the right hand perimeter of a field. When the fence on your right ends and the field opens out, you should continue straight ahead following a grass track across the centre of the field. Follow the track to descend to the other side of the field heading for woodland and a gate. Pass through the gate and continue downhill along a track across the centre of the next field, where there are superb views across the valley ahead to North Down and a white chalk track which is part of our route. The hamlet below is Upwaltham our next destination.

The track passes through a small wooden gate beside a large metal farm gate and continues ahead to soon pass a small pond on your left. After this go through a metal gate to reach the farm yard of "Upwaltham House Farm". Turn left in front of the farm and follow the track round passing between barns to meet the main road, the A285. Turn right at the road back to the house itself and then cross the road to join a track signposted  to Upwaltham 12th century church, St. Mary the Virgin. Follow the track to meet and pass through a small wooden gate on your right and continue along a fenced path to the church.

Upwaltham (OS. 943138 Map 197), *is barely noticeable if you are speeding past in the car on the busy A285. To walk through the village, or rather hamlet, Upwaltham suddenly becomes a place to be noticed. From the church yard where there is a seat, you gain the best view of the hamlet and it is hard not to stop here for a few minutes to contemplate what life must have been like here years ago in this remote sweeping valley. The large cultivated fields which now surround the hamlet were then dense woodland. The church where Cardinal Manning was once curate, is unusual in that it is only one of four in Sussex with a chancel that finishes in a half circle. Originally built in the 12th century, the church must also be one of the smallest in West Sussex.*

To visit the church pass through the small gate on your right. Our route however, is left through another small gate to join the track the other side. Turn right along the track passing behind the church and at a "T" junction turn left up North Down along a wider track. Ignore a track off to the right and continue uphill following the public bridleway signs. At the top of the hill ignore another track off to the right and continue straight on heading for the tree line. On reaching the tree line turn right on to a signposted public bridleway and follow the left hand perimeter of the field, with the trees now on your left.

The bridleway leads to a small wooden gate at a point where the field bends away to your right. Here there is a small grass area with several large beech trees. This is a wonderful place to stop and rest awhile. The immediate beauty of your surroundings is

4

complemented by the panoramic views which stretch to the North
Downs in the north and the coast to the south. The real beauty
however, is that this spot is relatively undiscovered and allows
you to escape the 20th century undisturbed. To continue, pass
through the gate and follow a path signposted as a public
bridleway, through woodland. The wood covers an area known as
Crown Tegleaze and at 255m is the highest spot on the Sussex
downs. Ignore a path later going off to the left and carry straight
on to eventually meet a track in front of a field.

Turn right along the track and pass through a small wooden gate
beside a larger gate to arrive at a large crossing track, the South
Downs Way and a signpost erected by the Cowdray Hunt. From
here you are again spoilt by the views. In the distance on your left
there is Blackdown, directly ahead Petworth and immediately
below, Graffham Common. Go straight over the crossing track,
thereby crossing the South Downs Way, and continue in the
direction of the sign to Duncton. The wide track you are following
curves right to descend gently. Below the escarpment of the hill,
though not visible, is East Lavington with its famous stud farm,
which has bred and trained many a successful horse. This area of
the downs is ideally suited for horseriding and it is highly likely
that you will pass several riders en route.

Follow the track ignoring all turnings off to eventually meet the
A285 after passing Duncton Quarry on your left. At the road turn
right and after approximately thirty metres, cross the road to join
the signposted public bridleway opposite. The bridleway goes
across the centre of a field with a lovely shallow valley on your
right (in the field) and to your left views over the Weald. At the
far end of the field, the path enters woodland, Duncton Hanger.
Incidentally, "hanger" is an old name for a steep tree covered
slope. Thankfully, the steep slope of this hanger is below to our
left, with our route running along the top. Stay on the main path
where in winter you may catch glimpses to your left through the
trees of Burton Mill ponds. Ignore a turning later off to your right
to continue ahead gradually going downhill.

Pass over a large junction of tracks still going straight on,
following the public bridleway sign and soon after join a wider
path. Continue in the same direction to meet a stile beside a gate.
There are lovely views here to your left of the Burton Mill ponds
and also of Duncton and its church. Go over the stile and continue
straight downhill to meet a road. Pass through a gate, cross the
road and go over a stile the other side. Follow the public footpath
sign to cross the right hand corner of a field to meet the edge of a
garden on your left. Continue straight on keeping the garden to

your left and pass a lovely brick and timber built cottage in the distance on your right.

Pass over a stile and go down a bank to meet a lane with a picturesque cottage on your left. Cross the lane and follow the path ahead crossing a small stream via a wooden bridge and continue on the path up a steep bank the other side. At the top of the bank you will pass an enormous yew tree - one of the largest I have seen - and then through a small wooden gate to reach a drive way belonging to the stables on your left. Go straight down the drive to meet a lane where you should continue ahead, do not turn right, to pass through the village of Barlavington. You will soon arrive at St. Mary's parish church opposite the estate and farm offices to the Slindon estate. Pass through the wooden gate into the church yard, signposted as a public footpath, and follow this round to the front of the church. There is an old tree stump here, now a seat, which is a lovely place to stop for a short rest.

Pass the front of the church and follow the path through the church yard to exit via a small wooden gate on to a track. Follow the track behind some farm buildings, ignoring the turning off to your right. Pass between a number of large metal silos after which you should turn right in the direction of the public footpath sign, to follow a wide grass track. This runs beside a line of scotch pines and then continues along the right hand perimeter of a field, going gently downhill. Near the end of the field, turn right to pass over a stile into another field which you should cross going diagonally left in the direction of the public footpath sign, to meet a wooden fence. Follow the wooden fencing on your left to reach a stile which you should cross.

After the stile go over a small brick bridge passing over a very pretty stream. The stream is a good opportunity in summer to cool off those steaming feet. Though be warned, even in summer the water which has only just come above ground from a spring below Barlavington Hanger, is icy cold. After your possible bathe or paddle follow the path uphill to meet a stile. Go over this and turn immediately left to follow the left hand perimeter of a field. As the trees on your left gradually end, take the first turning left over a stile at a public footpath sign. Follow the path ahead between shallow banks passing a modern house on your left, "Potcroft".

The path leads out to a drive way where you should continue straight ón with Sutton church in view ahead to your right. The drive soon runs between houses to meet a lane on to which you should turn right - there is in the migration season, a "Toads Crossing" sign here on your left. Pass "Bakers Cottage" on your left and follow the lane through the centre of the village passing St. John the Baptist church and then an old flint building on your left, the old school house with a weather vein on top portraying an indicative scene at the school! Welcome to Sutton.

Sutton (OS. 979155 Map 197) *is a slender village built on a ridge with views across the Weald and "Bignor Park", once home to the noted traveller John Hawkins. Many of the village's tudor buildings still remain, one of particular note is "The Rectory" originally the priest house and years ago home to the local rector, Aquilo Cruso. Aquilo Cruso is one of the more colourful characters in our country's religious history. Whilst at Sutton he was accused of having sympathies with the Pope. Being, an eminent hebraist, he prepared his own defence in Hebrew and consequently, his case was never disputed leaving him to continue his work. The church of which Cruso was once rector dates originally from the 11th century, though most of the building is of the 12th and 14th centuries.*

The lane eventually leads you to "The White Horse" pub, a well run free house serving a wide range of good food and offering the tired walker accommodation.

From the pub, take the signposted public footpath opposite the bus stop. The path starts beside a cottage "Orchard Thatch", and is signposted to Bignor. Follow the path between houses to meet and go over a stile into a field. Continue across the field in the direction of the public footpath sign (do not turn right), and at the other side cross another stile to carry straight on going downhill across the next field. At the far side go over a third stile and then a wooden bridge over a stream. In front of you here to your left is a lovely property which overlooks two ponds. This is the site of the original Bignor mill. Turn right after the bridge and follow the footpath bearing left to run alongside one of the ponds. Go over another bridge crossing a stream which feeds the pond already mentioned and turn immediately right to follow a path running between streams. Needless to say, with all this water surrounding you the going can get very wet and in wet weather care is needed if you want to avoid having an early bath!

After a short distance, cross another narrower footbridge over a stream to go gently uphill and then right to run above a small pond on your right, this time fed by a small waterfall. Leave the pond and cross a grass lawn taking care to keep to the path which is marked, as this runs through private property. Pass through a small wooden gate to reach a lane between some attractive cottages. Turn left on to the lane and follow this uphill to reach Bignor village.

Bignor (OS. 983146 Map 197) *is often overshadowed by its famous Roman villa and therefore ignored by travellers and guide books. For this very reason Bignor remains a peaceful untouched village well worth donating time to. The village has had some notable inhabitants, John Hawkins is probably the most famous. Hawkins, born in Cornwall, was a well known traveller and became an advisor to the gentry all over Europe. He moved to the village in 1806 taking up residence at "Bignor Park". Before Hawkins, "Bignor Park" belonged to Nicholas Turner, whose two daughters, Charlotte and Catherine were novelists. More recently, the house was home to John Hayward-Johnson, M.P. for Horsham in the early part of this century. The village church dates from the 13th century and was built on the site of an earlier church of which today only the font remains. Most of the church was rebuilt in the 19th century by George Edmund Street. Despite the 19th century restorations, the church has kept is earlier charm and has some interesting memorials if you have time to visit.*

The Church Gate - Bignor

Stay on the lane as it bends round to the right past "Manor Farm" and ignore a lane off to the left marked as a public footpath beside a lovely old Wealden timber cottage. After a short distace the lane bends sharp left and you should continue to follow it ignoring two more lanes (one ahead and one on the right) which join at this point. After approximately 75 metres leave the lane to join a footpath on your right which leads diagonally left across the centre of a field. First however, its worth making a short detour to visit Bignor Roman Villa. To do this stay on the lane for a further 50 metres and you will see the entrance to the villa on your left. You will have to retrace your steps to rejoin the route

Bignor Roman Villa (OS. 987146 Map 197) *lies just west of the then main road, Stane Street. The villa prospered from the same economic factors relevant today, rich farmland and easy access to a good transportation system. The villa first dates from around 190 AD and continued to grow over the centuries as trade prospered. With the hurried retreat of the Romans, this magnificent villa, one of the largest in England, fell into decay and incredibly remained forgotten until a local farmer hit a large*

*stone whilst ploughing in 1811. The farmer, George Tupper, had
probably hit a water basin or piscina, now on view in the museum.
The discovery led to much interest and a regular number of
tourists visited the mosaics. John Hawkins concerned that the
villa might suffer serious damage, enlisted the help of Samuel
Lysons, a specialist in Roman antiquities. In 1812, the first
building was consequently erected to protect the villa. The villa is
today still owned by the Tupper family who run it as a museum.
The main attractions are its magnificent mosaics which are some
of the best preserved in England. The whole villa reflects a life of
luxury which many people would envy today. Residents enjoyed
central heating, a steady supply of hot water and walk-in baths.
Reflecting on your own modest dwelling now is probably a good
time to continue our walk!*

At the far corner of the field, cross over a small wooden bridge and
continue ahead to cross a second bridge over a small stream into
another field. Turn left here to follow the left hand perimeter of the
field and after some distance look out for a gap in the hedge on your
left. Pass through this, turn right and take a narrow signposted
footpath which follows a small stream through scrub and woodland
to eventually arrive at a lane beside "Fogdens" cottage.

Turn right to pass between "Fogdens" and "Hatchetts" in the
direction of the public bridleway sign. If you wish to visit the
village of West Burton however, which I recommend, then ignore
the bridleway sign and continue straight on along the lane. West
Burton is a village with strong character and a discovery all its
own. In the late 18th century the skeletons of several elephants
were found nearby, why they were there still remains a mystery.

Continuing on our route, take a wide farm track heading towards
the South Downs. You will soon begin your ascent between banks
up the wooded side of West Burton hill on one of the ancient
tracks of the South Downs, quite possibly an old drovers road. In
wet weather it can become a stream and the going can be very
slippery - take care.

Near the top of the hill, which is a long time coming, the track
levels out to continue along the side of a steep valley. You
eventually leave the woodland to arrive at a wide crossing track
beside some corrugated iron barns. Go over the crossing track and
turn right thereafter to follow a track running parallel,
signposted as the South Downs Way. This then bends round to
the left, still going uphill, to join another track coming in from the
left. Bear right here, staying on the South Downs Way which is
signposted. You will once again enjoy excellent views across the

Surrey and Sussex Weald, to the south Brighton and the coast and to the east Amberley Mount and the line of the South Downs.

Follow the South Downs Way up Bignor Hill to pass through an old gate way beside a low stepped stone memorial. This is known as "Toby's Stone" and as the inscription explains, Toby is in fact James Wentworth Fitzwilliam Toby, 1885-1955. He was Secretary of the Cowdray Hounds, a member of the British Field Sports Society and Master of the Foxhounds Association. The other side of the stone remembers his wife Beryl who died in 1960. The stone represents a mounting block and intentionally or not, offers an excellent view from its top. Ignore a track off to your right and continue on heading for the aerial masts ahead to go over the brow of Bignor Hill and return to the car park from where our walk commenced.

ACCOMMODATION

The White Horse Inn, Sutton. Tel: 07987 221
On the walk, this fine 18th century inn has been tastefully refurbished retaining its local atmosphere. The rooms are extremely comfortable and the food and real ale are of equal quality.

Melrose, Graffham. Tel: 07986 541
Two miles from the walk, this friendly guesthouse is set in a beautiful downland village surrounded by the famous Graffham Common. From the guest house it is but a short walk along the South Downs Way to join our route at Tegleaze.

Youth Hostel, Arundel YHA, Warningcamp.
Tel: 0903 882204
Seven miles from the walk, this is a large hostel located in a Georgian house set in spacious grounds. The village is very peaceful but should you want more, it is but a short walk along the banks of the river Arun to Arundel. Camping is also permitted.

The Gumber Bothy, Bignor Hill. Tel: 0243 65313
(After 6.00 p.m.)
Half a mile from the walk, Gumber Bothy is a so-called camping barn or stone tent run by the National Trust. Accommodation is in an attractive converted flint barn, part of Gumber Farm. For the uninitiated, you will be required to bring your own sleeping bag otherwise you will be in for an uncomfortable night! Should you prefer to sleep under canvas, there is also a field in which you are permitted to camp.

THE AUGUSTINIAN AMBLE

Distance: 10½ miles (17 km)
Time: Allow approximately 5 hours
Map: Ordnance Survey Landranger Map 186

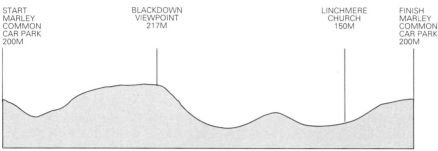

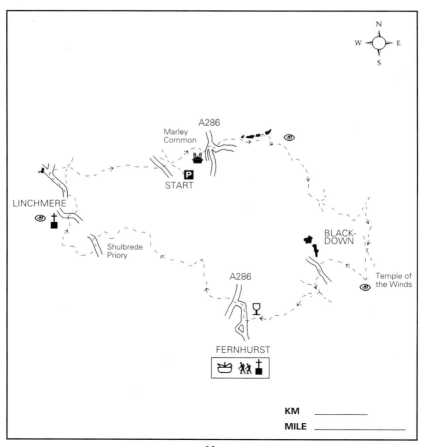

Walk Summary

The Augustinian Amble explores some of the best woodland West Sussex has to offer. It takes you along some of the oldest routes in the country, many of them used by smugglers when the Weald was mainly untamed forest. Apart from the woodland, you will also climb Blackdown the highest point in the county. One word of warning, the going can get very muddy and more than once I have found myself up to my ankles in mud. Make sure you wear those walking boots.

Start - OS. 887313 Map 186

The walk starts at the National Trust Marley Common car park. If coming from the south, take the A286 to Kingsley Green and take a lane west opposite Hatch Lane, signposted as a single track road. Follow this for approximately one mile to reach the car park which is signposted on your right. Do not make the mistake of stopping at the first car park on your left which has a view point. If coming from the north, take the B2131 to Camelsdale between Haslemere and Liphook and take a lane (Marley Lane) beside Arnolds Garage, south. The car park is on your left at the top of the hill. As an alternative, you can start from Fernhurst village green (OS. 900285 Map 186).

THE AUGUSTINIAN AMBLE

P

The beginning of the walk follows the Sussex Border Path. To join this, take the wide track going east from the car park passing to the right of a National Trust information sign for Marley Common, which is over one hundred and fifty acres of ancient sheep woodland. You will soon pass a grove of beech trees on your left which were planted by the National Trust, in memory of Betty Gregson (1912-1984).

At a crossing track continue straight ahead on the Sussex Border Path, which is signposted, to pass through mixed woodland. The path soon begins to descend and you should ignore all joining and crossing paths to stay on the Sussex Border Path. At one point you will pass between two posts and a bank which is probably the remains of an old boundary. Continue up and down some shallow dips and then over the crest of a hill to fork right still following the signs for the Sussex Border Path.

Ignore a crossing path immediately after the fork and go steeply downhill to shortly turn left following an even steeper path to reach some houses. The path twists left and then right before going down steps to run between houses. Cross a road and take a narrow hedged path at the end of which you should turn left to reach a main road, the A286. As a point of interest, on your right here is "Shrimptons Restaurant" which is well worth a visit in the evening if you are staying in the area.

Cross the main road, turn left and then right along Fernden Lane to pass over a small stream and continue uphill. Pass a private road on your right and continue until shortly after, you meet a gravel drive on your left. Take this, signposted Sussex Border Path, and follow the path as it bends round to the right to run between gardens and some very attractive properties. On meeting a lane continue straight ahead, do not turn left, still following the Sussex Border Path.

After approximately fifty metres the lane ends and you should continue straight ahead along a smaller path, still the Sussex Border Path, passing a lovely property on your left with a series of ponds. At a lane you can turn left for a short distance for a better view of the ponds. Our route however, turns right up the lane to pass "Vine Cottage". Follow the lane which progresses naturally into a drive, ignoring a footpath off to the right, and pass through a brick entrance to continue ahead. As the drive bends left, turn right along a narrow footpath and shortly after turn left along a small path, still the Sussex Border Path, going steeply downhill to the bottom of what can often be an extremely wet and muddy valley. Turn left along a fenced path, ignoring a path on the right and pass over a small stream to reach a drive way. Turn right to continue on the Sussex Border Path passing through the gates to "Valewood Farmhouse".

The drive bends round to the right with good views to your right across water meadows. You will shortly pass "Valewood Farmhouse" on your left after which you should take the first farm track going left, almost back on yourself, passing an outbuilding on the right. Ignore a gate on your right and continue to pass through another gate ahead into an open field. After approximately ten paces turn right uphill following the public bridleway signs. At the top of the hill it is worth looking back across the valley through which you have passed. Pass through another gate to rejoin the Sussex Border Path and follow the path ahead to cross a field. At the far side of the field, turn left to pass through another gate and follow the path as it bends right to continue between banks through mixed woodland, where laurels and rhododendrons are particularly prominent. Indeed, they can often be so dense as to meet above the path to form a tunnel and you cannot help suspecting that this could have been one of the infamous smuggling routes used all those years ago. When the path forks, follow the right hand fork still on the Sussex Border Path, along the side of a hill known as Ridden Corner. After approximately a quarter of a mile, you will reach another fork where you should bear left going gently uphill to meet and join a wide track. Turn right here still following the Sussex Border Path, to begin traversing Blackdown.

i **Blackdown (OS. 920295 Map 186)** *is the highest point in West Sussex rising to 917ft (280m). It gets its name from the dark heather and firs which dominate its summit and not as many believe, from the iron industry that once surrounded it. Through the heather, pass some of the oldest tracks in the county, one known as "Pen-y-Bos" dates back to celtic times when crossing this area would have meant a journey of some daring. Blackdown was infamous as a haunt for smugglers, it acted as a half way post from the coast to London and the down is said to have a cave used by the smugglers as a hideout and safe storage for their contraband. The down does have a more respectable association. In 1866 Alfred Lord Tennyson looking for a hideaway, bought some land on Blackdown and on 23rd April (reputedly Shakespeare's birthday), 1868, he laid the foundation stone to the great white house he called "Aldworth". Here he lived for twenty four years never tiring of the beauty that surrounded him, often reflected in his poems, until his death in 1892.*

On reaching a crossing track go straight across, where you will notice the terrain changes with a sandy base underfoot, the trees now predominantly spruce and an abundance of heather and bilberries growing beneath them. Continue on the Sussex Border Path, ignoring any minor joining or crossing paths. Ignore a track joining from the left beside a "No Horses" sign and carry straight on to meet a "T" junction. Bear left here ignoring the first bridleway immediately on your left, and follow the main track ahead. Soon after, you will pass a sunken track fronted by wooden rails, this is "Pen-y-Bos" and is probably the oldest track across the down. Do not turn on to "Pen-y-Bos", but continue straight on passing some small ponds and a marsh on your left. Just after these, take a wide track on your right signposted as a public bridleway, to finally leave the Sussex Border Path.

Shortly after joining the bridleway you will meet a fork where you should take the left hand track ahead, to follow the escarpment of the hill with superb views in places over the Sussex Weald. Ignore a bridleway on your right to reach another fork where you should take the right hand bridleway, do not be tempted to veer left as you will quickly find yourself going downhill. At the next fork turn left and continue to pass through two wooden posts to reach a stone seat and a famous view point.

Temple of the Winds (OS. 921292 Map 186). *The hilltop just above you is known locally as "Temple of the Winds" or "Temple of the Four Winds". It was Tennyson who gave this spot its full name in recognition of the winds which always seem to blow at its summit, though I can think of many other hilltops that better deserve this name. Tennyson however, did not entirely invent the name, this spot has always been called "The Temple". Its origin is unclear, but one explanation is that the Romans may have had a temple here. The prominence of this point has long been appreciated and in the 16th and 17th centuries there was a beacon near here, one of a chain to warn London of any invasion on the south coast. It would have been put to good use and in all probability, was lit at the threat of the Spanish Armada. A stone seat, erected in memory of Mable Elizabeth Hunter wife of Edward W. Hunter the donator of Blackdown to the National Trust in 1944, is set into the hill. A direction finder helps you to identify well known landmarks. Tennyson also appreciated this view point and built a summer house here. If you look carefully you can still see its foundations.*

From the view point go right along a narrow path and then immediately first right through a set of posts, take care not to miss this. Rejoin the track you were on and retrace your steps for a short distance until you reach a fork. Bear left here and then bend right to join the main track ahead. Do not turn left or right, but continue straight on. When the main track bends right in front of a wooden seat, leave it to continue straight on to go steeply downhill in the direction of a public bridleway sign. The bridleway leads down a slope which turns to grass to reach a cottage ahead, "Cotchet Farm". Beside you here, a spring bubbles into a trough before running away beside a lane.

Turn left at the cottage and walk along the lane to reach a "T" junction where you should turn left again. After approximately fifty metres take a signposted public bridleway on your right, passing through a farm gate into a field. Follow the left hand perimeter of the field to reach another gate through which you should pass and continue straight on following the fenced narrow path ahead along the left hand perimeter of another field.

The path descends gradually and then bears round to the left.

When I last walked this way, access was blocked at this point due to fallen trees from a storm. To avoid this you should turn immediately right up a steep bank where there is a narrow somewhat undefined path, going down a slope onto another path. Here you should turn left and follow the path round as it bears right, signposted as a public bridleway. As a guide you should now find a field on your left and woodland on your right.

When the path meets a drive way in front of a farmhouse, turn right to follow a footpath along the perimeter of the farm going downhill. At times, this path follows the same route as a stream and as such can be extremely wet in winter, particularly towards the bottom. Sometime later as the path forks, take the second turning from the left, signposted as a public footpath. Do not take the right fork which is in fact private property. Ignore a crossing path sometime later to continue downhill and ignore also any other paths near the bottom of the hill. The stream which has made your progress so muddy now runs parallel on your right.

The path finally leads down to another farmhouse with a large wooden barn, just before which you turn right to follow a signposted public footpath. After a short while, the stream rejoins your route but thankfully you are now above it as opposed to in it! Continue along the path to pass over the stream where another stream joins it from the right. Bear left here to follow a public footpath sign with the stream on your left.

Continue on the path now leading gently uphill and bear right ignoring a path on your left, to walk between fields. Ignore another footpath shortly after on your right and continue straight on. Pass over a small bridge again crossing the stream which, after heavy rains cascades down a series of steps, and follow the path along the perimeter of a playing field to reach Fernhurst village beside "The Red Lion" pub, a free house.

Fernhurst (OS. 899286 Map 186) *is almost two villages, one the older half, clustered round a village green and the other, the new village, built to trade off of the main route south, the A286. Fernhurst was in the centre of the iron industry and much of its surrounding countryside reflects that past with names such as "Furnace Wood" and "Ironhill Common". For refreshments the village is host to the excellent "Red Lion" free house, which is proud of its selection of real ales and excellent food.*

From the pub, cross the road and turn right to follow it up Hogs hill to meet the main road, the A286. Cross the A286 and join the drive ahead, marked as a public footpath and "2 Upper Cross Cottages". As the drive ends, take the tarmacced footpath to the right of a garage to pass a fairly modern housing estate. Stay on the footpath ignoring any turnings off and continue down some steps to cross a stream via a small wooden bridge and go uphill turning sharply right between shallow banks. On meeting a lane turn right and follow the lane steeply uphill for some distance, passing attractive cottages and properties on your right.

After passing "Updown Cottage" on your right, the lane ends to become a track. At this point you should take a public footpath on the left thereby leaving the track, and go uphill to meet a gate and stile on the left. Cross the stile and follow the track ahead, marked as a public footpath, to pass through a well established coppice of sweet chestnut.

The Chestnut Coppice. *This part of Sussex is famous for its*   *i*
chestnut coppices. The coppice was once used for an industry unique to this area, the making of cleft fencing. This fencing was popular for enclosing large gardens or even estate land. It takes eight years for a coppice to regenerate after felling, ready for the next harvest and so the work has to be strictly rotated if one is to avoid a serious cash flow problem. Felling is normally done in the autumn. The trees are cut about a foot from the ground and then trimmed. The bark is then removed, a process known as rinding, and the wood left in the open to season.

The path runs along the side of a hill with good views to the south. Continue straight on ignoring a path which joins from the left, still following the public footpath sign. After a short distance, pass through what appears to be an old boundary, continuing straight on and sometime later ignore another signposted footpath going off to the left. You may at this point be able to see the top of a hill close by on the left, topped with fir trees, its name Green Top Hill being self explanatory.

Stay on the path as it twists along the side of the hill ignoring any crossing or joining paths, still following the public footpath signs. Eventually, the path joins a wide track where you should continue straight on, still passing through coppicing. Shortly after joining the track, follow it as it bends left ignoring a signposted footpath off to the right and stay on the track until you eventually meet a "T" junction in front of some fields. Turn right here and pass through a farm gate to follow a track, marked as a public footpath, across the centre of a field.

At the other side of the field, follow the track to pass over a small stream and bear left to meet a lane beside a cottage. Turn left along the lane passing farm buildings on your right and "Shulbrede Priory" with its pond on your left.

i **Shulbrede Priory (OS. 876299 Map 186)** *was founded in 1240 by Ralph de Arderne and inhabited by Augustinian monks. Inside, the Prior's room is decorated with murals of farm animals with a story in Latin. The priory is now a private dwelling and is not open to the public. There are still ponds in the surrounding area which were used to support the priory with fish.*

Just after the farm buildings turn right on to a track marked as a public footpath. The track runs across a field to enter woodland where you should continue ahead, ignoring a path off to your left. Cross over a stream, shortly after which the track forks and you should now bear right along a public footpath which is signposted. Continue straight on heading for a house in the distance and ignore two paths off to the left.

Stay on the footpath to meet a field ahead where, on your right there is a pond and mill race. At the field bear left uphill towards the house, following the perimeter of the field. The path reaches a gate in front of the house through which you should pass. Bear right here to immediately pass through another gate almost adjacent, and follow the left hand perimeter of a field to reach and pass through a third gate. You will now join the drive way to the property where you should turn right, leading away from the house, passing a small fish pond on your left.

Follow the drive which gradually winds downhill between beech trees crossing over a stream and leading out to a lane beside "Corner Cottage". Turn right along the lane in front of the cottage for approximately twenty five metres and then turn left on to a narrow signposted public footpath through the woods. This soon meets a drive way on which you should continue straight ahead to pass through the gateway to "Linchmere Cottage". Pass to the left of the cottage and bear left to continue through woodland to another house. Bear left again, following the public footpath sign, to continue along a very old path between steep banks.

Ignore a path off to the right to continue ahead and shortly after again ignore a somewhat undefined path joining from the left. Soon after, the path joins a wide track where you should carry straight on, do not turn right, this still being marked as a public footpath. Bend round to the left with fields on your left to shortly see a grand stone property "Upper Covers", the first signs of the village of Linchmere. On meeting a lane turn right and follow this uphill to arrive at St. Peter's church on your left.

The church is well worth a visit particularly a walk around the building itself to the front where there are lovely views from the grave yard across the Sussex Weald. Inside the church which was once used by the monks of Shulbrede Priory, is a rare 14th century carving from the south of France, depicting the seven deadly sins. There is also a stone lamb resting at the base of the font. It is said that a lamb was once found in the church sheltering from a storm.

From the church continue along the lane to walk through the village. Look out for a large hollow oak on your left. Take a road on the right, signposted to Haslemere and Camelsdale, passing "The Old School House" and follow the road for a short distance to take the first gravel drive on your right. Bear left in front of a gate to follow the Sussex Border Path which is also signposted as a public bridleway.

After passing "Mare Barn Farm" on your right, the track meets a junction of footpaths. Our route continues straight ahead still on the Sussex Border Path, a pleasant part of the walk following a field on your left which dips down into a shallow valley surrounded by woodland. On long summer evenings this field is an abundance of rabbits. After leaving the field on your left, the path passes through mixed woodland. Ignore a stile and path off to the right and later a path leading off to the left, keeping to the Sussex Border Path to meet a lane.

Continue ahead still following the Sussex Border Path signs and as the lane bends round to the left, leave it to carry straight on along a track opposite "Manor Croft". The track leads to another lane where again you should continue straight on along the Sussex Border Path, running between houses. Again, as the lane bends left leave it to continue ahead and follow a sandy track passing "Marley House". Ignore any turnings off and continue straight on to arrive at a narrow tarmacced drive way on to which you should turn left to return to the car park from where our walk commenced.

ACCOMMODATION

Chelmsford House Hotel, Fernhurst. Tel: 0428 642633

Five hundred metres from the walk, this friendly hotel derives its name from oak panels from Chelmsford Cathedral, which now form the bar. Although on the main road, the rooms are surprisingly quiet.

Dawes Farm, Fernhurst. Tel: 0428 652286

One and three quarter miles from the walk, this charming old farmhouse maintains in the evening the beauty of some of the historic countryside through which you have trodden. Ideal if you plan to do "The Augustinian Amble" and "The Wet Common Waddle" in one weekend.

Youth Hostel, Hindhead YHA. Tel: 0428 734285

Four and a half miles from the walk, a simple youth hostel situated in the bowl of the Devil's Punchbowl. Basic but idyllic and I loved it. Camping is also permitted.

**Camping and Caravanning, Tilford Touring.
Tel: 025125 3296**

Eight miles from the walk, the site is in a particularly nice setting surrounded by Hankley Common, within walking distance of "The Duke of Cambridge" pub. The site is open all year.

SMUGGLERS SEVEN

Distance: 11 miles (17.5 km)
Time: Allow approximately 5½ hours
Map: Ordnance Survey Landranger Map 197

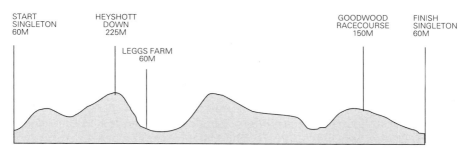

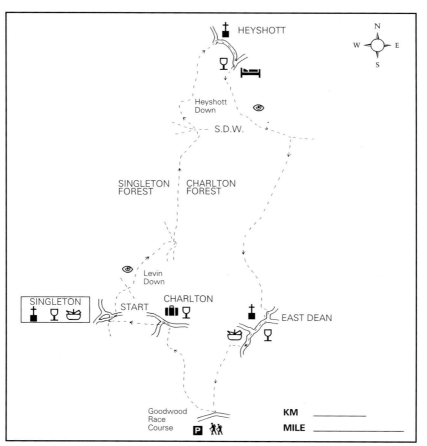

Walk Summary

Smugglers Seven takes you through the great forests of Charlton and Singleton, once popular refuges for smugglers. You will also explore several downland villages, each with their own particular charm, and pass the famous Goodwood racecourse.

The majority of the walk passes through woodland which is host to an abundance of wildlife, so keep your eyes peeled. There are several ascents, in particular Heyshott Down which is fairly tough but the views are just reward. The going can get muddy, particularly in Charlton forest so ensure you have good footwear.

Start - OS. 878131 Map 197

The walk starts from Singleton village. To be more definite, I recommend you start in front of "The Fox and Hounds" pub, which if you start in time, will still be open on your return for some well earned refreshment. Singleton is situated on the A286, half way between Midhurst and Chichester. The nearest railway station is at Chichester. An alternative starting point is the car park at Goodwood Country Park (OS. 896114).

SMUGGLERS SEVEN

Before starting the walk proper, it is well worth exploring your starting point, Singleton village. Alternatively, you could do this at the end of the walk, but by then all you will probably feel like exploring is "The Fox and Hounds"!

Singleton (OS. 878131 Map 197) *despite the busy A286, still preserves the peaceful charm of a remote downland village. Take only a few paces from the main road and you will find yourself wandering silent lanes bordered by enchanting flint cottages. The name Singleton is derived from an old Saxon word meaning "bundle of brushwood" or "thicket". For centuries, Singleton was surrounded by forest, much of it still remaining. This attracted the less desirable sectors of the population to settle here, finding the forest useful as a hideout. In particular, Singleton became notorious for smuggling, "The Drovers Inn" now a private house "Drovers", one mile north of the village, was renowned as a smugglers hideout and is said to have had hidden cellars connected by secret passages for the smugglers cause.*

Smuggling apart, Singleton was also famous for the Charlton Hunt, the most famous hunt in the country. A monument can be found in the church to Thomas Johnson, one of the most famous members of the hunt, buried here on his death on December 20th, 1774. Later, Singleton became well known for its association with Goodwood racecourse and attracted huge crowds on race days. This was not always to the delight of the local inhabitants who, by all accounts, had to put up with the equivalent behaviour of modern day football hooligans. More recently, Singleton boasted the first Womens Institute in England, formed in 1915 with Mrs. Leveson-Gower as its first President.

Even today, Singleton is a village known to most visitors to West Sussex, much of this due to the Weald and Downland Museum. Opened in 1971, this open air museum specialises in rescuing historic buildings to reconstruct them in their original glory. A visit is recommended and for details of opening hours telephone: 0243 63348. The village church is of Saxon origin and is also worth a visit. It was once owned by Earl Godwin, father of King Harold who died fighting the Normans in 1066. There is much of interest here, including some fine tombs and some unusual graffiti in the porch which is well worth examining. The church yard also contains many interesting headstones, one in particular marks the grave of two men killed by lightning on St. Roches Hill in 1790. For refreshments there is "The Fox and Hounds", Gibbs Mew, an excellent 18th century inn. The Post Office on the main road (once a toll house) sells basic provisions.

From "The Fox & Hounds" pub follow the road going north, or if you commence your walk from the main road, take the road which goes to the left of the village pond. Continue on the road following the signs for Charlton and East Dean.

Shortly after passing an antique shop and Singleton village hall on your right, take the signposted public footpath on your left, which passes to the left of a school. You will soon pass an old cemetery on your left. Pass through a gate to continue ahead going uphill along the left hand perimeter of a field, albeit at the time of writing the hedge is disappearing thereby leaving you almost walking along the centre of the field. As the hedge ends you should continue uphill, but now going diagonally right, heading for a stile in the hedgerow ahead. The path at this point becomes steeper as it climbs the slopes of Levin Down.

Cowslip

At the far end of the field, cross over two stiles passing a sign - "Boundary of Open Country". Thereafter, continue straight ahead to reach another public footpath sign. Here you will meet a large track, a public bridleway, on to which you should turn right still continuing uphill over Levin Down. Ignore a path to your left and continue ahead to reach a wooden farm gate, through which you should pass to enter open grass hillside. Here it is worth stopping for a moment to take in the view. To the west there are good views across the valley to Hat Hill, however the best view is to the south, of St. Roches Hill, easily identifiable by its rounded top and radio masts. To its left are the stands of Goodwood racecourse.

St. Roches Hill (OS. 877110 Map 197) is a landmark on many of the walks in this book and rightly so. This prominent hill popularly known as "The Trundle", has been a notable landmark for centuries. Its past as far as human influence is concerned, dates back to neolithic times when the hill was an important fort guarding the harbour at its foot. This role was later taken over by the Celts and later still by the Romans, before being abandoned. "The Trundle" however, remained an important landmark and was often used for gatherings. During the Civil War, it was used by local farmers in a mass protest at having to feed to the extent of ruin, soldiers on both sides. This reflects the conflict of loyalties in Sussex during the war. Later, "The Trundle" served as a lesson to wrongdoers, with a gallows on its summit. It was here that Tapner, a member of the infamous Hawkhurst Gang, was hung in chains. Up until the last century, a windmill also stood on the hill.

Today, radio masts ensure the hill's continuance as a prominent landmark and its popularity as a gathering point. With its varied history, it is not surprising that the hill is steeped in legend. One of the most popular is that the hill hides a great fortune left by the Vikings. Do not though get too excited, the Vikings left a guard, a ghostly calf sure to bring misery on any foolish prospectors. This loosely ties with another legend that a golden calf was buried on the hill. The name "St. Roches" dates from a chapel which once stood on the hill during the middle ages. This was administered by the church at Singleton.

Continue ahead along what can sometimes be a somewhat undefined track, to go over and then descend Levin Down. Through the gaps in the trees ahead "Broadham House" comes into view. If doubtful of your route, where the track becomes undefined head for the tree line at the other side of the field slightly to your left and as this veers away to "Broadham House", leave it to head for the gate in front of you. The view ahead at this

24

point is of Charlton and Singleton forests. Pass through the gate to meet a junction of tracks marked by a large signpost, originally erected to commemorate the Charlton Hunt.

The Charlton Hunt *or The Charlton Pack became, at its height in the early 18th century, the most famous hunt in the world. It consisted of some of the most well known members of the aristocracy at the time. Among them, the Duke of Monmouth, the Duke of Marlborough, Lord Grey, the Duke of Bolton, the Duke of Richmond and of less "blue" blood but perhaps most respected, Tom Johnson, whose memorial we have already discovered in the church at Singleton.*   *i*

The most famous hunt is well recorded and took place on Friday, 26th January, 1738. The hunt lasted over ten hours and started with a complement of twentytwo hunters, but at the kill only three remained. The hunt brought wealth and fame to this wild and remote area and the village of Charlton through which we later pass, boasted many a fine property built for the gentry as a base from which to enjoy their sport. The hunt declined after the death of the second Duke of Richmond, Master of the Hunt, and became the Goodwood Hunt. However, it could never regain its former glory and ended completely in the early 19th century.

Our route continues in the direction of Heyshott, which is signposted and is the second turning left at the junction. This is a well defined and fenced track running between fields descending gradually. As you follow the track, you will gain better views of "Broadham House" on your left. The track leads down to a valley where you should ignore a bridleway on your left and continue straight on to shortly pass through an old gateway. Here five tracks fan out in front of you. Our route continues along the track which is second from the right, signposted as a public bridleway. You now enter Charlton forest with the track continuing in a straight line as though going through a tunnel through the centre of the forest. As you progress, it becomes very apparent why the most infamous smuggling gang the south east has ever seen, chose this forest as their base.

The Hawkhurst Gang *were a large band of smugglers with a hard core of seven led by the ruthless Thomas Kingsmill. The gang were noted for their brutality and virtually dominated certain areas of the downs, making them almost mini kingdoms where few people dared to tread. The most famous act carried out by the gang was the raid on the Customs House at Poole. The raid is said to have been planned in Charlton forest, after a smuggled shipment of tea was seized and locked up at the Customs House. The raid on the house was successful but in the months which followed, the*   *i* *gang became nervous of capture and set out to silence all possible witnesses. Their first victims, the Customs House keeper and Daniel Chater, died slow and violent deaths. Daniel Chater was blinded before being thrown down a well to drown. The gang were eventually captured, though not before more fatalities, and were all hung for their crimes. Like St. Roches Hill, Charlton forest's history invited legend and the forest is reputed to be the home of several ghosts - maybe members of the gang or their unfortunate victims.*

Continue ignoring all crossing tracks and paths until you eventually meet an extremely wide crossing track, evidently well used by four wheel drive vehicles. Again, you should ignore this to continue straight on, still in the direction of the public bridleway sign. Soon after, the track appears to fork and you should follow the right hand and more prominent fork bending right, in the direction of public bridleway sign. Continue uphill until you meet a crossing track where you should turn left to leave the bridleway and join a signposted public footpath. As a guide, this junction has a farm gate on your right.

Follow the footpath which is lined ceremoniously by fir trees, to reach and cross a stile on to the South Downs Way. Do not follow the South Downs Way but cross this and then continue diagonally left across the field ahead in the direction of a public footpath sign. As you near the other side of the field, look out for another public footpath sign with a stile which can at first be difficult to see. Cross the stile and continue along the footpath ahead, going steeply down the side of Heyshott Down. This can be particularly slippery in winter or wet weather and care is needed. Near the base of the hill the path curves right going steeply down again and then sharply right at a public footpath sign, to descend through beech woods. On meeting a track at the bottom of the hill, turn left going north to run between fields eventually arriving at a wide track in front of a flint barn. Behind you are good views of Heyshott Down and our climb again later in the walk!

Continue ahead along the track passing to the left of the barn and on meeting a "T" junction, leave the track to continue straight on following a public footpath sign across a field. At the far end of the field you reach a lane on to which you should turn right. Follow this to enter the village of Heyshott and continue to arrive at the village church.

Heyshott (OS. 898181 Map 197) *lies almost forgotten straddling a common in the shadow of its namesake, Heyshott Down. Yet this silent village fathered one of the greatest pioneers of free trade and equal opportunity this country has ever seen, Richard Cobden. Born at Heyshott on 3rd June, 1804, Cobden later left the village*

to run his own business. *Always aware of his humble upbringing, he involved himself in public duties and eventually became M.P. for Stockport. His greatest triumph was the repeal of the corn duty in 1849 which touched every rural community. Richard Cobden built "Dunford House", three quarters of a mile north of the village, from monies donated by a grateful nation.*

The village church of St. James is supposed to have been built in the early 13th century, though a recently discovered kiln on the same site, throws some doubt on this and it is

St James Church

more likely that the church is of later origin. The church has changed little since Cobden's time, this being the place of his christening. His final resting place is however, at West Lavington. Heyshott was witness in 1850 to the last sermon of Henry Edward Manning (the once Archdeacon of Chichester) for the Church of England, before he changed his faith to become a Cardinal.

The name Heyshott is derived from an old term describing an area where heather grows. If you look carefully, you will find heather still growing in the area today. For refreshments, Heyshott has a good free house, "The Unicorn" which serves food as well as good beer.

Turn right in front of the church to follow the road through the village passing "The Old Forge" on your left and soon after, "The Unicorn" pub on your right. Continue along the road passing attractive properties and then more modern houses and as the road bends sharply left, leave it to continue straight on along a track which is marked as a dead end, heading once again for Heyshott Down. On your left at this point is the entrance to "Manor Farm", recommended accommodation. As a guide, you will shortly pass Heyshott Booster Station on your right.

When the track forks you should take the left hand fork to soon enter woodland, passing a Heyshott Down information sign on your right. Ignore a path leading off to your right at this point. Follow the track to begin your ascent of Heyshott Down where, at the next information sign, you should ignore another footpath off to the right to continue straight on along the public bridleway. As you continue to climb you will enjoy excellent views to your left of "Manor Farm" and the West Sussex Weald - a good place to take a breather! As you do battle with the ascent you may wonder why these hills were ever called "downs", when no matter what the overall gradient of your journey, you always seem to be on the up.

At the top of the hill the track leaves the woodland to arrive at open fields. Ahead of you is Charlton forest and to your left, some ancient burial mounds. Cross the field to meet another track, the South Downs Way, on to which you should turn left to follow this as it bends left and then right, passing the burial mounds on your left. Continue on until you meet a public bridleway signposted off to your right, which you should follow thereby leaving the South Downs Way. As a guide, you will pass through two old gate posts. This track now leads you back into Charlton forest and soon meets a wide crossing track where you should continue straight ahead still following the public bridleway. Ignore a track on the right and another on the left soon after.

When the track you are on forks beside a clearing and water tank on your left, take the left less prominent fork continuing straight on to reach another fork after approximately thirty metres. This time take the right hand fork, a grass track signposted as a public bridleway. This now takes you through beech woods where, soon after, you should look out for a public footpath forking right which you should follow - take care not to miss this. This leads you through more beech woods and later naturally joins a wider track where you should bear right to continue straight on. After approximately thirty paces, turn left to follow a narrower footpath, this time slowly descending through beech woods, to join a public bridleway coming in from the left where you should continue straight on.

Stay on the path as it runs along the edge of a steep sided hill, still passing through beech woodland, to reach a gate and a footpath going off to your left. Ignore the latter to continue ahead, passing through the gate into a field. Go straight on along the left hand perimeter of the field to pass through another gate on to a fenced path. The path leads you to a stile beside a fence over which you should pass to follow a sunken track downhill. Ahead of you now is the village of East Dean, our next destination.

The path you are on leads down to a metal gate through which you should pass on to a tree lined track. Just before the track meets a lane, turn first right into a car park for the church. Go through a small wooden gate to pass through the churchyard and at the other side leave it via another wooden gate to reach the lane mentioned earlier. The church of All Saints was built in the late 12th century, its simple design blending in well with its surroundings. If you have time, the church is well worth a visit. At the lane, turn right to pass "The Hurdlemakers" pub on your left, a free house serving food.

The Hurdlemakers and East Dean village (OS. 905130 Map 197). *Hurdlemaking was one of the main trades of this remote village. A hurdle is a rectangular portable fence constructed from woven hazel and strengthened by a diagonal bar. The hurdles were often used to construct sheep folds or temporary fields, restricting the rate of grazing. Their association with sheep meant that a shepherd was often better known as a "hurdleman".*

The poorer people of the parish would use hurdles to construct a basic home, covering the hurdles with clay to afford some protection against the elements. This process is well known as "wattle and daub". It is interesting to note that it is from this form of house building that the expression "mud slinging" is derived, the person constructing the walls being known as a "mud slinger". The versatile hurdle also gave rise to the popular sport of hurdle racing, a race in which one would have to jump over a set number of hurdles. This has evolved into the modern race hurdles in athletics today.

The village is now mostly owned by the Duke of Richmond and forms part of the Goodwood estate. The Richmond coat of arms is visible on several buildings in the village.

Shortly after the pub you will arrive at the village green and pond. Should you require provisions you can turn right here to visit the Post Office and general stores. Our route however, is left up the road signposted to Goodwood and Chichester. Go uphill for approximately a quarter of a mile and soon after passing the last house on your right, take a signposted footpath on the right which leads into a field. Go straight across the field keeping to the right hand perimeter, where on your right there are views over East Dean village. At the far side of the field cross a stile into another field and turn left to go straight uphill.

At the top of the field cross over a stile to enter woodland on Park Hill, the name a reminder that this was once part of East Dean Park laid out in 1154 by Henry II. Follow the path as it continues uphill until you meet a large grass clearing where the path can be somewhat undefined. You should continue straight on to the top of the hill and follow the path as it curves very gently left heading towards a gate. Pass through the gate to join a track ahead which leads naturally on to a wider track. Continue straight on and do not be tempted to turn right or later left.

Pass through the centre of a field, still on the track, to re-enter woodland and eventually meet a road opposite Goodwood racecourse.

Goodwood racecourse (OS. 895114 Map 197) *evolved from a popular hunt of the early 19th century which always started from this hill top. The popularity of the meets led the Duke of Richmond to build a private racecourse which became "Glorious Goodwood", so well known today.*

Turn right immediately before the road on to another track, signposted as a public bridleway. Follow this passing Goodwood racecourse on your left, descending gradually to meet a fork. Take the right hand fork to veer away from the racecourse continuing straight ahead. Soon on your right, you will enjoy lovely views over a lush green valley and Charlton village. In the distance to your right is East Dean.

Follow the track downhill to pass a saw mill on your left and a large brick building on your right, "The Old Mill", to continue thereafter between cottages arriving at a small triangular green with a war memorial. Continue straight on, bending round to the right, to visit the village and pub, "The Fox Goes Free", a popular free house serving food.

Charlton (OS. 888130 Map 197) *as previously mentioned, was once the home of the famous Charlton Hunt and at the hunt's height, around one hundred and fifty horses would have been stabled here. "Fox Hall" built as a hunting lodge by the Duke of Richmond in 1730, is one relic of those heady days. The village inn, "The Fox Goes Free" is another, which until recently was known simply as "The Fox". The modern name reflecting today's changing attitudes. Even Tom Johnson's humble cottage remains. It is now number "33".*

With many of the country's top aristocracy regularly meeting here, it is not surprising that business was often mixed with pleasure and it is at Charlton that the Duke of Monmouth is believed to have planned his unsuccessful rebellion in 1685. More recently, Charlton has had another claim to fame, it was in a room at "The Fox Goes Free" that the first meeting of the Womens Institute took place in this country. A plaque now records this historic event. Today, like her neighbour East Dean, Charlton is owned in the main, by the Duke of Richmond.

Turn left at the pub and follow the road, passing to the left of "The Woodstock House Hotel", to meet a small crossroads. Turn left here and continue for approximately fifty paces and then turn right to go over a stile to follow a public footpath across a field. This is marked by white topped posts along the way. The footpath eventually meets the corner of another field on your right. You should follow to the left of the fencing of this field heading directly for Singleton church.

Pass through a kissing gate behind some houses and follow the fenced path to run between gardens to reach a close. Continue straight ahead through a modern but pleasant group of houses, along the public footpath which is marked. The pavement takes you under a porch to shortly join a narrow footpath running between a garden on your right and a small field on your left. The path then leads you along the side of the church and leaves the church yard via a small black gate. Turn right here onto a narrow lane to lead back to "The Fox & Hounds" pub, the starting point of our walk.

ACCOMMODATION

The Woodstock House Hotel, Charlton. Tel: 0243 63666
On the walk, this charming hotel is so discrete that it could easily be mistaken for just another house in the village. Built in the early 18th century, the hotel has been pleasantly furnished to provide simple but quality accommodation.

The Fox Goes Free, Charlton. Tel: 0243 63461
On the walk, this picturesque and historic 18th century inn offers very comfortable accommodation in a beautiful setting. One night here and you will become addicted.

Manor Farm, Heyshott. Tel: 0730 813103
On the walk, this lovely old Georgian farmhouse is a must if you are looking for a relaxing break and want to be at one with your surroundings. The rooms are spacious and well furnished and come complete with excellent views.

Youth Hostel, Arundel YHA, Warningcamp. Tel: 0903 882204
Nineteen miles from the walk, this is a large hostel located in a large Georgian building in spacious grounds. The village is very peaceful, but should you want more it is but a short walk along the banks of the river Arun to Arundel. Camping is permitted.

Camping and Caravanning, Goodwood Club site, Singleton.   Tel: 0243 774486
Three quarters of a mile from the walk, this is a Caravan Club run site which has a superb position beside the Goodwood racecourse. The site is open during the summer months, though closed on race days so check ahead.

THE CHANCTONBURY RING

Distance: 11¼ miles (18 km)
Time: Allow approximately 5 hours
Map: Ordnance Survey Landranger Map 198

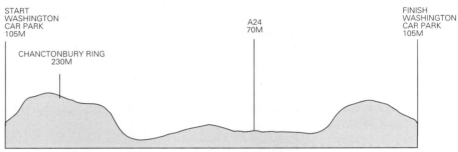

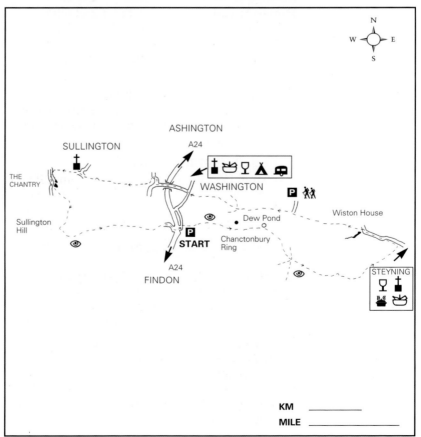

Walk Summary

The Chanctonbury Ring explores some of the most unspoilt downland scenery in West Sussex. The route follows in the footsteps of ancient man to explore the villages of our Saxon ancestors. On a clear day the views are breathtaking, on a rainy or misty day the downs are mysterious, the ghostly legends of which this area has plenty, becoming almost believable. The going is fairly easy though be ready for two steep ascents and one particularly long descent which can be very slippery in wet weather. The mud is prevalent in the woods at the base of the downs so, as ever, do ensure you wear the right footwear.

Start - OS. 121120 Map 198

The walk starts from Washington car park which is on the South Downs Way. To get there, from the A283 take the road south through Washington village past "The Frankland Arms" pub and follow the road uphill to take a left turn just before the road joins the busy A24. This is signposted, "South Downs Way" with a blue box "P" for parking and also as the entrance to Washington Lime Quarry. The car park is just a few metres on the right. An alternative start is from the car park near "Malt House Cottage" (OS. 146125 Map 198).

THE CHANCTONBURY RING

Leave the car park, passing through a metal gate to the left of an information sign. Go up the hill along a track following the signs for the South Downs Way, sometime on ignoring a footpath going off to the left. Shortly after this, ignore another track off to the right to continue straight on passing to the right of a brick building belonging to Segas. You will now ascend open downland, where behind to your right at a farmhouse you may see a plane as this field is often used as a private runway.

Approximately fifty metres after the Segas building, bear left on to a grass path signposted as a public bridleway, to pass through a small wooden gate with a "Sheep Grazing" sign. Go straight uphill to meet the remains of some old chalk earthworks. Continue uphill following a more prominent path between the mounds leading to a gate ahead. On your left you now have a good view of Washington sandpit and its windmill on Rock Common, once home to composer John Ireland.

Pass through the gate into a field and continue straight ahead in the direction of the public bridleway sign, following a line of posts. As you continue it is worth stopping to catch your breath and enjoy the views. At the far side of the field cross a stile and shallow bank to arrive at a chalkland dew pond.

33

i   **The Chanctonbury Dew Pond (OS. 133120 Map 198)**
*contrary to popular belief was only constructed in the 1870's. It
was later restored by the Society of Sussex Downsman to mark the
European Conservation Year in 1970. Although the dew pond on
Chanctonbury Hill was only built in the late 19th century, many
more found along the Sussex Downs are of a much earlier date,
some of them several centuries old. They were vital so shepherds
who couldn't keep taking their flocks to the base of the downs to be
watered. There is a constant argument as to how these ponds were
constructed and it is quite possible that a variety of methods were
used. Roughly, a pond was created by digging a hollow to a depth
of six feet. This was then lined with straw and protected by a large
layer of wet clay. The straw stopped the heat from the earth rising
to the surface at night, keeping the surface of the pond cool thus
causing the moisture in the air to condense. This ingenious method
of collecting water meant that even in the dry season, these ponds
would not dry up.*

Leave the pond via another stile opposite and head for the trig
point which is at the top of Chanctonbury Hill, 238m. This is a
good place for an early rest on the walk where you can enjoy
panoramic views. The grass hill to the south is Cissbury Ring, an
old hill fort, and beyond it the seaside town of Worthing. To the
east is Brighton and Truleigh Hill with its two aerial masts where
at the top there is a Youth Hostel. Continue by passing over a
shallow bank and ditch, known as a cross dyke and join a track
ahead, the South Downs Way, heading for a ring of trees, the
Chanctonbury Ring.

i   **The Chanctonbury Ring (OS. 139121 Map 198)** *is arguably
the most well known landmark in West Sussex, outshining even
the elegant spire of Chichester Cathedral and the grandeur of
Arundel castle. It is actually a neolithic dwelling and probably
had close connections with Cissbury Hill fort to the south, where
there were also some flint mines. The ring's striking appearance
which has made it such a famous landmark, visible from over
sixty kilometres distance, is due to the trees which colonise it.
These were planted by one Charles Goring who lived at "Wiston
House", visible below the hill. Goring planted them in 1760 when
he was just a boy and is said to have carried water up to them
daily to ensure their good health. His dedication paid off and by
his death at the age of ninety, the trees had fully grown creating
the landmark visible today. The ring has always been a religious
spot of some significance and this is borne out by the discovery of
the remains of a Romano-Celtic temple at its centre. Consequently,
myth and superstition surround the temple. It is believed that if*

you run round the ring seven times at midnight you will raise the devil and he will probably take you if you try this when unfit! This myth probably comes from a spiritual ritual which involved dancing around the ring. There is also the story of a Saxon ghost with a white beard who is seen hunting for his lost treasure. Funnily enough a hoard of coins was found here at the end of the last century. Whether you choose to believe these myths or not, the ring does have a certain presence and I for one would not want to spend the night up here alone.

Leave the Chanctonbury Ring going east along the South Downs Way to reach a gate beside a cattle grid through which you should pass. The track sweeps round to the left to reach a crossing track where you should continue straight ahead passing between fields. After some distance, another track joins from the right which you should ignore, still following the signs for the South Downs Way.

When the fencing on your left ends turn left following a signposted public bridleway, thereby leaving the South Downs Way. Take care not to miss this. Follow the perimeter fencing on your left to meet the tree line where you should turn right to continue with trees and the hill escarpment on your left and open fields on your right. After some distance, take a signposted public bridleway left leaving the field to begin your descent. The tree line on your left breaks here to afford superb views across the Sussex Weald and directly below the ruins of "Wiston Barn" and beyond, a pond belonging to "Wiston House".

Pass through some old wooden posts where there is a sign on your right, "Keep to the Bridleway" - take heed of this as either side there are unexploded shells. Staying on the path continue downhill through woodland. Half way down the hill, ignore a signposted public bridleway off to the right to continue straight on. At one point, the path opens out to your right giving views over the village of Steyning below, and beyond the South Downs and Truleigh Hill.

The path soon turns into a track leaving the woodland to run between fields with Steyning on your right. Just before you meet a lane, turn left on to a public footpath. If you wish to visit Steyning however, which I recommend, turn right instead and follow the public footpath which leads into Steyning. Steyning was an important Saxon pilgrimage town and is steeped in history reflected in its well preserved centre. It was also one of the reasons for the Norman invasion in 1066. There are not enough pages in this book to do Steyning justice. If I have wetted your appetite, then make sure you visit and buy a local guide book. As stated, our route is left along the public footpath to follow the right hand perimeter of a field heading west.

After some distance on meeting a footpath sign, turn right to join the lane. Turn left along the lane and follow this until it bends right. Leave the lane at this point turning left through a gap in the hedge and then right to follow the perimeter of a field. Take particular care not to miss this as the path can be somewhat hidden. Follow the perimeter of the field round to the left and then turn right in the direction of the public footpath sign, to cross a stream and continue through a narrow strip of woodland. On reaching a stile cross this into a field to continue ahead following the public footpath sign and follow the path as it bears round to the right. Cross another stile and continue ahead along the right hand perimeter of a field, at the other side of which are views right of "Wiston House".

i **Wiston House (OS. 155124 Map 198)** *pronounced "Wisson", is a splendid Elizabethan property now used as a conference centre. Its extensive grounds were once home to a herd of deer though today you are more likely to see men in grey suits than spot a deer. Wiston House was home to the Goring family and it was Charles Goring who planted the trees on the Chanctonbury Ring. There hangs a portrait in the house by Lawrence of Charles Goring holding a twig symbolising this act.*

Leave the field to continue along a wide track, still marked as a public footpath, to meet a lane. The best views yet of "Wiston House" are now to your right. Turn left to follow the lane passing under an old ornate brick and iron bridge and as the lane bends right towards a farmhouse, leave it to continue straight on to pass through a metal gate ahead on to a track, following the public footpath signs.

Iron Bridge - Wistone House

The track which is fenced on your right with trees on the left, continues in a westerly direction and soon passes through "Great Barn Farm" and ends at a metal gate through which you should pass to reach a "T" junction. Turn right here and then immediately left beside "Malt House Cottage" to follow the track ahead. Continue past "Two Malt House" and through a wooden gate following the track, which at first is hedged and then follows the left hand perimeter of a field before entering woodland. Take care not to miss the turning into the woodland. This is marked by a public bridleway sign and can be extremely muddy in wet weather.

Stay on the track to eventually meet an iron bar gate through which you should pass and continue straight ahead passing an old barn, "Owls Croft Barn" on your right. If the going is too muddy there is a smaller path on your left through the trees which runs parallel with the track you are on. The track soon narrows into a path with lovely open grassland above you, and continues along the base of the hill to reach another metal gate. Pass through the gate, ignoring a path going off to your left and go gently downhill to meet a crossroads at the edge of a field. Continue straight on to cross the field following the white posts. This route is confirmed by a public footpath sign. To your right now is "Locks Farm" and beyond, Washington windmill.

At the other side of the field you will pass through a gap to continue ahead. On meeting a hedgerow, turn left and follow the right hand perimeter of a field, keeping the hedgerow on your right. The path reaches a farm on the right where you should continue straight on along the right hand perimeter of the field, ignoring a signposted turning off to your right (this is in fact an alternative route into Washington). Continue straight on and at the end of the field cross a stile to follow a fenced path downhill to reach a lane and Washington village itself.

Washington (OS. 122128 Map 198) *like many other villages along the Sussex Downs derives its name from a Saxon chieftain. Literally translated, Washington means "home of the sons of Wasa". Unfortunately, little or nothing is known of this Saxon chieftain. Although the origination of the village was Saxon surprisingly no signs of a Saxon church have been found. The present church is in the main, a 19th century reconstruction although parts of the original 13th century church do remain. Before this, there had been another smaller church but this quickly proved to be too small and was demolished. Despite the reconstruction, the church today still has its Tudor tower built during the reign of Henry VII. The church has one or two interesting memorial tablets, the oldest and in my view the best, is one dedicated to John Byne of Rodwell House (which we pass later) who died in 1600. The tablet of marble depicts Mr. Byne with his wife and seven children kneeling in prayer. Another village building worth a mention is the village inn, "The Frankland Arms" (Whitbread). Though not always called "The Frankland Arms", the pub has always been popular with residents* *and travellers alike.*

So much so that the inn finds itself praised in an old Sussex drinking song:

> *They sell good beer at Haslemere,*
> *And under Guildford hill*
> *At little Cowfold as I've been told*
> *A beggar may drink his fill.*
>
> *There is a good brew in Amberley too*
> *And by the bridge also*
> *But the swipes they take in at the Washington Inn*
> *Is the very best beer I know.*

The inn which also serves good food is still as popular today, perhaps even more so. If you don't mind the crowds, why not test the merits of the song for yourself!

If you wish to visit "The Frankland Arms", turn right where the pub is visible. Our route is left along the lane to shortly turn right up a road called The Street. If the break at "The Frankland Arms" has effected your legs you can instead follow the lane uphill which will lead you back to the car park and our starting point. For those with more resilience follow The Street through the centre of Washington passing lovely old cottages and on your right a Post Office, which also sells basic provisions, to reach St. Mary's church.

Ignore a footpath on your right and carry straight on following the public bridleway signs to soon cross the busy A24 - suddenly reminding you of the hustle and bustle of the real world! At the other side of the bridge ignore a path going off to the left and follow the bridleway signs ahead where, in early summer, there is the instantly recognisable smell of ramsons a woodland plant often mistaken for wild garlic. At a fork, take the right hand fork which is signposted "Private Road - Rowdel and Rowdel Cottage - Public Bridleway and Footpath Only". On meeting the first property on your right, leave the lane as it bends right, to turn left along a signposted public bridleway. Almost immediately after, turn right along a fenced path to pass another property on your left. The bridleway leads round the property to bend left and then right before joining a track along the right hand perimeter of a field. Ahead of you here are good views of Sullington and Rackham Hill.

At the end of the field, pass through an old disused farm gate and continue ahead along the track, again keeping to the right hand perimeter of the next field. The track passes to the south of "Barns Farm", where you should go through a metal gate ignoring the tracks either side, to continue ahead between fences with the farmhouse on your right. The path bends round to the right behind the farmhouse and then left following the signposted public bridleway. You should ignore another bridleway off to the right.

On meeting a cantering track which is signposted, take care and cross this to continue ahead through a wooden gate into a field. Turn right to follow the right hand perimeter of the field in the direction of the public bridleway sign, where as you continue the hamlet of Sullington dominated by its tiny Saxon church, will come into view. At the end of the field go through a metal gate into a farmyard where you should bear right towards the church. You have arrived at the hamlet of Sullington.

Sullington (OS. 098131 Map 198) *is one of those secrets that is a delight to discover making all the effort of the last few hours more than worthwhile. On a summer's day it is easy to while away the hours here sitting and observing a Sullington day go by. Unlike many other downland villages, it is uncertain when Sullington first became a human settlement. Long before humans settled here an ichthyosaurus passed this way, its skeleton having been found nearby. The earthworkings on the nearby downs and some subsequent finds of flint arrow heads and tools, indicate that early man certainly had some sort of settlement near here. Human remains were also found on Sullington Hill, suggesting that this could have been an early burial site. Nearby on Sullington Warren, charred bones were found in huge clay jars. This was a form of burial used by neolithic man who burned their dead and then interned them in clay jars, burying them with their most treasured belongings in round or long barrows. This method of burial earned them the title of "Beaker people".*

The first church here was almost certainly Saxon, the one standing today being mainly rebuilt in the 13th century. The church stands so close to the manor house that they are connected with the church also acting as a farmyard wall. St. Mary's is one of the few churches in the county to have a squint. This would probably have been connected to a small cell outside the church. The cell would have held a hermit or anchorite locked up in the service of God, though it has been suggested that it could have been a lepers squint, there having once been a leper colony nearby. A better example of a squint and cell can be seen at St. James' church at Shere in Surrey. (See "10 Adventurous Walks in Surrey"). One other point of particular interest is the marble effigy of a knight. This is assumed to have been one of the de Covert family, although which member or from what date no-one is sure. The de Covert's, were lords of the manor from the early 13th century to the late

14th century when it became the property of Richard, Earl of Arundel. The manor house itself was built in the 11th century and in its farmyard stands a 115ft long tithe barn, one of the best remaining examples left in the country.

Turn left to pass in front of the church and continue ahead along a drive, passing "Sullington Manor" on your right. Pass another house on your right and at the end of the drive, pass through a gate to follow a track along the right hand perimeter of a field. At the end of the field, follow the track as it bends left to run down the side of a wooded valley. Pass through a gate into a field and turn right to pass a cottage on your right. Go through another gate on to a lane beside a small and unexpected waterfall. Turn left up the lane to reach a small hamlet known as The Chantry.

i **The Chantry (OS. 092129 Map 198)** *is a magical place which derives its name from a chantry chapel in the grounds of "Chantry House". A chantry chapel is a chapel dedicated to praying for the dead. The hamlet around "The Chantry" can be described as sleepy as opposed to dead. It comprises of several houses clustered around tranquil ponds surrounded by elegant woodland. The ponds are spring fed from the source of a stream called the Stor, the stream runs to Storrington where it feeds a mill, "Chantry Mill" before eventually running into the river Arun near Pulborough. Today the ponds are part of a garden to a modern house, but this has been tastefully added and does not take away from the character of the hamlet.*

Pass through two white posts to pass the two ponds divided by a low stone bridge and follow the lane ignoring a footpath off to your right. Just after "The Chantry", take a public bridleway on your left thereby leaving the lane.

The bridleway winds uphill through woodland to meet and pass through a small wooden gate and continues uphill between banks. This is an ancient track used for centuries by Drovers. On your right as you continue uphill there are some earthworkings known as cross dykes.

Continue diagonally up the side of the hill to pass through a metal gate still going uphill between banks. In the distance ahead is the church spire at Washington and beyond, the Chanctonbury Ring. The bridleway bends round to the right still going uphill. On meeting a track joining from the left, turn right on to this to continue your climb heading in a southerly direction. Soon after, the track will pass through some earthworks and sometime after this, you should ignore a second track joining from the left, to continue ahead along a less defined route across open hillside.

Head for a bridleway sign at the corner of the downland which is fenced and on reaching the sign turn left going downhill to meet a wide track.

Follow the track straight on, still in the direction of the public bridleway sign, to pass through a metal gate and head for another gate through which you should also pass. You are now back on the South Downs Way which you can at once recognise by the red faced hikers and mountain bikes with colourful riders. Turn left to follow the South Downs Way along the left hand perimeter of a large open field. You should now begin a long slow ascent and on reaching the crest of the hill you will see the chalk workings and the start of your walk ahead in the distance. Leave the field via a cattle grid to join a fenced track, where you should carry straight on following the South Downs Way for approximately one and a quarter miles to reach the A24. The last part of the way runs past houses and one friendly resident has had a tap put at the side of the lane to quench the thirst of the walker. Cross the A24 taking care to do this by following the South Downs Way signs and go up the other side still following the signs to reach the parking area from where our walk commenced.

ACCOMMODATION

Rock Windmill, Washington. Tel: 0903 892941
One mile from the walk, this windmill is as much a feature of the walk as it is good accommodation. Apart from the delight of staying near a windmill (the accommodation is in a modern extension), there is also a heated swimming pool.

Greenacres Farm, Washington. Tel: 0903 742538
Three quarters of a mile from the walk, this versatile camp site also has chalets and an outdoor swimming pool in which to relax after your day's exploration. A stay here is recommended.

Youth Hostel, Truleigh Hill YHA. Tel: 0903 813419
Five miles from the walk and 600ft above sea level, this Youth Hostel is sited in a modern building on the South Downs Way.

Washington Caravan and Camping Park. Tel: 0903 892869
Half a mile from the walk, this well run site lies beneath the Chanctonbury Ring, only five minutes walk from Washington village and "The Frankland Arms" pub.

N.B. There is a wealth of accommodation in Steyning. For full details, contact the Tourist Office at Arundel - 61, High Street, Arundel, W. Sussex, BN18 9AJ. Tel: 0903 882268.

THE WET COMMON WADDLE

Distance: 12 miles (19 km)
Time: Allow approximately 6 hours
Map: Ordnance Survey Landranger Map 197

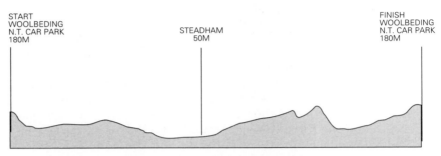

START
WOOLBEDING
N.T. CAR PARK
180M

STEADHAM
50M

FINISH
WOOLBEDING
N.T. CAR PARK
180M

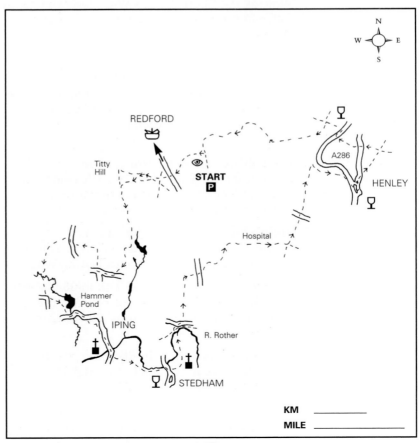

REDFORD

Titty
Hill

START
P

A286

HENLEY

Hospital

Hammer
Pond

IPING

R. Rother

STEDHAM

KM _____
MILE _____

Walk Summary

Centuries ago before the dark ages, the Sussex Weald was a wild impenetrable forest known to the Romans as "Anderida Silva", meaning "uninhabited place". Only the desperate or those with criminal tendencies would venture into the forest. The result today is that much of the Sussex Weald is common land, free of fencing and open for the traveller to explore just as it was all those years ago. The Wet Common Waddle follows many of the ancient tracks across some of the best preserved common land in West Sussex. The scenery is constantly varied and always pleasurable, the villages and hamlets you pass forgotten by the modern world, never failing to surprise.

Start - OS. 869261 Map 197

The walk starts from the National Trust car park at Woolbeding Common. The car park is quite remote and care is needed if you don't want to get lost before you start. From the north, take the A286 south from Haslemere and at Fernhurst take a road right (west), signposted "To Shopping Centre, Car Park, Toilets" and called Vann road. Stay on Vann road until you meet a "T" junction where you should turn left signposted to Midhurst, Linch and Milland. After approximately half a mile, take a left turn signposted to Woolbeding and St. Cuthmans. Stay on this road to pass through Redford village and shortly after, take a very narrow lane left signposted to Older Hill. Follow the lane for approximately half a mile to reach the car park which is on your right.

THE WET COMMON WADDLE

From the car park cross the lane and walk to the edge of the hill where there is a wooden bench. You are immediately rewarded with stunning views across Woolbeding Common, the Weald and beyond, Hampshire. From this position, it is easy to appreciate the magnificence of the once Anderida forest, much of the area still being wooded. Turn right to join a narrow path running along the edge of the hillside. On meeting a crossing path beside the lane, turn left to follow the signposted public footpath steeply downhill through Woolbeding Common predominantly made up of bracken and gorse.

Woolbeding Common (OS. 866264 Map 197) *is one of several commons stretching across the Sussex Weald, though few are arguably so beautiful. The word "common" denotes that the land belongs to the common people and therefore open to all, it is against the law to fence a common. For centuries people have relied on the common for their living. It was used in the main as grazing land, the abundant gorse or furze being cut and used as a winter fodder. The furze so splendid in early summer, was an important natural resource and furze cutters would collect this* *bush to sell to farmers as windbreaks and as already mentioned, winter fodder. The scene you see today would have changed little over the years though the sheep and furze cutters have long gone.*

On reaching the bottom of the hill, go over a crossing path to continue straight on still following the public footpath sign. As you progress, the bracken gives way to mixed woodland to soon reach a garden wall on your left, topped by wooden fencing. Continue straight on following the wall to arrive at "Barnetts Cottage" and a crossing path. Turn left passing in front of the cottage to go downhill and shortly cross a drive way continuing straight on, with Older Hill visible on your left.

Go downhill and cross over two more drive ways, one immediately after the other, to carry straight on following the footpath sign, ignoring another footpath off to your right. The path continues downhill through open woodland and bracken and shortly after, a pond comes into view on your left. At the next footpath sign continue straight on unless you wish to visit the pond, in which case, turn second left at this sign. Staying on our route you will shortly meet a lane with a sign for Redford on your right. If you are already in need of refreshment turn right here to enter Redford village, which has a Post Office doubling as a general stores. To continue our route, cross the lane and follow the signposted footpath ahead.

The footpath continues between young birch trees and can be extremely muddy. It soon reaches a small grass clearing with a signposted crossing path. Ignore this and continue straight on to arrive at a "T" junction, where you should turn right in the direction of the footpath sign. The going here is very very wet so care and good footwear are essential. After twenty paces you will meet another footpath sign where you should continue straight on, ignoring the signposted paths of to the left and right. As a guide, you will now pass a field on your right. Follow the path as it bends round to the left, ignoring a footpath off to the right. Carry straight on following the now familiar woodland interspersed with bracken, later ignoring another footpath off to the left.

The footpath gradually ascends to reach some houses and a drive at Titty Hill, behind which are the lower slopes of Dunner Hill. Titty Hill is reputed to have been a look out station for the Romans protecting the posting station at Iping Marsh. The Saxons later took it over and used it for the same purpose. Bear left to follow the drive and join the track ahead, ignoring the signposted footpath off to the right. Keep Dunner Hill on your right and after a short distance pass a sign on the same side - "Beware Adders". Ignore a track on your right and carry straight on later passing a public bridleway on the left.

44

Soon after a gated drive and prior to reaching a cottage, turn right at a fork on to an often extremely muddy track, signposted as a public bridleway, running between banks. Follow the bridleway through woodland and keep your eyes peeled sometime later for two ponds below to your left. The path at this point bears right to run between more steep banks and then sharply left. If you are walking this way when the ground underfoot is wet you will begin to understand why the roads of Sussex (of which this would have been one) were so notorious. It is also another reason why the countryside of Sussex has been so well preserved. It was quite common in the days before tarmac, for a cart to be abandoned in the mud blocking the route, one reason why you will often find two or more tracks running parallel to one another for a short distance.

i

Ignore a signposted footpath on your right and continue ahead for approximately twenty metres to meet a fork. Take the right hand fork going uphill, signposted as a public bridleway, and follow this as it bends right to reach open common land. On your right, some cottages and a few scattered farm buildings make up the hamlet of Tentworth. Continue straight on in the direction of the bridleway sign with views on your left of the South Downs. On meeting a tarmac lane join this to continue ahead ignoring any paths off to the left or right. Continue for approximately a quarter of a mile to meet another lane where you should turn right on to a marked public bridleway. This runs between shallow banks gently uphill with a field on your left and woodland to the right. It is obviously another very old and well used track lined with a crumbling stone wall now acting as an upmarket frontage to several rabbit warrens.

The field on your left gives way to woodland and the banks either side of the bridleway become steeper. After some distance, you will meet a signposted bridleway on your left which you should now take, to continue between shallow banks through woodland later giving way to fields. There are once again views across to the South Downs and soon, ahead of you to your right, a house comes into view. The bridleway passes to the left of the property and on meeting a gravel drive, you should bear left to continue down to a lane passing another cottage on your right, "Stubbsfield".

Turn right along the lane passing the remains of an old gas lamp on your left and continue for approximately twenty metres to meet a public footpath sign on your left, just before the lane begins to go downhill. Leave the lane to follow the footpath which runs above the lane for a short while before turning away to the left. The hill ahead of you to your right at this point is Hill Brow - the busy line of the A3. To your right below you is the hamlet of Robins.

The footpath begins to descend through woodland and if you look carefully, you will soon see a cottage ahead on your right. Shortly after this you will reach a fork, with the right hand fork clearly marked as a footpath. Follow the footpath as it descends behind the cottage to arrive at a track in front of another half timbered cottage with a stunning garden. Turn left here along the track, Moorhouse Lane, pass in front of the cottage and continue almost along the bottom of a valley. On your right at the very bottom is a small stream, Hammer stream.

Follow the track as it bends right and ignore another track going off to your left which is private. Thereafter, the track bends left again on its original course and descends into Hammer Wood, passing to the right of a pond, possibly an old hammer pond. Continue on to pass over Hammer stream and go uphill through Hammer Wood, ignoring a public footpath on your right. You will eventually meet a lane which you should join continuing ahead for a few paces, before turning left on to a signposted footpath passing through a gate way. You are now entering Hammer Wood proper.

i **Hammer Wood (OS. 844240 Map 197).** *You may have noticed by now the frequency of the name Hammer. This is a name left over from the iron industry which was at its height in the 16th and 17th centuries. The iron foundry in Hammer Wood was located beside a lake, Hammer pond, which we will shortly pass. The pond created the force to drive the great hammers which would break the iron stone. Another free resource, the great oaks which made up the wood, provided fuel for smelting the iron. At the time of the iron industry, the wood belonged to the Iping estate, owned by the Hooke family from Hampshire. Today the wood is a nature reserve and belongs to the Chithurst Buddhist Monastery.*

The footpath, more a track in appearance, runs along the top of Hammer valley now on your left, to meet a fork. Take the right hand fork, a signposted public footpath, to pass through a sweet chestnut coppice where the Hammer stream is still visible through the trees below to your left. The track winds through the coppice gradually bearing away from the stream. You should ignore any smaller paths off to the left or right to eventually arrive at a point above a horse shoe lake, the Hammer pond. Go straight on, downhill, passing to the right of the lake and towards the bottom, follow a fence on the right leading away from the lake to pass between two cottages.

On meeting a lane turn left to follow this over a bridge again crossing the Hammer stream, to "Aloka", a cottage on your left owned by the Buddhist Monastery. Continue up the lane between steep banks and when the banks give way to open fields, turn right over a stile and go diagonally left across a field enjoying superb views of the South Downs. (The footpath signposted on your left, the other side of the lane, runs along the course of a Roman road leading from Chichester to Silchester in Hampshire). At the far corner of the field pass through a gate into another field on your left and follow the right hand perimeter in the direction of the public footpath sign. On your right now is the village of Iping. Pass through a small gate at the other side of the field and then through a farm gate approximately twenty paces on on your right and continue across the centre of the next field heading for Iping.

At the far end of the field cross a stile and turn left along a track to meet a lane. Turn right along the lane to enter the village.

Iping (OS. 854229 Map 197) *derives its name from "Ippa" a Saxon chieftain who settled here after the Romans. Apart from the iron industry, Iping has mainly relied on the river and its mills for an income. The main mill, "Iping Mill" west of the river, now an enviable residence, was in action from at least the 15th century until shortly after the second World War, milling anything from wheat to paper. The church at Iping, St. Mary's, was rebuilt in 1840, with the tower being added in 1885. The earliest recorded church on this site dates back to the 12th century.*

Walk through the village, passing the "Mill House" to reach St. Mary's church. Ignore the footpath signs either side and continue along the lane to cross the river Rother via a stout 17th century bridge. Continue for approximately fifty metres after the bridge and join a public bridleway on your left. Follow the bridleway uphill along a brick path, to meet a stone wall and then a tarmac drive. Go straight on passing "Coachman's Cottage" on your left and after twenty metres, turn right and pass through an iron gate to continue ahead, along a signposted public bridleway which runs beside a field on your right. *It was hereabouts that the Reverend John Denham, Rector of Iping church, was brutally murdered by a local man, Aps, who killed his victim by stabbing him through the heart with a pitchfork. Aps was tried at Horsham and duly hung for his crime. The unfortunate Rector was buried beneath the chancel at Iping church. Turning to more pleasant matters, as you progress there are good views to your left of Titty hill and the earlier part of our walk.*

After some distance the bridleway meets the river Rother and follows the right hand bank to the village of Stedham. Keep your eyes peeled here for waterfowl, including kingfishers. You will arrive at Stedham beside another low medieval bridge.

Stedham (OS. 864226 Map 197) *like Iping derives its name from a Saxon chieftain, Chief Stedda. The building you immediately appreciate is "Stedham Hall" which stands high on the north bank as though on guard over the river crossing. The building as you see it today, was restored in the early 20th century to its original Elizabethan style. Before the 16th century, the hall was owned by a monastic hospital in Portsmouth called "Domus Dei" meaning "House of God". After the reformation, the hall passed to the Browne family. The village is worth exploring if only to find the popular "Hamilton Arms", a free house named after the Hamiltons of Iping. The pub offers good food as well as real ale.*

Cross the lane and turn right to follow a narrow sometimes overgrown path across a small green, heading uphill towards a half timbered cottage. Turn left in front of the cottage, to continue along a lane shortly meeting St. James church on your left. Follow the lane as it bends left to pass the entrance to "Stedham Hall" and later "Stedham Mill Farm" which sells free range eggs. Stay on the lane after the farm to descend to "Stedham Mill". This is an idyllic spot, the mill house having a beautiful terraced garden overlooking the mill pond, which is still protected by the old sluice. The mill itself ceased to operate around 1927 and was demolished.

Pass between the outbuildings at "Stedham Mill" and cross the river Rother by way of a narrow concrete footbridge, passing over the mill race. When the river is low there are stepping stones should you want to risk it. At the other side, continue ahead along the right hand perimeter of a field and at the far side go straight uphill, ignoring the paths off to your left and right. Go over a stile and continue uphill along a narrow path, taking time to look back and appreciate your last view of "Stedham Mill" and the river Rother. At the top of the hill the path meets a lane, on to which you should turn right for approximately twenty metres. Then turn left on to a signposted public footpath passing over a stile into a field and continue straight ahead across the field, keeping to the left hand perimeter. At the far side, pass through a gap in the fence and follow the left hand perimeter of the next field.

At the other side of the field, cross over a stile and turn right along a track signposted as a public footpath, heading for a farmhouse. The track passes to the left of the farmhouse, which belongs to the National Trust, and winds through undergrowth to meet Woolbeding Lane. Cross the lane and continue along the track opposite, signposted public footpath and "Pound Common", again National Trust land. Pound Common reaches to Woolbeding Common, the start of our walk. Ignore a crossing track almost immediately after and continue straight on to run through open bracken heading towards Woolbeding Common. The track goes down and up a dip passing to the left of a cottage and continues on across Pound Common, where heather and gorse now add to the bracken. You should ignore a signposted footpath on your right at the cottage which follows the perimeter of the property.

You will eventually meet a crossing path in front of some woodland. Turn right here, heading east and ignore a series of tracks soon after leading off to the left. Shortly after, look out for a footpath sign on your right pointing left, this is a short cut back to our starting point should your legs be tiring! Our route however, continues straight on to soon pass a National Trust sign for Woolbeding Common. Ignore all turnings off to the left and right and continue ahead where you will soon see the King Edward VII hospital on your left.

After approximately half a mile, you will reach a crossing track with a public footpath sign where you should turn left. Follow this across Great Common heading for two houses ahead. Over to your right Great Common runs into North Heath, where in 1799 two men were hung in chains after their execution at Horsham. Their crime was to rob the mail coach to Portsmouth. It was one of the last occasions that criminals were hung in chains in this country. At the far side of the common as the track bends right, leave it to continue straight on along a narrow signposted public footpath, passing to the left of a house. Stay on the footpath to arrive at a road opposite a bus stop with a memorial seat to Frederick P. Neale. Cross the road to continue along the signposted footpath opposite, another ancient track, between banks covered with brambles and trees.

i

Go straight over a crossing track, staying on the footpath, to eventually enter woodland and gradually descend. The footpath again runs between banks and descends Verdley Edge to arrive at some houses. You should continue straight on along a drive and turn sharp right at a house sign "Verdley Edge", to pass in front of "The Lodge" along another gravel drive. You will then pass the cottage "Verdley Edge" with an ornate clock tower above the garage. Soon after, the path re-enters woodland and progresses uphill between more steep banks to later reach a fork. Take the right hand fork, still going uphill, and ignore all minor turnings off to follow the path to the top of the hill. As the path levels out it follows the side of the hill to shortly meet a main road, the A286.

Cross the road and take the footpath opposite downhill to reach a gravel drive to a house, "High Wood". Go straight across the gravel drive and take a narrow somewhat hidden path the other side downhill to cross a wooden plank bridge on to a lane. Turn left to follow the lane (the original A286) down into Henley village, which clings to the steep slopes of Verdley Hill with views across the Weald to Blackdown. Pass "The Duke of Cumberland Arms", a free house serving food with a stream running through the garden. Ignore a footpath off to the right opposite the pub and shortly after, pass a cottage on your right, "Old Smugglers", a hint to the history of the village. Immediately after the cottage, turn right on to a drive signposted as a public footpath, leading to "Woodland" and "White" cottages.

Pass to the left of the cottages following the footpath signs, to join a narrow path ahead. Follow this, later ignoring a signposted turning off to your right. The path, which now becomes wider, follows an old stone wall on your right for approximately a third of a mile to reach a junction of tracks. Turn left here along a track, signposted as a public footpath. On meeting a lane turn right and then almost immediately left, to follow another track signposted public footpath through mixed woodland, Henley Copse, once part of Henley Common. Follow the track, ignoring a path off to your left, to eventually turn right in front of a timber yard, still in the direction of the public footpath sign. As the path continues it shares its route with the course of a stream and as such is extremely muddy. Thankfully, the stream soon disappears into a ditch on your right, shortly after which you should cross over another two streams before arriving again at the A286.

Cross the road and turn right passing a lovely farmhouse on your right offering B&B, "Dawes Farm". Soon after you will arrive at a drive way on your left leading to "Lassams Farm", signposted as a public footpath, which you should now take. Just before the farmhouse which is on your right, take a fork left across a green again signposted as a public footpath. This passes to the left of the farm pond complete with ducks and leaves the green to enter woodland, descending to cross a stream via a wooden bridge. Continue up the other side to meet a gravel drive way in front of two cottages. Turn left along the drive and on reaching a small tarmac lane, go straight across in the direction of the public footpath sign, passing in front of "Upper Lodge Cottage".

Continue for some distance to meet a large house on your right, "Stable Cottage", where you should turn left down a track, a public footpath. Ignore a track off to the left almost immediately after and continue straight on gradually descending to pass over a stream. Follow the path uphill now passing through a sweet chestnut coppice and on meeting a crossing track soon after, turn right to pass to the left of a pond. Thereafter, continue ahead, ignoring a turning uphill on your left to follow wooden fencing on your right.

You will soon meet a stile which you should cross into a field where you should turn left to follow the left hand perimeter going uphill. This field is particularly attractive in spring, being lined with rhododendron bushes. At the top of the field it is worth stopping for a rest and to take in the views behind over to Bexley Hill.

Cross a stile and continue ahead passing a footpath on your left to soon join a track which you should follow for approximately thirty paces. At a public footpath sign, fork left on to another track which leads along the side of Telegraph Hill through mixed woodland, mainly young conifers. Ignore all turnings off and follow the track which later bends left going steeply uphill. Half way up the hill, leave the track, turning right on to another track, signposted as a public footpath to follow the side of the hill. On your right the low hill topped by fir trees is Green Top Hill.

Go over a crossing track and continue straight on to shortly enter a conifer plantation. Behind you at this point are good views of Blackdown and Fernhurst village. Again ignore all turnings off to reach another track behind a house. This is the beginning of Older Hill. Continue straight on along the track, do not turn right, and ignore another turning on your left soon after. You will soon see "Older Hill Kennels" ahead to the right and then reach a "T" junction where you should turn left on to a narrow tarmac lane. Follow this back to the car park, our starting point.

ACCOMMODATION

The Spread Eagle, Midhurst. Tel: 073081 6911
Two miles from the walk, this is a fine 15th century hotel with a colourful past. A secret passage used by smugglers still exists. The bedrooms maintain the character of the building, which is addictive. You will return, I promise.

Dawes Farm, Fernhurst. Tel: 0428 652286
On the walk, this charming old farmhouse maintains in the evening the beauty of some of the historic countryside through which you have trodden. Ideal if you plan to do "The Wet Common Waddle" and "The Augustinian Amble" in one weekend.

Camping and Caravanning, Graffham, Great Bury. Tel: 07986 476
Seven miles from the walk, this is a Camping and Caravanning Club site situated in the heart of the beautiful Lavington Common. The site is well spread and it is easy to find a remote spot away from other campers, even when the site is busy.

THE BLUEBELL PUDDLE

Distance: 12¹/₂ miles (20 km)
Time: Allow approximately 6 hours, more if you wish
to visit the various points of interest en route.
Map: Ordnance Survey Landranger Map 187

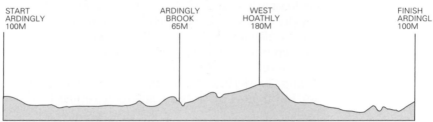

START	ARDINGLY	WEST	FINISH
ARDINGLY	BROOK	HOATHLY	ARDINGL
100M	65M	180M	100M

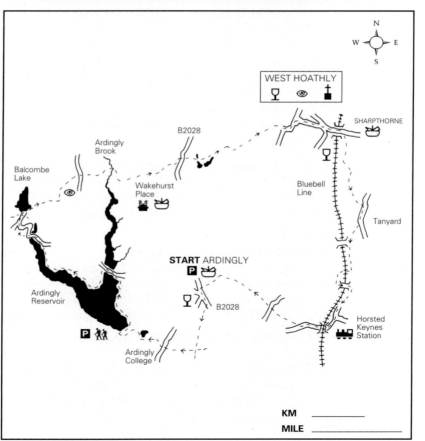

Walk Summary

The Bluebell Puddle is situated in the north east corner of the county, close to the borders of Surrey and Kent. Consequently, the countryside is more in keeping with those counties than the chalk downland one normally associates with West Sussex. As the title suggests, the walk is never far from water which dictates the appropriate footwear. The route also passes some magnificent properties and explores some of the lesser used paths in the county. As a finale you will follow the line of the Bluebell Railway, with its carefully restored steam engines.

Start - OS. 347295 Map 187

The walk starts in front of "The Ardingly Inn", opposite which there is a public car park. Ardingly is situated a few miles north of Haywards Heath on the B2028. Alternatively, you can start at the public car park for Ardingly Reservoir (OS. 334288 Map 187). The nearest railway stations are at Balcombe and Haywards Heath, both stations are on the well served London to Brighton line.

THE BLUEBELL PUDDLE

Before commencing the walk, it is worth getting to know the village at which we start and hopefully finish!

Ardingly (OS. 347295 Map 187) *is famous for its college and "Wakehurst Place", both later visited on our walk. The village church on the lane to Balcombe has some fine brasses to the Culpeper and Wakehurst families. One of the brasses is to Nicholas Culpeper, the brass records that this man had a wife, ten sons and eight daughters, which must be some kind of record. For lovers of cricket, Ardingly was the birthplace of Thomas Box one of the greatest wicket keepers of all time. For refreshments Ardingly has two good pubs, "The Ardingly Inn", a free house, and "The Oak", Pheonix. Both serve food and "The Ardingly Inn" also offers accommodation. As well as pubs, there is a cafe and a village stores which sells a wide range of provisions.*

From "The Ardingly Inn" cross College road which is to the left of the inn and pass the Ardingly Village sign, the site of the old toll house demolished in 1923. Turn right along the B2028, signposted to Lindfield and Haywards Heath. Shortly after passing Ardings Close on your left, turn right along a small lane or drive way signposted "Little Platte" and "Chinook". Follow this round to meet another sign to "Stable Cottage" and continue until the drive ends in front of a gate. Turn left at the gate, which at the time of writing is blue, to follow a hedged path to reach a stile.

Cross the stile and continue straight across a field, keeping to the left hand perimeter. There is a fine view ahead of you now of

53

Haywards Heath. At the far left hand corner, cross another stile and carry straight on, this time across the centre of a field. Pass over a concrete drive, still going straight on, to cross a stile beside a gate. Go across the next field in the direction of a public footpath sign, where as a rough guide you should follow the base of a very gentle valley with the more prominent slope on your right. Just before the end of the field near woodland, bear right to cross a stile ahead to follow the left hand perimeter of the next field, still in the direction of the public footpath sign. After approximately forty metres you will reach a stile on your left beside another footpath sign. Ignore this and turn right to go across the centre of the field.

At the far side of the field cross a stile beside a metal gate and continue straight ahead along a track through Sandgrove Wood. Ignore all joining and crossing paths and stay on the track to eventually arrive at some tennis courts and a small car park. Carry straight on to join a tarmac drive passing between the tennis courts, which belong to Ardingly College now in view ahead. Cross the road in front of the college and continue straight ahead to pass through the entrance gates.

i Follow the drive ahead to shortly pass a college information sign mapping out the grounds. Ardingly College was opened in 1870, its main feature being its chapel completed in 1833. The college was founded by Canon Woodward who also founded two other colleges, the most famous being at Lancing. Go straight on passing the main college buildings on your left and continue along the drive way as it bends round behind the college to shortly pass to the right of the Tuck shop. The drive then bears right to go downhill passing new accommodation blocks on your left to meet Saucelands pond with its picturesque cottage.

Stay on the drive passing to the left of the pond and follow it as it bends left in front of the cottage. You now follow the drive to its end which is at another cottage, where you should turn left over a stile to cross the centre of a field in the direction of the footpath sign. Go over another stile to arrive at a car park for visitors to Ardingly Reservoir, and head for the information sign.

i **Ardingly Reservoir (OS. 334288 Map 187)**, *as the sign will tell you was formed by the construction of an earth embankment across the southern part of Shell Brook, a tributary of the river Ouse which flows south east from the reservoir. The length of the dam is 920ft (280m), it can hold 1,050 million gallons (or 4,773 million litres). The waters conceal a Roman road and the old Ardingly mill which worked iron here from 1574 until the late 17th century.*

From the information sign, continue straight up the bank ahead of you to reach the edge of the reservoir with a valve tower, which regulates the flow of water, on your left. Turn right to follow the perimeter of the reservoir to eventually reach a road, where you should turn left. Follow the road over a bridge across the reservoir and at the other side, turn left again going over a stile and follow the perimeter of the reservoir once more, this time along a signposted public bridleway. The bridleway follows the perimeter of the reservoir for approximately one and a quarter miles to eventually rejoin the road.

At the road turn left and continue downhill to reach a small bridge with a flood gate separating the reservoir from a mill pond on your right. This is one of those forgotten corners of England and it is worth pausing to appreciate your surroundings. Stay on the road to reach "The Mill House" a rambling building completely at ease in its surroundings and look out for some steps going uphill on your left. Go up the steps taking time to look back over the pond and "The Mill House" and note as you ascend that some of the steps are actually old mill stones.

At the top, go over a stile and pass through a gate immediately on your right and then turn left to follow a marked public bridleway. This now takes you through woodland winding gently downhill and then uphill slightly to once again reach the road. Pass through a small wooden gate, cross the road and turn left to follow it and after a few steps, leave it as it bends left, turning right on to a drive way to "Woodward's Farm". This is also signposted as a public footpath. Ahead of you now is Balcombe Lake.

As you reach the lake, unless you want refreshments ignore a footpath and stile on your left which leads up to Balcombe village. Continue straight on following the drive with the lake on your left and go uphill where the drive changes from tarmac to concrete to run between fields. Follow the drive as it bears left until you reach a public footpath sign on your right. Turn right here with "Woodward's Farm" now in view and go over a stile beside a gate keeping to the left hand perimeter of a field. At the far left hand corner of the field turn left over another stile to continue straight across the centre of the next field, going gently uphill.

As you reach the brow of the hill veer right away from the farm buildings on your left and head towards three metal gates. At the gates, cross over a stile beside the centre gate and continue ahead following the footpath sign, along the right hand perimeter of a field. At the far side of the field you gain excellent views over Balcombe and its forest where several prehistoric skeletons were discovered. Go over another stile and straight on along a drive, do not turn left into the farm. Note the house on your right which has a miniature railway running through the garden.

The drive leads out to a lane on to which you should turn right and after approximately twenty paces, left over a stile. Follow the right hand perimeter of a field passing a large house, "The Oaks", on your right. There are good views ahead now of Tilgate Wood and the grounds of "Wakehurst Place". At the bottom right hand corner of the field turn left in the direction of the footpath sign, still following the field perimeter and at the next corner, turn right and descend to pass through a wooden gate. Go downhill along a narrow path through Tilgate Wood, which can be steep and slippery in places so care is needed.

At the bottom, cross two narrow wooden bridges over Ardingly Brook. The brook and its valley are particularly pretty and if you can stand the mosquitos it is a place worth stopping. The brook once maintained a mill and hammer pond and flows south to the consuming mass of Ardingly Reservoir. Go up the other side of the valley and follow the path which after a short distance, turns right to lead downhill again crossing a tributary to the brook. At the other side of the bridge you will see a footpath sign which informs you that you are entering Wakehurst estate, owned by the National Trust. You must keep to the footpath at all times as access to the gardens from this route is prohibited.

Continue uphill to reach a tall metal gate, part of the perimeter fencing for "Wakehurst Place". Pass through the gate to follow the footpath signs across the parkland uphill. Cross over a stile still going uphill and pass through another tall metal gate and continue ahead along a fenced footpath passing through a deer farm, the reason you now discover for the tall fencing and gates. Go through two more gates to reach a drive way with some cottages on your left and "Havelock Farm" on the right. Continue straight on following the drive which shortly bears left away from "Wakehurst Place", still signposted as a public footpath, to reach the main road the B2028, beside a cottage. If you wish to visit "Wakehurst Place", turn right along the road and first right again to reach the main entrance.

Wakehurst Place (OS. 339315 Map 187) *is a fine Elizabethan mansion built by Edward Culpeper in 1590. The house is now in the hands of the National Trust, who lease the estate to the Royal Botanic Gardens, Kew. The name "Wakehurst" is derived from the Saxon words "Wak" meaning "moist" and "Hyrst" meaning "wood". Before the Saxons, the area was well populated by people from the iron age period and later the Romans who had a road which ran through the*

estate from Aldrington to Croydon. The Wakehursts first moved here in 1205 and quickly established themselves as the most important family in the area. In the 15th century, Richard and Nicholas Culpeper (regarded by some Wakehursts as lesser stock) married the two heirs to the estate, Margaret and Elizabeth Wakehurst.

The estate consequently passed to the Culpepers and it was Edward Culpeper who built the current house. Generations of Culpepers continued to live there, the most famous being Nicholas Culpeper, the herbalist. His herbal studies started after the sudden death of his mistress. Rejecting the church he chose to study occult philosophy, based on Hermetica. He later joined the Society of Apothecaries and after years of studying, himself became an Apothecary. He went on to publish several books including "English Physician" and "Culpeper's Herbal", still popular today. Unlike the rest of his family, Nicholas spent most of his life in the East End of London where he died. Unfortunately, you cannot visit his grave as this is now covered by platform 11 of Liverpool Street Station.

Wakehurst Place later passed out of the Culpeper family when the last heir, William, sold it in 1694 to pay off his gambling debts. The estate finally passed into the hands of the National Trust as a donation on his death in 1963, by Sir Henry Price. He also left a considerable endowment. In 1965, the Trust leased the estate to the Royal Botanic Gardens and today one can visit the house and enjoy the gardens, both of which are a unique experience. Wakehurst Place also has a shop and a small restaurant which make it a convenient rest point.

To continue our route turn left along the busy B2028, taking great care as you go. Pass "Stonehurst Nursery" and continue on to meet two cottages on your right. Take the public bridleway, sometimes difficult to see, passing through a wooden gate between the two properties. Follow this downhill to arrive at a large track on to which you should turn left in the direction of the public bridleway sign. Ignore a track going off to the left which is marked "private" and continue on to meet another public bridleway sign, just prior to meeting a lake visible ahead. Turn left here passing beside a pond on your left and at a crossing track, ignore this to carry straight on staying on the public bridleway. You will now begin to climb up the side of a valley with a stream running through the valley bottom to your left.

The valley is both unusual and one of the most picturesque in this part of West Sussex. Either side rhododendrons fight with majestic trees for prominence, in early summer their flowers turning the valley into a celebration of colour. At the far side a huge sandstone rock face guards an ancient fort. It is protected on three sides by the rock face, the fourth by a ditch and bank over six feet high. The fort is believed to be Andreds Wald and was the site of a fierce battle between the Britons and the Saxons. Several primitive weapons were discovered at the base of the rocks. Amongst the rock buttresses, stands a rock known as "Big upon Little", so called because its huge bulk juts out from the cliff with seemingly nothing to support it.

The track becomes steeper as you go and eventually meets some houses, where you should ignore a footpath going off to the left. This path leads down into the valley and up beside the rock face to pass beside the hill fort. If you have time, its worth exploring this for a short distance. Our route however, follows the track which bends left, to pass between some fairly modern buildings belonging to "Philpots Manor School". Ignore a track going off to the right. Pass a red telephone box on your right and continue straight on heading for West Hoathly, the church spire of which is visible ahead.

The track continues for approximately three quarters of a mile, to meet a tarmac lane between two cottages. On the left though not easily visible is "Lower Barn", an old tithe barn now an amateur theatre. A tithe was the name given to one tenth of the total crop produced by a parish to support the church. Do not turn right, but carry straight on along the lane passing "West Hoathly Bowling Club" to enter West Hoathly itself.

West Hoathly (OS. 363326 Map 187) *stands proud on a hill overlooking the Weald, the spire from its church being a landmark for miles around. In Saxon times the village was known as "Hafocunga Leaghe" and with the coming of the Normans it changed to "Hoadelie". It was the Normans who built the present church in 1096, the church and the village being administered by the priory at Lewes. The monks had charge of the village for over four hundred years until the 16th century when the growth of the iron industry changed everything.*

Like everywhere else in the Weald, the seemingly never ending supply of timber was ideal for the furnaces required to smelt the iron. Until now, West Hoathly had been little more than a forest clearing with a few peasant farmers. The iron industry turned it into a bustling village, its forest receding as the trees were cut down for fuel. The local people resented their forced change of life and many scuffles broke out between the iron workers and the farmers.

Progress finally conquered and with it the money enabled people to

*build some fine houses, many remaining to this day. One of the
oldest and most interesting buildings in the village is "The Priest
House", which the monks built as an estate office in the mid 15th
century. The house is now a museum and for opening times
telephone: 0342 8104789. Another building of note is "The Manor
House", the next house on from "The Priest House". It was built in
1627 by the Infields, owners of several iron foundries, as a dower
house on the site of the original manor. Over the gate way are the
initials of James and Katharine Infield. The original manor once
belonged to Thomas Cromwell and when he was beheaded, Henry
VIII gave it to Anne of Cleves in an attempt to console her after
their divorce.*

*The church as you might expect, is not without interest. Inside one
can see the workings of the original clock, they are amongst the
oldest in the country being produced in the early 16th century.
Facing the church is the excellent "Cat Inn", Beards of Sussex,
which serves good beer and food in comfortable surroundings.*

Turn right in front of the inn and follow the lane to leave the
village. Where the properties on your left end go up some steps on
the same side and turn right to follow the public footpath above
the road. There are excellent views to your left here of the North
Downs and in places to your right, the South Downs. The church
spire nearest you in the distance on your left is Turners Hill. In
the woodland before this, is "The Gravetye Manor", built in 1598
by Richard Infield.

The path meets a small car park with allotments on your left. You
should continue straight on following the path passing the
allotments to shortly descend some steps to meet another road
and "The Vinols Cross Inn", a free house. Until the reformation
this crossroads was known as "Image Cross", the name "Image"
being forcibly changed to "Vinols", a local farming family. Cross
the road ahead and turn right passing to the left of the pub, to
follow the pavement downhill into Sharpthorne. Look out for a
small grass play area on your left with a round brick tower. The
tower is in fact a chimney/flue from a railway tunnel which runs
beneath you. At a garage on your right, turn right to pass
between the garage and The Royal British Legion Club. Behind
the club, look for a small footpath on the left which you should
follow, signposted as the West Sussex Border Path.

The footpath runs between hedges heading south and after some
distance meets a stile. Cross the stile into a field where there are
superb views ahead across the South Downs and on your right,
the church spire of High Brook. You may at times hear a forced

hissing sound, be reassured this is not a dragon but the steam trains of the Bluebell Railway! Go straight on keeping to the left hand perimeter of the field and descend to meet and cross a stile. Cross a farm track and go over another stile ahead to go straight across the next field.

At the end of the field cross a stile, bear right to go over a stream and then over another stile into a field. Go diagonally across the field to reach the far corner, where there are views behind across to West Hoathly and Sharpthorne. Go over a stile at the corner of the field and cross the next field keeping to the right of the trees in the centre. To your right is "Northwood House". On meeting a track at the other side of the field, look out for the public footpath sign at a stile which you should cross to go diagonally right across another field, heading for two disused brick farm buildings. At the far side, cross two small stiles into the next field and go straight on keeping to the right hand perimeter. Ahead to your left now is an old oast house.

The path you are on soon bends round to the right to meet a stile beside a metal gate. Go over the stile and turn left to go uphill along a narrow lane. On reaching a wider road beside a stone house, turn right and follow the road for approximately three hundred metres to pass "Saxons" which offers B&B. Just after "Saxons" look out for a white concrete drive way marked as a public footpath, opposite the entrance to "Tanyard". The footpath runs up beside "Vox End" and then past a stone outbuilding. After the outbuilding, turn left in the direction of the footpath sign to cross a stile into a field.

The path now follows the left hand perimeter of a number of fields linked by a series of stiles, to finally reach a stile beside a bridge over the Bluebell railway line. Do not cross the bridge but go across the lane and over a stile into a field, where you should continue straight on along the right hand perimeter with the railway line on your right. Approximately half way across the field look out for a footpath sign and stile on your right, which you should cross to go over the railway line, taking care to look in both directions first. Thereafter, turn immediately left to follow the railway until you meet a stile on your right. Incidentally, the hill on your left at this point is Cinder Hill, obviously a name given after the railway was built. Go over the stile and continue ahead to a gap in the hedge on your left and cross another stile on your left into a field. Keep to the left hand perimeter of the field looking out for a stile on your left, which you should cross to reach a wide fenced path.

Follow the path, almost going back on yourself, which leads uphill to a bridge. From the bridge you gain a good vantage point over Horsted Keynes station, usually busy with steam locomotives. Go over the bridge and ignore a path off to the right, to go into the station car park. Turn right through the car park and follow the track down to the station. Unfortunately, the train cannot take you back to the start of your walk, but a platform visit would be well worth the expense. Should you want more details on the Bluebell Railway and its timetable, telephone: 082 572 2370.

To continue our route pass to the left of the station and follow the road round to meet another road where you should turn right. It is safer to walk on the left hand verge of this road. Follow the road round passing under a bridge, ignoring a footpath off to the left, and continue through an "S" bend after which you should take the footpath signposted on the right. Cross the field going uphill in the direction of the public footpath sign and at the top of the field, pass through a gap in the hedge to continue straight on across the next field. The path here can be somewhat undefined and as a guide you should bear slightly right heading for the tree line ahead, to the left of which there is a signposted footpath.

Go over a stile and go straight on downhill to meet another stile. Cross this to go down a bank, crossing a stream and go up the other side bearing gently right. There is a pond on your left. You are now going through a private garden so take great care to follow the footpath signs to reach the other side, where you should turn right towards the house passing through a kissing gate on to a lane. Cross the lane and turn right proceeding uphill and after approximately twenty paces, turn left up some narrow steps. Go over a stile and continue straight ahead along the left hand perimeter of a field. As you continue a large property, "Brook House" comes into view.

At the far side of the field go through a kissing gate and carry straight on across the next field with "Brook House" on your left. As you near the far side of the field you will see a cricket pitch and pavilion on

Cricket Pavillion, Brook House

your left. Turn left through a kissing gate to arrive at the cricket pitch where there is seating offering a pleasant place to rest. Turn right to pass in front of the pavilion and leave the cricket pitch via another kissing gate to go straight across a field, following the right hand perimeter going downhill (west). Continue to meet a small wooden gate. Pass through the gate and continue downhill along a narrow path through woodland. At the bottom of the valley the path crosses the brook via an old brick bridge and goes through another kissing gate into an open field.

Continue straight on going uphill towards Ardingly and pass to the right of a house, "Withyland", immediately after which you should turn left through a small metal gate. Follow the path leading steeply uphill through woodland and shortly after, pass through another gate into a field. Here you have your last chance to look back at High Brook and its elegant church spire. Continue straight on uphill following the left hand perimeter of the field to pass through a kissing gate. Go over the next field with the houses of Ardingly (at last you might say!) now in view, to go through another kissing gate on to a tarmac drive. Follow the drive ahead to reach the High Street beside a sweet shop on your left. Turn left along the road to arrive at "The Ardingly Inn" and the car park from where our walk commenced.

ACCOMMODATION

The Ardingly Inn, Ardingly. Tel: 0444 892214
On the walk, a friendly inn run as a hotel set in the heart of Ardingly village. The inn is popular locally.

Saxons, Nr. Sharpthorne. Tel: 0342 810821
On the walk, this cottage is in a peaceful setting ideal for those looking for quiet. There are good views from your room which is comfortably furnished.

Youth Hostel, Crockham Hill YHA. Tel: 0732 866322
Fifteen miles from the walk, the hostel is a fine Victorian house in two acres of ground. Camping is also permitted.

Camping and Caravanning, Crowborough. Tel: 0892 664827
Ten and a half miles from the walk, this is a Caravan and Camping Club site situated on the edge of Ashdown Forest. Open in the summer only the site comes complete with squash and badminton courts, a swimming pool and fitness room - so you will not be bored. If all this sounds just a bit too much, Crowborough has some excellent pubs.

THE BOSHAM TACK

Distance: 12½ miles (20 km)
Time: Allow approximately 6 hours,
more if you are a boat watcher
Map: Ordnance Survey Landranger Map 197

| START
ITCHENOR
FERRY - Sea Level | BOSHAM
CHURCH
5M | WEST ITCHENOR
CHURCH
10M | FINISH
ITCHENOR
FERRY - Sea Level |

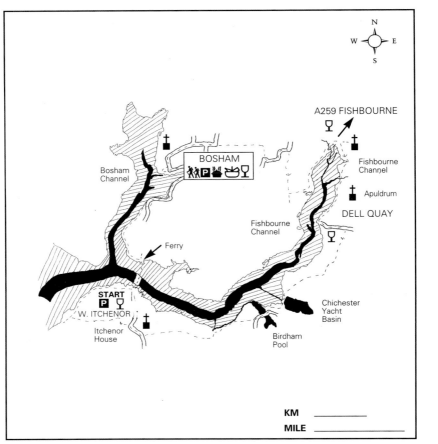

Walk Summary - Essential Reading!

The Bosham Tack is a walk which requires advanced planning. To complete the walk it is necessary to take a ferry from West Itchenor across the Chichester Channel. The ferry is seasonal so to be certain it is running, it is essential to check in advance. As a rough guide, the ferry runs from April to September at weekends and from July to August, daily. For timetable information, telephone: 0243 512479. As the name suggests, this is a walk which follows a coastal route, in fact the sea is rarely out of view. The route takes you around two of the creeks which form part of the famous Chichester harbour. You will be treading land which has always been at the forefront of the defence of Britain and the villages through which you pass, consequently have a colourful history. Unlike the other walks in the book, the Bosham Tack is without any hills however, do not under estimate it.

Start - OS. 799013 Map 197

The walk starts from West Itchenor village. To get there take the A286 from Chichester. At Birdham, ignore the B2198 and stay on the road which turns into the B2179. Shortly after this, take a turning on your right signposted to West Itchenor. The road leads to the village where there is a public car park. Alternatively, you can start at Bosham (OS. 806040 Map 197), where there is also a car park though be warned, this can get very congested. The nearest railway station is at Fishbourne.

THE BOSHAM TACK

Please ensure you park in the public car park. Leave the car park and turn right to reach the main road. Turn left and follow the road to reach the Harbour Office on the sea front.

West Itchenor (OS. 799013 Map 197). *The view from the harbour is of hundreds of small boats. This reflects the history of Itchenor which for centuries has been a harbour to vessels entering the Chichester Channel. The idyllic setting you see today was almost destroyed when in Georgian times, a businessman tried to turn the village into a ship building centre to rival Southampton. Unfortunately for him and thankfully for us, the first launch was a disaster and resulted in a serious accident. After this, the businessman gave up his ideas and Itchenor survived. For refreshment, there is "The Ship Inn", a free house which serves food, the bar as you might expect, is decorated with sailing memorabilia.*

At the sea front, take the ferry from the end of the jetty (do not mistake the boat tours for the ferry, or you will end up following your route by sea!). If you cannot find the ferryman, ask around. At low tide the ferry will drop you off at a causeway which you follow inland to reach the shore line. Be prepared to get your feet wet! At high tide you will be dropped at the beach.

At the other side, turn left to follow the coastline round heading for Bosham. (If however, the tide is in, follow the signposted public footpath inland beside a Chichester Harbour Conservancy sign. Follow the path until you reach a road and then follow the road ahead for three quarters of a mile, to rejoin the coast opposite Bosham). Assuming the tide is low, follow the coastline inland along the Bosham Channel. The channel is a haven for water birds which live comfortably with the yachts. Amongst the most common, are curlews, oyster catchers, shell duck, brent geese and the noisy blackheaded gull. Bosham village will soon come into view and beyond it, Kingley Vale. Pass a small jetty before reaching a road in front of a house (this road is the alternative high tide route mentioned earlier). Continue ahead on the road following the coastline, where again at high tide when the road is flooded, there are signposted footpaths running slightly inland, behind houses.

Follow the road or footpath depending on the tide, right round the end of the channel to reach the centre of Bosham village. At low tide, there is a safe causeway which you can take across the mudflats cutting out some of the distance.

Bosham (OS. 805038 Map 197) *although small has a history that most cities would be proud of. So much so, that I can only touch on it here and if you want to know more, I suggest you buy a local guide book.*

Bosham or "bozzum", as the locals pronounce it, has for centuries been a main guardian of the channel that leads almost to Chichester's heart. Around the time of the Spanish Armada, Bosham's importance was so great that it was even granted an Admiral to oversee the defence of the channel. The first settlers to make Bosham a place of some importance were the Romans, who reputedly built a palace here for Vespasion himself. After the Romans, the Saxon King Canute built his palace here and it is at Bosham that Canute is said to have tried to hold back the sea. Another famous Saxon, King Harold, sailed from Bosham for his disastrous visit to the Duke of Normandy, which ultimately led to the Norman invasion and Harold's death. The famous Bayeux tapestry depicts Harold travelling to Bosham and praying for the success of this journey.

The village church is one of the oldest in West Sussex and stands on the site of a Roman Basilica. The church today is mostly Saxon, Bosham being one of the first villages in Sussex to accept Christianity. The Venerable Beed, an eminent churchman of the 7th century, described in his book a small monastery in Bosham run by an Irish monk, Dicul, who worked hard to convert the local population.

During renovation work in 1865, a small stone coffin was discovered which is strongly believed to be that of King Canute's eight year old daughter. In 1954, further renovation work uncovered another Saxon coffin, this one containing the bones of a powerfully built man who had suffered from arthritis. It is highly probable that this was Earl Godwin, King Harold's father. After the excavations, the coffins were replaced in their original position and the site repaved.

Like most ports, Bosham comes complete with an excellent pub in "The Anchor Bleu", which is a free house and being a tourist centre, there are also a number of small shops and cafes where you can restock.

View of Bosham

On reaching the main road through the village, Bosham Lane, which literally ends at the shore, cross this to take a narrow road beside a tea room on your left. Continue to shortly pass the Post Office on the right and then "The Anchor Bleu". After the pub, bear right passing to the left of Bosham church to arrive at Quay Meadow, a pleasant green overlooking the creek with an old mill and mill stream. The meadow belongs to the National Trust and is a peaceful place to rest awhile. Return through the church yard to leave this via two iron gates east of the church and continue along a shaded fenced path to rejoin Bosham Lane beside "Bosham Walk", an Arts and Crafts Centre.

Turn left at Bosham Lane and follow the road heading away from Bosham village. Keep to the road as it bends right in front of "The Mill Stream Hotel" and continue to later pass "The Berkley Arms"

pub, a Gales pub which serves food. Stay on the road ignoring all turnings off until it finally bends left, where you should leave it to continue ahead along a track beside the entrance to "Rectory Farm", signposted as a public footpath. The track leads to a field where you should continue ahead along the right hand perimeter, with glass houses on your left. This whole area as far as Lancing, is famous for its glass house industry. The first glass house, or greenhouse, was at Worthing, built from glass left over from the construction of the ill fated Crystal Palace. This new form of gardening attracted visitors from all over Europe and the idea quickly caught on.

i

The path continues in a straight line to reach a line of poplar trees which you should follow, ignoring a signposted footpath off to your left. As you progress, there are good views left of Kingley Vale and ahead, the spire of Chichester Cathedral. At the end of the poplar trees, the path meets a private road which you should cross continuing straight on along a wide track. After approximately one hundred metres, turn right along another track signposted as a public footpath, heading towards "Stonewall Farm" which is visible. You are now walking between two spires, that of Bosham church on your right and Chichester Cathedral on your left.

Pass through a gate in front of "Stonewall Farm" to meet a lane where you should turn left. Follow the lane which bends left and then right until you meet a large white house. Turn right at the house to pass to the left of "Beggars Roost" along a signposted footpath. Continue ahead to reach a field and there carry straight on in the direction of the footpath sign, across the field heading for a hedgerow in front of you. Go the left of the hedgerow following the right hand perimeter of the field to later skirt a pond.

At the far side of the field turn left ignoring a footpath off to your right and continue along the right hand perimeter of the field, which eventually gives way to mud flats beside Fishbourne Channel. Follow the path as it bears left along the shore line to go over a small wooden bridge crossing a small inlet. After a short distance, the path leaves the mud flats to go along the top of a man made dyke. From here you will enjoy some of the best views yet across the water of Chichester Cathedral. You will later enter a nature reserve where the path drops to run alongside the dyke.

At the far end of the channel follow the path as it bears right to cross a small footbridge and enter a pleasant area of tall rushes. Follow the path through the rushes from where there will occasionally be a rustle or deep quack, reminding you that the rushes are home to a wide variety of birds. The path leaves the rushes to arrive at a mill pond and Mill Lane. The old mill is on your right overlooking the pond. Should you require refreshments, turn left here along Mill Lane into Fishbourne where you will find "The Bull's Head" pub, a free house serving food and also offering accommodation. Though you will not have time to visit now, Fishbourne has a Roman palace which is well worth coming back to see.

Our route however, is across the lane to pass through a kissing gate and join a signposted public footpath also signposted to Fishbourne church. The path follows a mill stream on your left and after a short distance, passes through another kissing gate to reach Fishbourne Meadows. These meadows were once part of the Roman harbour associated with Fishbourne palace to the north. When later reclaimed they would have been used for grazing and hay.

At an information sign for Fishbourne Meadows, bear right over a small wooden plank bridge, heading back towards the coastline thereby leaving the footpath to Fishbourne church. After a short distance, go over a larger bridge and pass through a kissing gate into a field where you should continue straight on with the coastline on your right. On meeting an inlet, go up some steps and cross over a stile to follow the top of the dyke as it bears right. Ignore a footpath off to your left which is a route to Fishbourne church, and follow the dyke around the inlet to take the next footpath left leaving the dyke and going over a stile. Go straight across a field to rejoin the dyke at the other side. Continue ahead, again along the top of the dyke heading for Del Quay which is visible in front of you, to later pass over a stile into a field. Ignore another footpath off to your left.

Go across the field where at the other side, there is a footpath left which leads to Apuldram church which I recommend you visit. (Should you wish to do this, take the footpath left to pass through a small gate. Go straight on along the right hand perimeter of a field to reach the church - you will have to retrace your steps to rejoin our route).

Apuldram (OS. 842032 Map 197) *is basically a church and two houses, "Manor House Farm" and "Rymans", the village that* *surrounded them having disappeared. Originally, Apuldram was the centre of the salt pan industry which at its height, had over three hundred salt pans in Sussex. This started in Roman times and lasted at Apuldram right up until the mid 19th century. The salt pans immediately surrounding Apuldram covered as much as three acres.*

"Rymans" has a squat medieval tower which has an interesting story attached to it. This was built in 1410 by William Ryman. At the time Ryman was building the tower, the Bishop of Chichester was trying to raise money to build a bell tower for Chichester Cathedral. Struggling to find the cash, the Bishop saw his opportunity in Ryman's tower. He contacted the King and suggested that a fortified residence in the area was against the country's interests. The King agreed and stopped the construction of the tower and left with a lot of unwanted stone, Ryman was then persuaded to donate the stone to the Cathedral. The resulting Cathedral bell tower is still known as Ryman's Tower.

The church at Apuldram dates from the early 12th century and was almost rebuilt around 1250 AD. It was built on the site of an old burial mound.

Our route however, is not left, but straight on through a gap in the hedge into the next field to follow the right hand perimeter. At the time of writing, the farmer had planted a line of trees - our route passing between the newly planted trees on the left and the coast on the right. At the end of the field go over a stile and continue ahead along the water's edge to later run between a boat yard and the water to arrive at Del Quay.

Del Quay (OS. 835028 Map 197) *was made the main port for Chichester by the Romans, a position which it held until 1822 when a canal was opened bypassing Del Quay to reach the river Arun at Ford. At its height, Del Quay was the ninth most important port in England and sent two ships to beat off the Armada. For this service, Queen Elizabeth I granted Del Quay special harbour rights. The main reason for the construction of the canal was the poor access overland to Del Quay from Chichester. This has not changed and I advise you not to bring your car here!*

i

Sailors being a thirsty lot, one of Del Quay's few buildings is a pub. This is "The Crown and Anchor", Chef & Brewer, which overlooks the harbour.

Turn left up the road to pass to the left of the pub and follow the road inland for approximately a quarter of a mile, until you meet two drive ways either side of the road. Turn on to the right-hand drive, which is signposted as a public footpath and follow it until you reach "New Barn Farm". Pass to the right of the farm house and continue straight on on a track along the left hand perimeter of a field.

The track eventually becomes a fenced path running between fields and later enters woodland, Salterns Copse, which is managed by Apuldram's "Manor Farm". Ignore a turning off to your right and continue straight on to arrive at a small car park beside the Chichester Yacht Basin. Go straight on and cross the lock ahead via the footbridge, where you may have to wait a few minutes until the lock gates are closed. At the other side, follow the road ahead until it bends left beside a canal. This is the Chichester Canal which put Del Quay out of business. It was designed by John Rennie, its purpose to form the last link in a one hundred and sixteen mile waterway from London to Portsmouth. The canal opened in 1822 and remained in operation until 1855 when the railways took over.

Leave the road here and turn right in the direction of the public footpath sign, following the canal on your left and passing the Chichester Yacht Club on your right. Follow the path left over the canal by way of the lock gates, Saltern Lock, which is still operational. At the other side of the lock follow the narrow path ahead which leads into a small car park. Follow the buildings on your right and after the last building, turn right along a narrow footpath to meet a lane. Go straight across the lane following the signs to Birdham Pool and Shipyard.

Follow the narrow lane between two ponds, Birdham Pool, where there is an old tide mill (a mill with its wheel turned by the tide), said to be haunted by a ghost "Old Stevens". Pass the boat yard and as the lane bends round to the left, leave it to turn right on a drive way signposted as a public footpath and also "Harbour Meadow". Follow the drive and leave it soon after to turn left on to a signposted public footpath, which runs along the right hand perimeter of a field. The views to your left here are of Birdham village and church.

At the far end of the field the path runs alongside a brick wall to reach a lane where there are good views across the water to Itchenor, our starting point. Cross the lane and continue ahead along a fenced footpath running in front of some magnificent sea view properties. After a short distance, the path runs inland between the properties and then bears right to reach a road. Continue straight on along the road and follow it as it bends left to meet a "T" junction. Turn right at the "T" junction and ignore a footpath off to the left, to pass through a wide gate ahead on to a concrete drive, still going straight on. The drive leads to "Westlands Farm" which sells free range eggs.

Follow the drive to reach the farm and then pass between the farmhouse and a small pond to follow a track which leads into a field. Cross the field along the left hand perimeter ignoring a footpath going diagonally right. At the far side of the field, pass through a gap in the hedge and continue straight on along the left hand perimeter of the next field. The path you are on shortly becomes the dividing line between two fields. At the far end you will arrive to the left of a large barn where you should continue straight on staying on the path to reach a road. Turn right along the road and pass Itchenor church on your right. The church was built in the 13th century and contains a magnificent 13th century font. The church sits on a low mound which in the 17th century, did not stop the local farm animals from almost destroying the graveyard.

Just after the church leave the road turning left on to a drive way to "Itchenor Park", also signposted as a public footpath. Follow the drive which shortly bends round to the right, immediately after which you should pass through a gate on the left and turn right to follow a fenced path. At the end of the path go over a stile to rejoin the concrete drive way where you should turn left to pass to the rear of "Itchenor Park House", hidden behind trees. After the house, pass a cricket pitch on your left and stay on the drive, which becomes a farm track, until it bends left. Here, you should leave the track to turn right over a stile and cross a field following the left hand perimeter.

At the far side of the field, cross another stile and turn right to follow the shoreline back to Itchenor. Just prior to Itchenor itself, the path meets and crosses Chichester boat yard, to join a narrow footpath back to Itchenor harbour front. This last stretch is one of the nicest parts of the Chichester Channel coastline and is a pleasant way to end a most enjoyable walk.

ACCOMMODATION

The Mill Stream Hotel, Bosham. Tel: 0243 573234
On the walk, the Mill Stream Hotel as its name suggests, has a mill stream running through its garden. The setting is very relaxing.

The Ship Inn, West Itchenor. Tel: 0243 512284
On the walk, this comfortable and popular inn allows you, unlike day visitors, to enjoy the harbour at night when the boats are moored and the sea takes on a different feel.

Youth Hostel, Arundel YHA, Warningcamp.
Tel: 0903 882204

Sixteen miles from the walk, this is a large hostel located in a Georgian house set in spacious grounds. The village is very peaceful, but should you want more it is but a short walk along the banks of the river Arun to Arundel. Camping is also permitted.

Camping and Caravanning, Nunnington Farm,
West Wittering. Tel: 0243 514013

Two miles from the walk, this is a convenient site well run and in attractive surroundings.

A STING IN THE TAIL

Distance: 12½ miles (20 km)
Time: Allow approximately 6 hours, more if you
are short of stamina
Map: Ordnance Survey Landranger Map 197

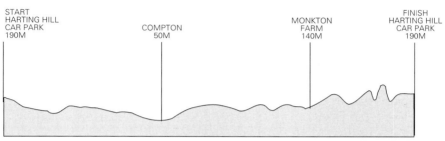

START
HARTING HILL
CAR PARK
190M

COMPTON
50M

MONKTON
FARM
140M

FINISH
HARTING HILL
CAR PARK
190M

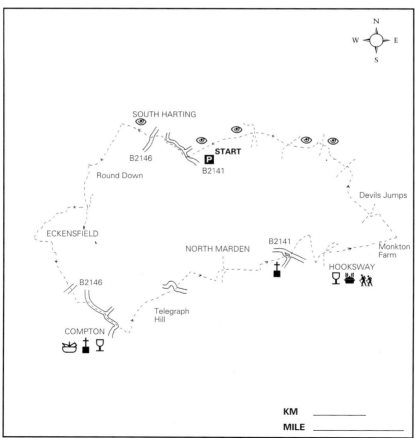

SOUTH HARTING

START
P

B2146

B2141

Round Down

Devils Jumps

ECKENSFIELD

NORTH MARDEN

B2141

Monkton
Farm

HOOKSWAY

B2146

Telegraph
Hill

COMPTON

KM

MILE

Walk Summary

A Sting in the Tail takes you through some of the most picturesque downland scenery in West Sussex. For some of the route you follow the escarpment of the South Downs via the South Downs Way. The majority of the route however, leaves the well known to explore the little known paths which connect some of the remotest hamlets in south east England. The route is fairly easy going until the end, when you negotiate Beacon Hill and the Harting Downs which will put your fitness to the test, hence the walk's title. The effort is not however, without reward.

Start - OS. 791181 Map 197

The walk starts from the National Trust car park at the top of Harting Down. The car park is signposted "Viewpoint" off of the B2141, one mile south of South Harting. An alternative starting point and a good one if you want to get the "sting" over first, is the hamlet of Hooksway (OS. 815162 Map 197). The nearest railway stations are at Petersfield or Chichester.

A STING IN THE TAIL

From the National Trust car park at the top of the hill walk straight ahead to the edge of the hill overlooking South Harting. The view is immediately breathtaking. The three counties of Hampshire, Surrey and West Sussex lay at your feet, dominated in the foreground by the tall slender spire of St. Mary's, South Harting. From this position it is easy to see why the church shares the title "Cathedral of the Downs". *Although we do not visit South Harting, it is worth a mention and has three good hostelries should you require refreshments at the end of your walk. The village which is large and airy compared to many of its neighbours is much noted for its literary associations. Gilbert White of Selbourne owned several properties around Harting and in 1880, Anthony Trollope move here in the hope that it might relieve his asthma. Unfortunately, he enjoyed Harting for just two years finding time to write four novels before his death in 1882. His grave can be seen at St. Mary's church yard.* Now determined to explore South Harting at the end of the walk, turn left along a wide grass track, heading west, to follow the South Downs Way, which is signposted.

Follow the track as it enters woodland to shortly meet a road, the B2141, which you should cross and follow the path the other side. This descends slowly through woodland overlooking the B2141 to meet another road, the B2146, which you should again cross to join a track ahead, still the South Downs Way. Stay on the track as it bends round to the left, do not be tempted to continue on the footpath ahead. The track continues between fields, ascending gradually, where behind you there are good views of a ruined tower on the appropriately named Tower Hill. This is simply a folly and is in the grounds of "Uppark House".

At the top of the hill ignore a path on your right to continue straight ahead along the South Downs Way. There are continuous good views to your right and just below to the north of South Harting, is a low unusually shaped hill. This is Torberry Hill once an iron age hill fort. Local legend would have you believe that the hill was formed by a spoon belonging to the devil.

The track begins to descend where you should then take the first turning left over a stile, thereby leaving the South Downs Way. Turn right after the stile for approximately twenty paces to turn left at a public footpath sign over another stile and follow a narrow and very pretty path through woodland, which acts as a windbreak between two fields. In spring and early summer the floor is a carpet of lily of the valley and ramsons.

The path eventually meets and crosses a stile, a farm track and then a second stile to continue straight on. On your left now is a slope with more dense woodland which soon gives way to a large field. The path now runs along a fairly steep slope before meeting another stile. Go over the stile and follow the footpath sign ahead along a wide track which curves gently right. Ahead of you at this point is West Harting Down, a wooded hill owned by the Forestry Commission.

Ramsons

Pass a small man-made pond on your left and then the remains of an old flint wall to continue ahead along the right hand perimeter of a field heading for West Harting Down. You will shortly leave the field to enter woodland, where you should take the track on the left signposted as a public footpath. After approximately thirty paces you will join another track marked as a public bridleway, where you should bear left to continue straight on. The track you are on now climbs slowly uphill with fields just visible through the trees on your left. Ignore a path off to your left which, as a point of interest, leads you to "Uppark", a National Trust Property.

i **Uppark (OS. 780177 Map 197)** *like South Harting is not strictly on the walk, but is worth a mention and well worth a visit if you are staying in the area. "Uppark House" is a fine brick building, of which you will have good views later in the walk and was designed by Talmer a pupil of Inigo Jones. It was built by the Earl of Tankerville in the 17th century and in 1745, purchased by Mathew Fetherstonhaugh, who made it the seat of his family. The house has two famous associations, Lady Hamilton lived here for a while and Sarah Wells, mother of H.G. Wells, worked here as a housekeeper. Her son only stayed at "Uppark" for a short time in his 14th year, but in that time produced a paper which he called "The Uppark Alarmist". Later H.G. Wells used "Uppark" as a model in his work "Tono Bungay", changing the name of the house to "Bladesover". The house unfortunately, was partially destroyed by fire in 1989 and is currently under restoration.*

Unless you wish to visit the property, our route continues straight on to reach a metal gate. Pass through this and cross a semi-tarmacced track to continue ahead, passing through a green metal gate to follow a grass track marked as a public bridleway. After approximately a quarter of a mile, you will reach a junction of tracks where you should turn right following the public bridleway sign. This track passes through woodland and crosses a shallow valley until it meets a "T" junction where you should turn left. Immediately after, at a fork, take the right hand track and follow this as it veers right to climb very gradually uphill enjoying good views of the surrounding area. As the track begins to descend again ignore a track on your right and continue straight on to reach the small hamlet of Eckensfield, consisting of two houses and a converted barn.

At a "T" junction turn left to pass in front of the converted barn and follow the lane to later bend right and then left between fields. It is worth stopping occasionally to look back at the view and the picturesque hamlet of Eckensfield. As a point of interest, the land beyond (to the west of Eckensfield) used to belong to "Lady Holt Park". The house which has long since disappeared used to belong to the writer John Caryll. It was in the park that Galley an excise officer, was brutally murdered by the Hawkhurst Gang in 1747 (see "Smugglers Seven").

Shortly after the lane has bent left, turn right over a stile to join a marked footpath. Cross a narrow field to go over another stile and continue ahead following the left hand perimeter of the next field. Compton Down is now visible directly ahead. At the far left hand corner of the field, cross a stile passing through undergrowth to go over a second stile into a field. Go straight across the field heading just to the left of the bottom of Compton Down. The farm visible in the valley on your right is "Cowdown Farm", its name describing the area perfectly.

At the far end of the field go over a stile to cross a narrow lane and a second stile ahead into a field. Continue diagonally left across the field to cross a stile at the far side. You will then cross a lane and yet another stile ahead into another field. Go straight on across the field going downhill to meet the base of Compton Down. On nearing the fence on your left, follow this to reach a farm gate where you should turn left over a stile to continue along the right hand perimeter of a field. At the end of the field, cross over a stile to meet a road, the B2146. Turn right and follow the road for approximately half a mile into the very pretty village of Compton.

Compton (OS. 778148 Map 197) *lies either side of the B2146 with a small green at one end and a square with a well at the other. Like all good villages the local pub is situated close to the church. It is believed the original church was Saxon, though the building you see today is Norman with much 19th century renovation. The village surprisingly for its size, has two schools. For refreshments there is the village stores or if you feel the need to treat yourself, try "The Coach and Horses", a free house offering a wide variety of good beer and well prepared food.*

i
t
■
Ψ
🍺

On reaching the small village green, follow the road round to the right in the direction of the signs to Chichester and West Marden, ignoring a turning on the left. The road passes through Compton village to meet the local pub, "The Coach & Horses", where you should turn left thereby leaving the B2146. Follow the lane which passes in front of the pub and to the right of "Compton Village Stores". Immediately thereafter, take the right hand fork (the left fork leads to the church only) and follow this to pass Compton Up Marden school on your right to then join a public bridleway ahead. On your left at this point is an entrance to Compton church. Our route however, follows the bridleway gradually uphill to reach a junction of tracks. Here you should bear left to cross a stile ahead and go uphill along a narrow path. You will shortly reach a track, a public bridleway, on to which you should turn left.

The bridleway hugs the wooded side of Telegraph Hill to eventually reach a field where you should follow the left hand perimeter continuing straight on to meet a track coming from the summit of Telegraph Hill beside a long mound. The mound is a neolithic long barrow some 210m long used by early man to bury their dead. The mound has long caught the locals imagination and legend has it that this is the thumb of a local giant, hence the name Bevis' Thumb, which is even printed on the Ordnance

i

Survey map. There is a hill east of Bevis' Thumb also with a mound on top, called Apple Down, the odd mound this time being nothing more than a modern day reservoir.

Cross over a lane and continue ahead to go over a stile beside a farm gate and follow the right hand perimeter of a large field, in the direction of the public bridleway sign. There are good views now to your left of Uppark Hill and "Uppark House". Approximately two thirds of the way across the field, look out for a footpath signposted on the right. Cross over a stile to join this and follow the left hand perimeter of a field, where there are more good views ahead to your right of Apple Down and below it "Fernbeds Farm". At the far left hand corner of the field cross over a stile slightly to your right, to follow a small path round to the left and cross a second stile into a field. Go across the field, keeping to the left hand perimeter, to reach the far left hand corner where you should cross another stile. Turn immediately left along the perimeter of the field and continue for approximately 150 metres to reach a public footpath sign pointing right. Follow this to cross the field going diagonally left and at the far side, go over a stile to follow a narrow path through woodland. This winds between trees which thin out to form a windbreak between fields.

Stay on the path as it descends and when the tree line breaks and three fields meet, continue straight on. Should the footpath be too overgrown or less prominent, then simply follow the perimeter of the field on your left. On the same side now are good views of "Telegraph House", at one time a semaphore station and later owned by Earl Russell, Minister of Transport during the First World War. His brother later turned the house into a school. At the end of the field, ignore a footpath sign going off to your right and continue straight on to cross a stile into another field following the right hand perimeter. Ahead of you is the small hamlet of North Marden, our next destination.

On reaching the right hand corner of the field, go over a stile and continue straight ahead to cross a long narrow field. At the far side, turn left to follow the right hand perimeter of the field in the direction of the public footpath sign and after approximately 50 metres just before the end of the field, turn right. Follow the public footpath sign, to cross a stile and go uphill along the left hand perimeter of another field. The footpath leaves the field via a metal gate and continues through a farmyard to reach the gate to North Marden church.

i
†
■

North Marden (OS. 808161 Map 197) *is one of the smallest hamlets in West Sussex, it is also one of the most remote. There has probably never been more than thirty people living here and this*

*century it has not risen much above ten. It is therefore, quite
surprising that this small cluster of dwellings has such a beautiful
and well preserved church. The church which is unusual in that the
chancel ends in a semi-circle, was probably built in the 12th century
from Caen stone. The beauty of this church and its setting is well
worth taking time to absorb and it is easy to see why the small band
of local parishioners continuously work to preserve its charm.*

Pass through the gate into the church yard and turn right to
follow the path between fences to reach a farm track on to which
you should turn left. The farm track leads to a small road where
you should turn right for a short distance. As the road bends right
and after the last outbuilding on your left, turn left up an
unmarked path leading to the main road, the B2141.

Cross the B2141 with care and continue straight ahead along a
fenced public footpath between fields. This eventually leads to a
track on to which you should turn right to wind slowly downhill
until you meet a lane. At the lane, its worth taking time to stop and
enjoy the views ahead of a particularly attractive valley and beyond,
St. Roches Hill. Turn left to follow the lane downhill to the small
hamlet of Hooksway and "The Royal Oak" pub, a popular free house
serving food. If you are really hungry there is also a restaurant
called "The Hideaway", though judging by the number of people who
flock here at the weekend, it could be called "The Discovery".

Pass through the hamlet passing the pub and restaurant on your
left, after which you will meet three paths the far right of which is
our route, marked as a public footpath. This is not immediately
visible so take care in selecting the correct route. Follow the path
through woodland going steeply uphill, the path later narrowing
before widening again. Soon after, take care to look out for a
signposted footpath on your left which you should follow. As a
guide, the footpath now follows close to a field on your left. The
distance from Hooksway to this point is approximately one mile.

Follow the path as it narrows again winding through woodland to
join a wider path coming in from the right. Do not turn right but
continue straight on to reach a kissing gate through which you
should pass into a field. Go along the left hand perimeter of the
field following the public footpath sign and at the far side, pass
through a metal gate to continue along the left hand perimeter of
the next field. There are now good views on a clear day to your
right, of Chichester Cathedral spire. At the corner of the field, go
over a stile and continue downhill into a picturesque valley
heading towards a flint outbuilding, "Monkton Farm". Turn left in
front of the outbuilding and follow a wide track to go over a stile
beside a metal gate. On your right a fenced enclosure hides the
ruins of "Old Monkton".

i **Old Monkton (OS. 830164 Map 197)** *was once a medieval settlement now protected and a nature reserve. It originally belonged to the monks of Waverley Abbey, being served by the chapel of Chelegrave until the mid 17th century. The settlement had a well which was accessed by a donkey wheel. The woodland running along the side of the valley hides the terraces which were created for growing vegetables. The settlement was finally deserted around the late 16th or early 17th century, except for one farm which lasted the ravages of time until the First World War when it was sadly demolished.*

Continue along the track which once served the settlement, along the bottom of the valley heading west. Shortly after passing through a metal gate into a field, turn left to follow the left hand perimeter fencing in the direction of the public footpath sign. At the corner of the field, pass over a stile beside a gate and follow the track ahead for a short distance to meet a crossing track. Unless you wish to visit the Devils Jumps (a series of burial mounds) which are right, continue straight on going over the crossing track and follow the signs for the South Downs Way. The track now passes through woodland which was particularly badly hit during the storm of 1987, the only benefit being the superb views to your left.

i Continue straight on to shortly pass a small flint memorial to a pilot, Hauptmann Joseph Oestermann, and as the track descends ignore another wide track off to the left, staying on the South Downs Way. Soon after, the track forks and either route is acceptable as they later rejoin. The track goes down the side of Treyford Hill and then bends left gradually climbing again to reach a "T" junction. Turn left and then first right, passing through a small wooden gate to join a narrow fenced path between fields, still following the South Downs Way.

At the end of the field, ignore a bridleway on your right to continue ahead. Your route now takes you slowly uphill, marked all the way as the South Downs Way, to bend right following the perimeter of a field. There are good views as you go of Treyford village at the foot of the downs. The path meets a small crossroads where you should continue ahead, still following the perimeter of the field and then meets another smaller junction where you should bear left. You should now follow the South Downs Way signs all the way to the top of Pen Hill.

On reaching the top you are confronted with the beginning of "the sting in the tail", the descent and the steep climb straight up the other side to the top of Beacon Hill, 795ft. After resting awhile to gather your breath and recover from the shock, follow the South

Downs Way to the bottom of the valley and then leave it to half walk and half climb up the side of Beacon Hill. You soon begin to realise why iron age man chose this hill as a site for a fort. The panoramic view from the top of the hill is however, reward enough for the effort. A direction finder (a memorial to Nicholas Bothwell) helps you to spot local landmarks. Blackdown to the north, Stoner and Butser Hills, South Harting and Petersfield to the west. Kingley Vale, Chichester Harbour and Portsmouth to the south and the South Downs escarpment to the east.

From the trig point and direction finder take the main path ahead to pass through a wooden gate and descend steeply down the side of Beacon Hill. This can be extremely slippery in wet weather and you will regret it if you haven't got good footwear. At the bottom you will reach a junction of tracks where you should continue straight ahead, at this point rejoining the South Downs Way. Do not turn left at the junction on to the South Downs Way or you could find yourself retracing your route! Follow the track straight ahead to climb East Harting Down and continue along the top of Harting Downs admiring the views as you go. This eventually leads you to the car park and our starting point.

ACCOMMODATION

The South Downs Hotel, Rogate. Tel: 0730 821521
Five and a half miles from the walk, this is a large comfortable hotel complete with croquet lawn, indoor swimming pool, sauna and gym. If exercise seems too much like hard work after your exertions on the downs, the hotel has a large bar in which to relax and a good restaurant to restock.

Compton Farmhouse, Compton. Tel: 0705 631597
On the walk, this large flint farmhouse has a beautiful setting beside a village church. Apart from a pleasant bedroom, accommodation includes a private sitting room.

Youth Hostel, Arundel YHA, Warningcamp.
Tel: 0903 882204
Twenty one miles from the walk, this is a large hostel located in a Georgian house set in spacious grounds. The village is very peaceful, but should you want more it is but a short walk along the banks of the river Arun to Arundel. Camping is also permitted.

Camping, Goodwood Club Site, Singleton. Tel: 0243 774486
Ten miles from the walk, this is a Caravan Club run site which has a superb position beside the Goodwood racecourse. The site is open during the summer months though closed on race days, so check ahead.

THE TWO CASTLE WAY

Distance: 13 miles (21 km)
Time: Allow approximately 7 hours, more if
you wish to stop at one of the many
excellent pubs en route
Map: Ordnance Survey Landranger Map 197

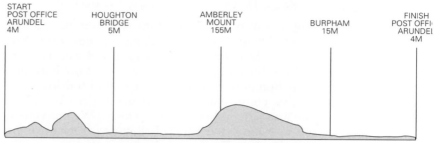

START
POST OFFICE
ARUNDEL
4M

HOUGHTON
BRIDGE
5M

AMBERLEY
MOUNT
155M

BURPHAM
15M

FINISH
POST OFFI
ARUNDE
4M

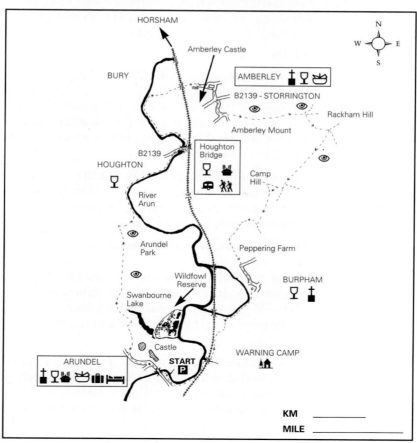

Walk Summary

The Two Castle Way literally connects two castles, that of Arundel and Amberley. The first half of the walk follows in the main, the river Arun, whilst the second half returns over the downs following tracks which are centuries old. The walk is surrounded by history as well as beauty and never fails to surprise. The going can be a real contrast between seasons. In summer the paths are dried and cracked and tire the feet, whereas in winter you may often find yourself ankle deep in mud. Refreshments are readily available with local hostelries conveniently situated along the way. Don't however, forget the climb up Amberley Mount. A touch too much of the local brew and this hill can seem like Everest!

Start - OS. 019070 Map 197

The walk starts in front of Arundel Post Office on Mill road at the northern end of Queen Street bridge. Arundel is well connected by the A27 which runs east to west along the coast. The A29 connects from the north with the A284 making the final approach. Arundel also has a railway station. An alternative starting point is Houghton Bridge (OS. 027118 Map 197), which also has a railway station, though confusingly it is called Amberley.

THE TWO CASTLE WAY

Before starting out it is worth knowing a bit about Arundel.

Arundel (OS. 015070 Map 197) *is one of the most famous towns on the south coast, visited all year round by tourists from all over the world as well as England. It is the castle which dominates the town that is the main attraction. This "Neuschwanstein" of West Sussex was largely rebuilt in Victorian times, the southern battlements of this period adding to the grandeur of the castle. The site has been a stronghold since recorded history began. First the ancient Britons and then the Romans set up camp here guarding the Arun (then the Tarrant), which at the time was the only safe access into darkest Sussex.*

The original castle was built by Alfred the Great. After the conquest William the Conqueror awarded the castle to Roger de Montgomerie who enthusiastically set about turning it into one of the most impregnable strongholds in Britain. The castle walls survived two sieges, one by Henry I in 1102 and a second by Stephan in 1139. There was a third siege in 1643 by the Roundheads which unfortunately, reduced much of Montgomerie's handiwork to rubble. To achieve such devastation the Roundheads set their guns up on the tower of St. Nicholas church. The destruction was such that the keep built by Alfred the Great is the only easy recognisable part of the original castle to survive. Up until a relatively short time ago, the keep was famous for its owls who made their home here. So revered were they that many of them were given names, often after a public figure of the time. One legendary West Sussex figure associated with the castle is the giant Bevis. The story goes that he was a warder here and to keep up his strength, he would eat a whole ox and drink two hogheads of beer every week. This awesome being would ride about Arundel Park on his equally giant horse Hirondelle. The giant is said to have been buried under a mound in the Park (his thumb on Telegraph Hill, near Compton - see "A Sting in the Tail"), and as a memorial a castle tower named after him.

The castle today is the seat of the Duke of Norfolk as it has been since the 16th century. With such a spectacular monument it is easy to forget the town of Arundel, which has an attractive collection of buildings and an equally fascinating past. A walking book can never do the town justice and I recommend you leave several hours or even another day to explore Arundel proper, employing a local guide book to search out its history.

From the Post Office, go up the High Street to enter the town square with its war memorial, once the site of the town well. Pass the "Norfolk Arms Hotel" on your right and continue uphill to follow the castle walls. At the top of the hill follow the road round to the left and take the first turning right to continue beside the castle walls. Follow the road to pass the church of St. Nicholas of Arundel on your right, where the Roundheads launched their successful siege in 1643, and Arundel Cathedral on your left. The Cathedral, built in 1873, is a modern building compared to much of the town. It was built originally as a church, being granted Cathedral status in 1965. After the Cathedral, pass "The St. Mary's Gate Inn", a free house, and continue along the road keeping the wall on your right to later pass a cemetery on your left and shortly after, St. Philips Catholic Primary School.

Just after the school take the road on the right still following the castle wall, leading to Arundel Castle Cricket Club and Foundation. After the Arundel Park sign, take the left hand fork and ignore any crossing tracks and follow the drive to meet a red gate. Pass through the gate, passing a gate house on your right, and continue straight on between banks ignoring any turnings off. Follow the drive to later ignore a turning left and shortly after continue straight on over a crossing track where ahead of you a flint tower, Hiorne Tower, will come into view.

Immediately after the crossing track turn right on to a somewhat undefined and unmarked grass track to continue diagonally across open grassland. At the other side, cross over a gallops to turn left on to a track. The gallops form part of an extensive training ground for racing horses, the John Dunlop racing stables being situated on the estate. Go over a stile beside a gate and follow the track downhill. The track gradually descends down the side of Mill Hanger valley where to your right Swanbourne lake attracts a melee of tourists. You are now entering Arundel Park proper, part of the Norfolk Estate, a Park which has attracted many painters over the centuries including Turner and

Southdown Sheep

Constable. The Park once boasted several herd of deer though these sadly have disappeared. Stay on the track to reach a crossroads at the bottom of the valley.

Ignore all the wide tracks to take an undefined path diagonally left uphill heading for the fence ahead. This is marked by a public footpath sign. On meeting the fence bear gently right towards another footpath sign ahead. Cross over a stile and continue straight on along the top of a hill with the valley bottom on your right. Contrary to the direction of the footpath sign (at the time of writing), the path runs along the top of the hill and does not wander back down into the valley. Continue straight on until you eventually meet a track in front of fenced woodland, Dry Lodge Plantation, where it's worth stopping to enjoy the fine views behind the coast. Turn left on the track which follows the perimeter of the woodland round to the right. On your left now you can see the boundary wall of Arundel Park and one of the gate houses.

As the track bends left away from the woodland, leave it to carry straight on downhill, in the direction of the public footpath sign, heading for a wooden gate. From here one gains one of the best views of the Arun valley and Amberley Wild Brooks. The villages of Amberley, Houghton and North Stoke lie at the bottom of the valley protected by the South Downs, which stand guard to the east and west. Go over a stile to the left of the gate and follow a track downhill. On eventually meeting another track at a "T" junction, turn right and continue downhill. At a farm gate and fence turn left, keeping the fence on your right. This is a narrow path winding downhill through typical chalk scrubland.

After some distance, go over a stile and descend to meet a boundary wall on your right and follow this downhill until you meet a gap in the wall, through which you should pass to turn immediately left and follow the path down to the river. Turn left here to follow the Arun upstream. Being tidal you may wish to check your map to reassure yourself which is up or downstream.

Centuries ago, the river was a lot wider and supported a variety of craft sailing to Amberley. Today, the valley has been drained and turned over to agriculture, the consequential narrowing of the river and the strong tide reputedly providing the Arun with the second strongest current in Britain. The path along the bank is idyllic and on a sunny day with the local wildlife putting on a show, it is hard to resist forgetting your adventure and finding a spot to watch the world go by.

Take heed of the firing range sign on your left and follow the river as the path bends round to the right with good views across the Arun to North Stoke village. The path passes close to a chalk quarry where you should ignore a footpath off to your left to continue along the river bank. After the quarry, ignore another path off to the left which leads to Houghton and stay on the path to shortly meet a metal gate. If you wish to visit Houghton with its famous 800 year old inn, "The George and Dragon", a free house, pass through the gate and follow the track uphill. The inn is reputed to have refreshed Charles II on his flight to the coast. What is certain is that the inn was later a smugglers hideout and had a tunnel leading to the river, where contraband was offloaded for its perilous journey across the Weald to the appreciative people of London. Returning to our route, take a narrow path right just before the metal gate. This continues to follow the river upstream and is a lot less defined than the well trodden path before Houghton, "The George and Dragon" obviously being the last stop for most people.

The path which is muddy in winter and overgrown in summer (be prepared), ends by passing over a small bridge into a field. Once in the field, continue straight on following the river bank heading for Houghton Bridge, dominated by a huge chalk pit now a museum. At the other side of the field go over a stile and ignore a path off to your left and continue ahead along the top of the river bank to reach the main road, the B2139. Go over a stile and turn right to pass over a stone bridge. At the other side, a collection of buildings huddle between a railway station and the river. They include a welcome pub, "The Bridge Inn", a free house, and a riverside cafe. There is also an excellent museum which demonstrates the history and workings of the numerous chalk pits found on the South Downs. Once huge barges would dock at Houghton Bridge to transport the chalk and lime from the quarry up the Wey and Arun canal to London.

Just before the railway bridge turn left on to a drive which is signposted as a public footpath. As the drive bends left leave it to continue straight on going over a stile into a field, still following the public footpath sign. Follow the footpath along the top of a bank with a holiday caravan site on your left. Cross over another stile and follow the path still on the top of the bank, once again following the river now on your left. Follow the river the other side of which a prominent track, the South Downs Way, descends to the village of Houghton, and pass over two stiles some distance apart before turning north with the village of Bury now across the water on the western bank. To your right, beyond Amberley, rises the Amberley Mount a reminder that not all of your walk is along the flat banks of a river. Stay on the riverside path until you are almost directly opposite Bury church on the far bank and here turn right at a public footpath sign, to cross a field heading for Amberley and its castle. At the river bank there is also a footpath sign pointing towards Bury. Unfortunately, taking this route today would involve a swim, the ferry which serviced the path since the days of Charles I, having now ceased.

The fields all around you are reclaimed land dissected by drainage ditches as opposed to hedges. This whole area of rich water meadows is known as Amberley Wild Brooks. From May to July they are ablaze with meadow buttercups and this could account for the name Amberley which when divided reads "Amber" (yellow) and "Ley", an old word (still used today) for meadow. The buttercup was believed to be a great medicinal plant and was often crushed and mixed with salt as a cure for the plague.

Go straight across a meadow passing over a small bridge. Cross a stile beside a gate and carry straight on across the next field, still following the footpath sign. The ground underfoot here is very marshy and good footwear is essential. At the far end of the field, cross over a stile to bear left heading for a gate and a footpath sign ahead to your left. On reaching the gate, go over a stile and follow a path along the right hand perimeter of a field. At the other side of the field go over a stile and cross a railway line with care, and over another stile to follow the track ahead beside a low chalk cliff. On reaching the walls of Amberley castle, continue straight on to shortly meet a lane which leads uphill into the village of Amberley.

Amberley (OS. 030132 Map 197) *is justifiably known as the prettiest village in West Sussex. The amazing thing is that few people seem to be aware of this and it is not overrun with tourists. Like Arundel, Amberley has a castle though unlike Arundel, this does not dominate the village. The castle is a well preserved ruin now a hotel, and stands on the western side of the village overlooking the Wild Brooks. The main entrance is along a drive from the B2139. It is almost disappointing however, to learn that Amberley castle was but a manor house later fortified.*

The house which is the base for the hotel was built in the 12th century by Ralph Luffa, Bishop of Chichester, who also built the present Chichester Cathedral after the original Cathedral was destroyed by the sea. The house became the seat of the Bishop of Chichester and high above the main entrance stands a Latin cross serving as a constant reminder of the castle's connection with the Church. It was Bishop William Rede who was responsible for building the fortifications around the house. These were started in the late 14th century after permission had been granted by the then King, Richard II. It is likely that the walls were constructed for protection against dissatisfied peasants rather than possible invaders. Further additions were made by Bishop Rede including the Great Hall which is now only a ruin. Bishop Sherbourne was the last Bishop to hold Amberley up to 1536, when the castle was leased to a succession of tenants.

During the Civil War, the castle was the home of the powerful Goring family who were devout Royalists. At this time, there was a covered trench from the castle to "Houghton House" at Houghton, probably used as an escape passage. The castle was taken by the forces of General Waller and the Gorings were forced to leave. It is not without surprise that we learn the castle is supposed to be haunted. A white lady is said to walk the walls at night, although it is possible that any modern sighting of a ghost could simply be a hotel guest taking the night air!

Amberley has another ghost which is said to haunt the vicarage. This is a young girl and during building work earlier this century, skeletons of a young girl and old woman were found. The village itself is very well preserved and its beauty has been captured over the centuries by several well known artists. The church like the manor house, was built by Bishop Luffa, though there was an earlier church.

Follow the lane through Amberley village passing the village pond with seating overlooking Amberley Wild Brooks. Pass the church and look out for a pottery on the right which is well worth a visit and note the names of the houses as you go, many denoting their origins. The lane eventually meets a "T" junction where you should turn right. If however, you wish to visit the village shop or pub, "The Black Horse", Friary Meux which serves food, then take a detour left. For our route follow the road south to pass the primary school on the left and continue straight on to meet the busy B2139. Cross the road to go up Mill Lane opposite and as the trees give way on your right, you will enjoy clear views across to Bignor Hill and Blackdown in the distance. As the lane nears the top of the hill, you will naturally join the South Downs Way. Do not turn right here but continue straight on to pass "Highdown", a large house on your left. After the house turn left on to a wide path uphill, still signposted as the South Downs Way.

The path you are now on leads up to a small wooden gate through which you should pass to continue uphill. The path, which is fenced, leads on to a much wider track where you should carry straight on. Shortly after, go over a stile and go straight uphill, staying on the South Downs Way, keeping the fence to your left. Ignore a bridleway off to your right. Near the top of the hill, Amberley Mount, go over a stile beside a gate and at a bronze age tumulus you have almost a full view of the entire walk.

Continue straight on along the South Downs Way, which is fenced with open fields either side. As the path begins to ascend Rackham Hill you will reach a crossing track signposted as a public bridleway, where you should turn right passing to the left of some trees. You are now at the highest point on the walk. To your right there is a grass covered mound known as Rackham Bank. This can act as a pleasant place to rest and enjoy your last views of the Weald and the North Downs. Below you incidentally, you can see "Parham House", a fine Elizabethan mansion with a deer park and heronry, one of only a few left in the country.

Follow the path to the left of the trees and ignore a path going off to the right shortly after, to continue ahead along the southern slope of Rackham Hill until you meet a "T" junction. Turn right at the "T" junction and follow a track downhill to almost immediately meet a gate. Pass through the gate to continue on the track which proceeds downhill in a south westerly direction. This part of the route is one of the highlights of the walk. The track is obviously ancient, probably used by the ancient Britons, Romans and Saxons alike. The track is lined with typical chalkland scrub and a sprinkling of gorse, which in early summer makes a pleasant change to the regular green and white of the downs. All around are open views of the southern side of the downs rich in ancient field systems and tumuli. Over to your left "Lee Farm" nestles below Harrow Hill. Today it is hard to imagine that this was once the site of a leper colony, a chalk track leads from the farm to the village of Burpham. This is still known as "The Lepers Path".

After three quarters of a mile, the track bends round to the right where you should leave it to carry straight on along another track, signposted as a public bridleway. After some distance, ignore another public bridleway off to your left and continue for a further fifty metres to take the next signposted public bridleway right and follow this as it bends left by a copse, ignoring a bridleway going off to the right. The track now starts to descend with the copse on your right and on a clear day views of Arundel castle ahead.

Continue straight on to join a track coming in from the right. Over to your right on another hill are a collection of disused barns, this is Camp Hill, the name a clue to its past. After approximately half a mile, turn right over a stile to join a marked and fenced public footpath downhill - take care not to miss this. The path runs between fields to reach another stile. Go over this and cross a farm track and over another stile to proceed steeply downhill, following a fence on your right. Take great care as this path is extremely steep.

At the bottom of a valley go over a stile and turn left to pass through a gate way and follow a track ahead signposted as a public bridleway. This runs along the side of the valley with water meadows on your right. Ignore a footpath off to your right opposite a small quarry and shortly after ignore another path right, to continue straight uphill to meet a gate. Pass over a stile beside the gate and continue ahead along a track following the left hand perimeter of a field. At the brow of the hill is "Peppering Farm" and on your right and now much closer, Arundel castle. Pass to the left of the farm yard to meet a lane where you should continue straight ahead, ignoring the turnings off to the left and right. Pass to the left of "The Garden House" and stay on the lane to reach Burpham church, St. Mary the Virgin.

Take the signposted footpath on the left which leads into the churchyard and continue on along a tarmac footpath on the right hand side of the church. The church yard is particularly well kept and is maintained by the "Cecil Hay Legacy 1982". A path, Marjorie Hays Path, leads round to the southern entrance of the church yard and then out to "The George and Dragon" pub, a free house built in 1736, and the centre of the village.

Burpham (OS. 040089 Map 197) *is at once refreshing and not just because of its fine hostelry! Its quaint church and narrow lanes bordered by picturesque cottages hide a wealth of local history. The village started as a settlement for ancient Britons and later became a Saxon stronghold, its situation ideal to guard the river Arun against marauding Danes. The village church still has traces of Saxon architecture, though much of the building dates from the 12th and 19th centuries. Like the church at Sullington (see "The Chanctonbury Ring"), St. Mary's has a squint. This was for lepers who could watch the service without supposedly infecting those inside and through which they could receive the priest's blessing. There is a track leading from Burpham over Perry hill to "Lee Farm" where there was a leper colony.*

Like other worthy downland villages, Burpham's past wouldn't be complete without its smugglers and like other local villages again, it was the village inn in this case "The George and Dragon", which was the safe house for contraband. This was brought from the river up a series of steep steps known as Jacob's Ladder.

After perhaps a taste of some legal refreshment at "The George and Dragon", you should continue on along what is supposedly the old smugglers route. To do this, pass in front of the pub and follow the signposted public footpath into a park passing in front of a pavilion. Keep to the left hand perimeter of the cricket pitch, where in the valley on your left now is this village of Wepham. Although not easily visible, you are also now passing through the centre of an old fort, supposedly built or strengthened by Athelstone, a Saxon chieftain, to guard the Arun against the Danish.

At the far end of the park pass through a small wooden gate, ignoring a path off to your left, and carry straight on along a fenced path. To your right just after the gate, is a seated view point. The path continues high above the banks of the river Arun and eventually descends Jacob's Ladder to cross over a stile into a field. Ignore a signposted footpath on your right to cross the field along the top of a bank, once again following the river Arun on your right. At the far end of the field, go over a stile to continue along the bank to reach and cross two more stiles over a small inlet. Carry on along the top of the river bank which here is lined with rushes and as such is a haven for wildlife.

At the next set of stiles, cross the first stile only and turn immediately left on to a signposted public footpath. Go down the bank and over another stile and continue straight on across a field, keeping a hedgerow to your left. At the other side of the field, go over another stile and turn immediately right along a public footpath and after approximately thirty metres, pass through a gate way and continue diagonally left away from the ditch on your right. You are now heading for a line a poplar trees, still following the public footpath signs.

On meeting the poplar trees cross over a stile and continue ahead along a fenced path. Pass through a kissing gate and carry straight on between hedges and ignore a path coming in from the right. The path soon runs behind some houses, these belong to the village of Warningcamp so called as it supposedly once housed a military camp, its purpose to provide advanced warning of an attack on Arundel castle. Do not turn through the gates on your left as these are private, but continue along the path to eventually meet a track which you should follow ahead to reach a tarmac lane. Turn right and cross the railway line immediately after which you should turn left to reach and cross a small brick bridge and thereafter a stile. There are excellent views now of Arundel castle and the Cathedral beyond.

Continue ahead along the top of a bank again following the river Arun. Follow the river to eventually enter Arundel after passing through fencing beside an old brick barn. The river here provides moorings to a number of boats, where under a century ago, this would have been busy with sailing ships carrying coal, chalk, timber and even salt. Trade came to an abrupt halt when a low railway bridge was built over the Arun south of the town. Pass a car park on your left and thereafter a miniature amusement park and swimming pool to eventually reach a driveway. Do not turn left here, but go through two white posts and continue between houses to come out at a bridge over the Arun. Turn right and cross the bridge to arrive at the Post Office, the starting point of our walk.

ACCOMMODATION

The Norfolk Arms Hotel, Arundel. Tel:0903 882101
On the walk, the Norfolk Arms Hotel is a Georgian coaching inn built over 200 years ago. It is situated on the eastern side of the main square immediately below the castle's battlements. Staying here means indulging not only in comfort but part of Arundel's past.

St. Mary's Gate Inn, Arundel. Tel: 0903 883145
On the walk, this excellent free house is situated beside the Cathedral at the top of the town. It is named after the original town gate, now inside the castle walls. The bedrooms are of a very high quality and most have views over the town.

Youth Hostel, Arundel YHA, Warningcamp.
Tel: 0903 882204
Five hundred metres from the walk, this is a large hostel located in a Georgian house set in spacious grounds. The village is very peaceful, but should you want more it is but a short walk along the banks of the river Arun to Arundel. Camping is also permitted.

Camping & Caravanning - Ship & Anchor Marina, Ford.
Tel: 0243 551262
Approximately two miles from the walk (2½ if you walk along the river) this is a very relaxed site based round a good traditional pub which can be recommended on its own. Facilities are good and are built so as not to take away from the pleasant location of the site.

N.B. Arundel has a wealth of accommodation. For full details contact the Tourist Office at Arundel, 61 High Street, Arundel, W. Sussex,   BN18 9AJ. Tel: 0903 882268.

UP MARDEN DOWN

Distance: 14½ miles (23 km)
Time: Allow approximately 7 hours, more
to fully appreciate the views
Map: Ordnance Survey Landranger Map 197

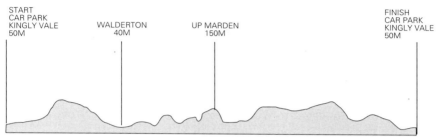

START
CAR PARK
KINGLY VALE
50M

WALDERTON
40M

UP MARDEN
150M

FINISH
CAR PARK
KINGLY VALE
50M

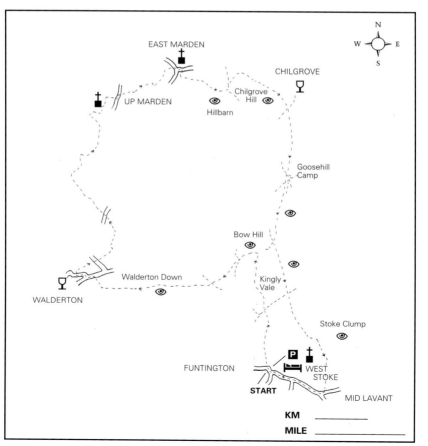

EAST MARDEN

CHILGROVE

UP MARDEN

Chilgrove
Hill

Hillbarn

Goosehill
Camp

Bow Hill

Walderton Down

Kingly
Vale

WALDERTON

Stoke Clump

FUNTINGTON

WEST
STOKE

START

MID LAVANT

KM _____

MILE _____

Walk Summary

Up Marden Down is a good description of what to expect on this walk. Not only is it the longest, but it also has some of the steepest gradients of any of the walks in the book, gradients that you would find hard to better on a mountain! The rewards for all your efforts are constant good views and the excitement of exploring some of the most untouched countryside in West Sussex. If you time your walk so you near the end at sunset and the weather is right, you will be treated to a spectacular display over Chichester harbour. I suggest you do not attempt this walk if you are unfit and even if you are fit, take plenty of provisions with you and allow plenty of time. Enjoy yourself!

Start - OS. 825088 Map 197

The walk starts from the car park for Kingley Vale at West Stoke. To get there take the road west on the bend of the A286 at Mid Lavant, signposted to West Stoke. Go through West Stoke and after passing the church, turn right to meet the car park. Alternatively, take the B2178 and at East Ashing take the turning north signposted to West Stoke. It is only three quarters of a mile from here to the car park. The nearest railway station is Fishbourne which is two and a half miles from the walk. However, if you don't relish walking to the start, it will probably be easier to get transport from the station at Chichester, only a short distance away.

UP MARDEN DOWN

From the car park at West Stoke take the wide track going north signposted public footpath. Join this by going over a stile beside a metal gate and continue between fenced fields heading for the impressive hill ahead, Bow Hill. After three quarters of a mile, pass through a tree line where there are the remains of an old stile, ignoring paths off to your left and right, and follow the track ahead which forks shortly after. Either route is acceptable, although the left hand path is usually easier in wet or muddy conditions. The left hand and more narrow path continues ahead winding through woodland and sometime after, rejoins the original wider track to continue straight on.

Pass over a crossing track and continue ahead over a stile into a grass clearing. You are now in Kingley Vale National Nature Reserve which is signposted. Continue ahead passing to the left of a small wooden hut, a field museum which is worth a visit. The track now follows in part, a nature trail on which there are leaflets available. At a fork take the right hand path to leave the track you are on, following the arrows on a green post, part of the nature trail. Continue on passing post "3" on the nature trail and

at the next post marked "4", turn right along the trail to enter a
yew grove called Druids Grove.

Druids Grove (OS. 824106 Map 197) *is a magnificent grove of*   *i*
yew trees which is the centre of a forest of yews, the largest in
Europe. Their dense canopy and dark twisting trunks make this a
mysterious place and you cannot help feeling just a little nervous.
Legend has it as the name suggests, that this was a meeting place
for druids and witches who would weave their spells under the
yews' protection. It was a pagan belief that the yew tree would
ward off evil spirits, which is why yew trees are so common in
graveyards. Another theory is that the yew trees were planted to
commemorate a battle fought here against the Vikings in 859 AD.
It has also been said that they were planted to guide pilgrims on
their way to Canterbury. Whatever their origin, they remain as a
souvenir of the past when much of southern England was yew
forest. The yew tree used to be protected as a provider of the raw
resource for the army's most common weapon, the longbow. Sadly,
as more complicated weapons came into vogue the yew tree lost its
protection and is now relatively rare. It is interesting to note that
there is a male and female yew tree, the female recognised by its
red berries which, contrary to popular opinion, are not poisonous.
It is the pips inside which can make you very ill and for this
reason, I recommend that you do not try any.

Follow the path through the grove to rejoin the original path and
continue straight on to naturally join a wider path, leading to the
southern slope of Bow Hill. You should ignore all other signs for
the nature trail marking points of interest. On reaching the open
hillside, marked by another Kingley Vale information sign, go
over a stile beside a wooden gate thereby leaving the nature trail.
From here for the first time, you can appreciate the full beauty of
Kingley Vale and the horseshoe slopes of Bow Hill which enclose
it. Over to your left is the older forest, these trees are
approximately one hundred and twenty years old and one of
several generations of yew to cover this hillside.

Continue straight on going up the grass slope of Bow Hill. The
shallow banks which you cross are in fact field boundary remains
of Celtic man. Follow the fence on your right uphill to reach a
stile where its worth stopping to admire the view over the
Chichester basin. On your left looking back is a small dew pond
and in the distance the spire of Chichester Cathedral. Go over the
stile to enter the yew forest ahead, the hill becoming considerably
steeper as you go. However you are rewarded at the top with
more excellent views. On a clear day Hayling Island and even the
Isle of Wight can be seen. At the top of the hill itself there is a

memorial stone to Sir Arthur George Tansley FRS, who was the first Chairman of the Nature Conservancy which formed the Kingley Vale Nature Reserve. It is said that the stone marks the spot from where Sir Arthur believed the best view in Britain could be obtained. You can form your own opinion, but you must admit on a clear day there are few places that can offer a view with such content.

Facing the memorial, turn left going west along the path following the top of the hill. Note the two round burial mounds or tumuli, the Devils Humps, on your right which will act as markers throughout your walk.

i   **The Devils Humps (OS. 821112 Map 197)** *are bronze age burial mounds and are associated locally with the supernatural. Their dead would be cremated and buried, sometimes in urns, in the mounds with their most precious belongings. This practice as with the tombs in Egypt, led to grave robbing and these were no exception hence the concave tops. Successive conquerors overran the south of England but no matter how dominant their reign, they feared these ancient burial sites. Even when the site could have been of military advantage they rarely built there, preferring a secondary site away from the spirits that were said to guard the burial mounds. With the coming of Christianity, cremation was condemned and the now familiar grave yards sprang up. It is a peculiarity that modern civilisation has once again turned to that most ancient of pagan rituals, cremation.*

From the tops of the tumuli you can gain more good views of the surrounding area, looking south over the Chichester basin and north to Harting Down and Beacon Hill. Just before the burial mounds you will reach another wide track on to which you should bear left and continue to follow the perimeter of the hill. Take care not to take the left hand path going downhill but stay on the track clearly signposted as a public bridleway. This runs through typical chalk woodland and can at times be very muddy.

Pass over a crossing track still following the public bridleway sign, until you eventually meet a "T" junction at the edge of a field. Turn left here along a wide track still a public bridleway, to go downhill for a short time and then bend sharply right to continue along the field perimeter. Ignore a small path and then a public bridleway off to your left and stay on the track which soon naturally enters woodland. Carry straight on ignoring any further turnings off to the left or right and follow the track to eventually leave the woodland via a gate. Continue along the right hand perimeter of a field where there are excellent views to your left of the sea, Hayling Island, Portsmouth and, on a clear day, the Isle of Wight. You are now on Walderton Down.

At some old flint outbuildings turn right along a public bridleway which is fenced and on reaching the tree line turn left to descend gradually through woodland. Ignore all minor paths and stay on the track as it winds downhill to meet a wooden one bar gate and a Forestry Commission sign for Walderton Down. Continue straight ahead downhill to reach a lane where you should turn left to enter Walderton village. At Cooks Lane turn right and follow this uphill. If however you feel like a little refreshment, then pass Cooks Lane and continue ahead to reach "The Barley Mow" a free house serving home cooked foods, which comes complete with a skittle alley.

To continue our route, go up Cooks Lane for approximately a quarter of a mile and turn right on to a marked public footpath between houses. Follow this between fences to reach a stile which you should cross and then turn right to follow the perimeter of a field. Shortly after, cross another stile and continue to follow the left hand perimeter of the next field to cross a third stile, a small narrow lane and yet another stile ahead into another field. Continue straight on across the field to meet a stile at the far side. It is worth stopping here to look back at the views of Walderton village and just beyond on the top of a hill a tower, Racton Monument.

The Racton Monument (OS. 776093 Map 197) *is a ruined tower probably built by Lord Halifax who lived at "Racton Manor", now sadly demolished. Its most obvious purpose was as a view point across the Channel, there being several others like it with the same purpose in most counties along the south coast. The local explanation is much more colourful. This maintains that it was built as a signal tower to guide smugglers when the way was clear. This would often be after the local excise men had been entertained by the Earl until they were senseless. Sadly for his efforts, he was later hanged. True or not, modern living and the EC hasn't changed many peoples' attitudes and I suspect the Earl would find as many sympathisers today as he did when he was alive.*

Go over the stile to follow the field perimeter climbing gently uphill. You will shortly leave the perimeter hedge and cross the middle of the field to reach the trees directly in view. At a "T" junction turn left and follow the marked public bridleway downhill, shortly leaving the woodland to follow the right hand perimeter of a field and reach a lane. Cross the lane and continue up the bridleway ahead between trees. At a fork take the right hand path and continue your climb. At the top, the bridleway naturally joins a more prominent track and you should continue ahead and shortly after, ignore a large track going off to your right. Carry straight on to leave the woodland and follow the track between fields.

Where the track bends left, leave it to turn right following the signs for Lye Common marked as a footpath only. Pass "The Keepers Cottage - 3, Lye Common" and then a second smaller and equally attractive cottage on your right, before going over a stile beside a metal gate. This part of the walk is particularly attractive especially in early spring, the path being dotted with snowdrops. Follow the footpath to meet a crossing track. Here you should continue straight on downhill and on nearing the bottom of a valley turn right along a signposted public footpath.

Snowdrops

The footpath runs along the bottom of the valley which is beautiful in that it is relatively untouched and thus a haven for wildlife whose presence can be felt and heard all around and if alert, seen. After approximately fifty metres turn left at a footpath sign and follow the path as it climbs gently to run along the right hand perimeter of a field, with woodland on your right. At the end of the field, the path once again enters woodland, Grevitts Copse.

Soon after, leave the path as it bends right and continue straight ahead along a slightly less prominent path, marked as a public footpath. Carry straight on and follow the path as it descends into a small valley and continues up the other side to meet a "T" junction. Turn right here to follow the public footpath and on reaching a stile, go over this into a field, turning right to follow the perimeter for some distance. As you walk along the perimeter, follow the path as it naturally passes into another field adjacent, this time to follow the perimeter left to reach a stile, with Up Marden and its church on your right. Cross the stile and turn right up what appears to be an old lane, a public bridleway, to the village of Up Marden.

i
†
■
Up Marden (OS. 796141 Map 197) *appears at first to be no more than a farm yard. Even the entrance to the church is tucked away*

between farm buildings. Its is the remoteness of this village, one of the smallest in Sussex, that makes Up Marden so special. It was the Romans who first formed a permanent settlement here, they built a villa the site of which is now a local farm. They were followed by the Saxons who named the village "Maere-Dun", meaning "Border Town", the village being on the border of the separately run kingdoms of the south and west Saxons. Maere-Dun came under the rule of King Aethelwealh, who in turn reported to King Wlfhere of Mercia. At this time Christianity was sweeping across Europe, after already wooing mighty Rome. Aethelwealh, with help from Wlfhere, quickly embraced it. Despite this, a church is not reported in Up Marden until as late as the 11th century, four centuries later. The building you see today is mostly 13th century and has hardly changed since it was built. In its early history, the church came under the wing of Lewes Priory, later sharing responsibility with Shulbrede Priory (see "The Augustinian Amble"). Serious illness and the general decline of these priories meant that responsibility later passed to the priory at Easebourne. The church since has survived a fairly turbulent history, the people of Up Marden not being noted for their Christian morals. Today it remains as one of the most unspoilt churches in West Sussex. It is easy to fall in love with this unassuming little village, its life still dictated by the seasons. A book of poems by Helen Jackson is for sale in the church and it describes perfectly the village and church through the year.

After the church pass in front of "Up Marden Farm" with its dovecot and pond, to reach a lane. Turn left and shortly after, right on to a public footpath opposite the entrance to "Up Marden Farm" and follow the footpath signs downhill along the right hand perimeter of a field. There are excellent views here to your left of the edge of the South Downs and Beacon Hill, an iron age hill fort.

At the far end of the field, the path descends very steeply through woodland and great care is needed if you are to avoid your first attempt at tobogganing! On nearing the bottom you will reach a crossing path which you should ignore, to continue straight on downhill to go over a stile into a field. Follow the right hand perimeter of the field to cross a second stile and turn right. Follow the perimeter of the next field round heading towards the village of East Marden. As you near the village there are good views on your right to Bow Hill and its two burial mounds. At the end of the field, cross a stile and go diagonally right across another field in the direction of the footpath sign. Go over a second stile to arrive at a narrow lane opposite "Cobbersfield Cottage" and turn right to arrive at the small village green with an old thatched well. Welcome to East Marden.

East Marden (OS. 807146 Map 197) *is another of those unspoilt downland villages. The village is dominated by the well on the green and the church of St. Peter which overlooks it. Small though it is, East Marden once supported a famous girls school, which later moved to "Telegraph House" a few miles away. The school, "Battire House", is now a private residence. The church probably Saxon, has a relatively modern treasure. The organ which is carefully preserved, once lived at St. James' Palace and was the property of Prince Albert.*

Turn left at the green passing the church on your left, following the sign for Chilgrove, Midhurst and Chichester. Shortly after, at the village pond, turn right on to a narrow lane in front of "Postman's Cottage" and follow this past houses to continue as it bends round to the left through a farm yard. Go straight on, ignoring a footpath off to your right, to cross a stile beside a hanger type barn and walk along a fenced track between fields. At the end of the track, go over a stile and follow the left hand perimeter of a field to go over another stile on to a narrow winding path, passing an old brick building on your right. Follow the path uphill and cross a stile turning right immediately thereafter, to climb up the steep side of East Marden Down. You will probably find it necessary to pause at least once to catch your breath. Use this to look back across to East Marden and beyond to Butser Hill, the highest point in Hampshire unfortunately topped by an aerial mast.

At the brow of the hill, head for the remains of a kissing gate ahead, now a stile, and go over this on to a narrow path to meet a drive way in front of a cottage. Turn left on to the drive passing a large property on your right, "Hill Barn", after which you should turn right on to a track marked as a public footpath. Just before the track enters a field, leave it to pass over a stile on your left on to a public footpath. The path passes to the right of some farm buildings to join a drive where you should bear right. Pass two bungalows, the latter being "Farm Cottage" and go over a stile into an open field and continue straight ahead. You are now on Chilgrove Hill with the village of Chilgrove very much hidden below in the valley on your left. To your right again, is Bow Hill and the Devils Humps.

At the far end of the field, cross a stile into another field and continue straight on to pass to the left of the trees ahead. After the trees head towards the right hand corner of the field and go over a stile beside a wooden gate. You can if you are hungry now, turn left to follow the track down into Chilgrove where you will find "The White Horse Inn", an 18th century free house. Although run more as a restaurant, light meals are served in the bar and in the summer there is sometimes a barbecue. The restaurant serves excellent food, though you must be prepared to pay for it. The wine cellar is famous and has won several awards. If however, another down and up seems too much for some refreshment, then continue on our route by turning right after the stile and then immediately left. You should now follow a wide track to reach three gates where you should pass through the small wooden gate on the far left and continue ahead. The track will take you along the backbone of Bow Hill to eventually arrive back at Kingley Vale.

The going is nearly all through woodland and after three quarters of a mile the track arrives at a house on your right, surrounded by high perimeter fencing. On your left, though hidden by the wood, is an old iron age hill fort known as Goosehill Camp. Pass the house and go through a gate ignoring a public bridleway on your left to continue ahead. You will immediately meet two bridleway paths initially running adjacent to each other. Take the left hand bridleway and continue to go straight on. After a short distance, you will meet a marked crossing track, where you again continue straight on to follow a wide grass track still along the top of Bow Hill.

As you near the summit of Bow Hill, you will see St. Roches Hill (The Trundle) with its aerial masts in the distance. Soon after, the spire of Chichester Cathedral, seen in the very early stages of our walk, will again be visible to your left. Keep to the main path marked as a public bridleway and do not be tempted to take the unmarked path on the left at this point. Shortly after, on reaching a crossing path at a Kingley Vale information sign, turn left to begin your descent.

The path leads downhill with more superb views and soon leaves the open downland to run between fields. Again you are treated to more views of Chichester harbour and also the early part of the walk. Go straight over a crossing track to continue along a fenced path still running between fields. You can if you wish turn right at the crossing track to rejoin our original route at the field museum. From there you can retrace your steps back to the car park. This will avoid some road walking but you will also miss one of the best views on the walk. To continue our route however, follow the path gradually uphill between fields and then through a small area of woodland to eventually reach the top of the hill with a wooded copse known as Stoke Clump. The trees were planted by one John Browning in the early part of the 19th century. Before this, there used to be a windmill on the hill. From the top of the hill you will probably gain the best views on the walk over Chichester harbour. If the weather is right and you have timed the walk well, it is a fantastic sight to watch the sun set over the harbour.

From Stokes Clump the path gradually winds downhill between fields, to eventually meet a road. All the time you are descending the spire of Chichester Cathedral will gradually disappear from view. At the road, turn right heading for the village of West Stoke.

West Stoke (OS. 829087 Map 197) *lives in the shadow of Chichester and indeed, in the 13th century it was known as "Stoke Juxta Chichester", "juxta" meaning "near" or "close by". The village church, a picturesque building with a squat tower, stems from the 12th century being almost completely rebuilt a century later. Over the main door is the Royal arms, a reminder that the Crown is the head of the Church of England. The church has a fine memorial to Adria Stoughton, Lord of the manor during the late 16th and early 17th century. Note the children at the base of the memorial, four of them are carrying skulls. This was a blunt but common way of showing that a child had died and we can only assume from this that four of Stoughton's children had died by the time the memorial was erected.*

On entering the village there is a B&B, "Cherry Tree Cottage", should you feel you can go no further and booking in for the night and a hot bath is the best idea you have had! Continue through the village, pass the village church and follow the road downhill to turn right and reach the car park, our starting point.

ACCOMMODATION

The Hunters Inn, Lavant. Tel: 0243 527329
One and a quarter miles from the walk, this inn named after the famous Charlton Hunt, is conveniently situated on the A286. The inn is unaffected by the busy road and a stay here will guarantee a pleasant rest after the vigours of your walk.

Cherry Tree Cottage, West Stoke. Tel: 0243 573822
On the walk, the house is set at the foot of the downs waiting with a warm welcome after the final descent of your walk. The interior has been tastefully decorated and the accommodation has excellent views of the local countryside.

Youth Hostel, Arundel YHA, Warningcamp.
Tel: 0903 882204

Fourteen and a half miles from the walk, this is a large hostel located in a Georgian house set in spacious grounds. The village is very peaceful, but should you want more it is but a short walk along the banks of the river Arun to Arundel. Camping is also permitted.

Camping, Goodwood Club Site, Singleton. Tel: 0243 774486

Three quarters of a mile from the walk, this is a Caravan Club run site which has a superb position beside the Goodwood racecourse. The site is open during the summer months though closed on race days, so check ahead.

SOME FURTHER ADVENTURES

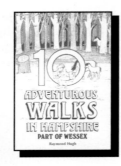

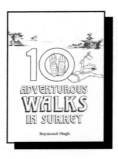

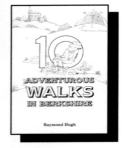

10 MORE ADVENTUROUS WALKS IN SURREY	**10** ADVENTUROUS WALKS IN THE SOUTH CHILTERNS	**10** ADVENTUROUS WALKS IN WEST KENT

KEEP UP TO DATE

If you would like a full list and to be kept updated on all the outdoor publications available from Morning Mist, please send a postcard with your name and address to Marketing, Morning Mist Publications, PO Box 108, Reigate, Surrey RH2 9YP.

BUILDING
YOUR FUTURE

A step-by-step guide
to **building a £1 million+**
construction business

GREG
WILKES

RETHINK PRESS

First published in Great Britain in 2019 by Rethink Press
(www.rethinkpress.com)

'Greg Wilkes has written a must-read for anyone looking to grow their construction company profitably. He has vast experience of the highs and lows of the industry and has demonstrated that he knows what it takes to be successful.

Applying the principles outlined in this book will greatly assist growth-hungry business owners looking to run a finely tuned operation.'

— **Daniel Priestley**, CEO/Founder of Dent Global and four times bestselling author

Contents

Introduction

Some say entrepreneurs are born. Some say they can be made, that you can teach someone how to be a successful entrepreneur. Both these statements have some truth. I do believe entrepreneurs have slightly different character traits to other people; they're a bit more daring, certainly ambitious, and confident in their own ability. Without a doubt, some people are born with the desire and character traits that are essential for being a successful entrepreneur. More than most, they can take risk, handle stress, and can manage and get the best out of people. Fortunately for some, they seem to have been born with these character traits, or developed them early on in life.

From a young age I knew I would work for myself. At around ten years old I started learning how to make

1

money, from having multiple paper rounds to setting up a gardening and car washing business, and then on to a window-cleaning round in my teens. It wasn't so much about earning money, although that was a nice bonus; it was the accomplishment, the sense of satisfaction that I could do this all by myself. And I loved the buzz of winning new work.

Fast forward ten years, I had a trade apprenticeship behind me and I was starting out on my own in the real world. As I was unsure of my abilities, I set up with a business partner and we decided to tackle loft conversions. Things started well; we built up the business quickly and I was earning good money for a twenty-year-old. There was a real boom in loft conversions in the early 2000s; everyone was doing them and we had jumped on the bandwagon at just the right time.

However, I wasn't fully comfortable with what we had achieved. Yes, I was earning well, but I was grafting hard. Back then, I was physically on the tools every single day and trying to fit paperwork and sales quotes in during the evenings. I was working ten- to twelve-hour days and it was tiring, both physically and mentally. But at the time I was young, energetic and full of enthusiasm and drive to keep the business growing, so I was quite happy to put in the extra hours.

As the business continued to grow, juggling full-time hours on the tools and all the paperwork proved a challenge. We decided to hire a business adviser to help us grow further, but in the right way. We were turning over around £400k per year but that wasn't quite enough. At twenty-two I was about to get married, was purchasing a new home, and I needed to earn a bigger wage.

The decision to hire our first business adviser was a pivotal decision, and a vital one. Having an outsider look at our business with fresh eyes and see what we were doing right and wrong was the best money we ever spent. She advised us that we were spending too much time working *in* the business rather than *on* it. It seems obvious now with all the books I have read since then – like *The E-Myth*[1] – but at the time it was a breakthrough for us. She suggested that one of us come off the tools and start focusing on running the business properly.

So that's what I did. My business partner carried on working on the tools and I concentrated on the sales and developing relationships with our key suppliers, mainly local authorities and architects. This decision paid dividends and it wasn't long before my business partner had also come off the tools to help out with the office paperwork.

---

1   Gerber, M (2001) *The E-Myth Revisited: Why Most Small Businesses Don't Work and What to Do About It* (3rd edn). London: HarperBusiness.

We were now in a position where we were earning quite well, were building a successful business, and were not having to do physical work on the tools each day. Our transit vans were traded in for pickup trucks, and I was loving it.

But things changed for us when we hit a turnover of around £650k.

For some reason, we just completely stopped growing. I was selling what I could but the business flatlined for a few years. We didn't have the right processes or people in place to take on much more work, so psychologically we were holding back. This started to become a problem once I had kids and needed a bigger home. I needed to earn more money, significantly more, but the business was no longer meeting my needs.

I started to grow resentful of it. My business partner and best friend was quite happy with how things were. And I can understand why. It wasn't stressful, and we were earning enough to meet his needs – he had no reason to want to grow. But for me, with a growing family and an in-built drive to make this business a huge success, I was growing frustrated.

As the years slowly ticked on with growth going nowhere, things came to a head. We were now both spending more than the profits the business could realistically generate and we were slowly but surely driving it into the ground. I made the difficult decision to split from my business partner. I can't stress enough how emotionally challenging this was, as we were (and still are) extremely close, so it felt like a betrayal in many ways. This is one of the reasons it took me so long to make the decision, when I should have done it years earlier.

I knew we couldn't continue on as we were and we had both started to move in different directions. I wanted to make the business much bigger; he, understandably, didn't want the unnecessary pressure. So, in 2013, we split. I bought my partner out of the company and was then free to take it in any direction I wanted. I was now financially committed to making things happen, as I'd had to take out a large loan to cover the buy-out. It was a risk, as we had run the company into a bit of debt, but I was convinced I could turn it around, cover the loan payments and make the business profitable again. I remember feeling excited, but also found it daunting that the failure or success of the business was now all down to me.

At this point I'd already consumed a lot of books on how to grow a business, and it was time to start putting the things I'd learned into action. One by one, I slowly implemented strategies and started to see changes. Sales were increasing without spending any more on marketing and my profit margins were growing.

The first year after the split I managed to turn over nearly £700k, which wasn't bad considering I was on my own and things were only just starting to settle. I must admit, though, I was working extremely hard and putting in long hours, but I was building a valuable foundation that would set me up well going forward.

The next financial year, things really started moving. I was now being viewed as a bigger company and started pitching for larger contracts. The contacts I had nurtured over the years had also grown and were taking on bigger projects, and I was now their preferred supplier. I needed to take on more admin staff to cope with the workload, so I converted my garage into an office and we all crammed in there.

Looking back now, it must have been an awful working environment compared to the offices I now have, but at the time it was exciting. New contracts were being won and our turnover was increasing month on month. Very suddenly I started to see the fruits of my labour, and that financial year I hit £1.2m in sales. We had increased revenue by 70% in just one year. This was a huge jump in both turnover and profits; all the effort I'd put in to laying a good foundation the previous year had now paid dividends.

I couldn't believe how easy it had been to smash through the £1m mark once I had put the right systems in place. And once I had sailed past £1m in revenue,

I had further funds to invest in building a great team around me. This then gave me more freedom and money to take holidays and enjoy some stress-free time with my family.

Having a great team was key to growing even further, and once we had passed the £1m barrier it was easy to get to £2m, then £3m and beyond in the years that followed. Our growth was staggering, and that brought a whole host of new problems that I had to learn to deal with and overcome.

I'd grown to a large company quite quickly and it seemed I was taking on new staff every few months. Unfortunately, some of my hires were awful. I had a member of staff steal money from me, and one even stole a lucrative contract worth hundreds of thousands of pounds for himself. Others were just not performing and trying to pull the wool over my eyes. Our business reputation began to decline as projects started to go wrong. I'd gone from making consistently good profits to losing money month on month. In all honesty, I'd started to lose control of it all. I was in unfamiliar territory, and it was too late to bring things back around as we were now entering a recession.

In the end, after a period of sustained losses, one problem after another and a dishonest client knocking me for a lot of money, the debts became unsustainable. I was over-leveraged and had to declare the business bankrupt.

This was one of the hardest decisions of my life. I'd spent years building this business up and now it was gone in an instant. I had lost my contracts, lost the trust of some great partners, and was left with nothing but a pile of debt. It was an absolutely awful time and one I never want to repeat. The stress and worry this caused me, my family and my employees were immense.

As you can now see, I've had success, but I've also experienced great failure. Without a doubt, my biggest lessons in business have been learned from my failures.

I always take comfort from this Michael Jordan quote when he was asked what made him so successful:

> 'I've missed more than 9,000 shots in my career.
> I've lost almost 300 games. Twenty-six times
> I've been trusted to take the game-winning shot
> and missed. I've failed over and over and over
> again in my life. And that is why I succeed.'[2]

I love that quote, as it shows there is no need to fear failures. They can and most likely will happen if we are pushing ourselves beyond our comfort zones. Failures are part of growing and learning. If you are in fear of failing, it can lead you to inaction and staying where you are in life. You end up never making progress.

---

2   Quoted in Goldman, R and Papson, S (1998) *Nike Culture: The Sign of the Swoosh*. London: Sage Publications, p49.

Nevertheless, my failure still hurt. I thought for a long time about what I wanted to do next. Should I get into a new industry, or go and work for a company? It didn't take me long to realise that if I'd have gone to work elsewhere, I would never have been satisfied. I couldn't end my career in construction with a loss like that. I needed to prove to myself that I could make a success of things.

I picked myself back up and decided to start all over again, but this time I would do it differently. I went back to my business books, did copious amounts of studying, a few intense courses along with high-level coaching sessions, and began to form a new strategy out of everything that had worked and everything that hadn't. This eventually became my DEVELOP principles, which I would use in my new business to grow in a controlled and sustainable manner.

And it worked. I managed to achieve over £1.5m of sales in the first year, starting from scratch. My DE-VELOP principles worked, and they continue to do so. It was much easier running my second £1m business than my first. I'd found the secret to running a highly successful construction company that gave me more time, freedom and money.

I decided I wanted to share this strategy with others, so I started coaching, which then led to me writing this book.

When I look back now, I find it frustrating that I wasted so many years stagnating at £600k. If I'd have implemented the DEVELOP strategies back then, I would have been five years ahead of where I am now and my first business would never have gone into liquidation.

But life's about moving forward and learning from the past. And I've learned some valuable lessons on the highs and lows of owning a construction company. My failures have helped me hone my strategy to enable me to put a system in place that really works.

I don't want you to learn the hard way.

I'm convinced that teaching you these strategies and learning from my past successes and mistakes will help you avoid the pitfalls that come with growing a business and sail past a £1m turnover. Let's jump right in and get the foundations in place to start this transformational journey.

1
Succeeding In A Tough Industry

Is it possible for you?

Although entrepreneurial qualities are inbuilt, success in business is about more than just having the right qualities. Running a truly successful company requires principles that can be taught.

I've read and dissected hundreds of business books and invested thousands of pounds in business coaches over the last fifteen years because I have a burning desire to understand the secret to success in business. But I've realised that this is something that I will be learning for a long time to come.

If you asked Jeff Bezos of Amazon or Mark Zuckerberg of Facebook, they would tell you they are still learning. Business changes and adapts to the times we live in and we need to be constantly open to ideas and strategies to get us ahead of the game. The principles of business stay the same, though. Having run a successful construction company for the last fifteen years and worked with many small businesses, I've come to understand these principles and have seen them in action. The DEVELOP principles I'm going to outline in the next chapters will be the same principles that even Jeff Bezos and Mark Zuckerberg would have followed when they first started out.

Although this book has mainly been designed for those within the construction and service-related industries, no matter what industry you are in, if you apply the principles found in this book, they will take your business to the next level.

What does the next level look like for you? If you've picked up this book, I hope your next level is to smash through £1m in annual sales turnover. What's so significant about this number? First, achieving a £1m turnover with a decent profit margin lets you invest funds in building a small and efficient team around you. This is crucial if you want more time and freedom as it will help remove you from the daily firefighting, which is draining and stressful. It will also allow you to be rewarded financially for your efforts – rightly so, with all the risk and pressure you have to take on when running your own company.

Some say the £1m figure is a psychological barrier to growth. Many cannot pass through it, no matter what they try. Without a doubt, many find that reaching £1m turnover is a goal they just cannot achieve and, as such, they settle for a business that doesn't grow. Often, this leads to them feeling frustrated, never being able to take a back seat in the business, and working all the hours under the sun for little reward and satisfaction. Sound familiar?

The £1m barrier is not only a psychological one. Even with a burning desire to grow the business, there can be real physical barriers that cause a business to stagnate. The purpose of this book is to identify those barriers and burst through them.

By applying the DEVELOP system, one by one, those barriers will be pushed aside and you can comfortably move past the significant £1m turnover milestone and, once you're on the other side, you'll be amazed at how quickly you can double your turnover again.

Many say turnover is vanity and profit is sanity. I 100% agree. There is no point having revenue of millions year on year if you can't make a decent profit; however, in the construction and service industry, without significant turnover those profits will generally be meagre.

The aim of this book is to show you how you can create significant turnover within your business and enjoy the profits that will come alongside that. We will identify how to remove the barriers to growth, and how to mentally overcome the fears many business owners face. If you apply the principles found here your business will grow, no doubt. Depending on how driven you are, it may grow faster than you expect.

I recommend reading this book through once fully and then going back and working through a section of the DEVELOP programme at a time, ideally in the order set out.

So, let's begin. First, let's discuss why the construction industry is a tough nut to crack and why many business owners in this sector struggle to make decent money.

Construction industry challenges

Why did you choose to get into construction? I often ask my coaching clients this, and I get mixed responses. Many tell me they just fell into it. Some didn't perform well at school but were grafters. Not having decent grades meant there weren't many options available to them except to learn a trade, and they knew that, once qualified, they could earn decent money at quite a young age. Others loved working with their hands, creating things, and enjoyed working outdoors. Some could never see themselves stuck in an office environment. Some just wanted the freedom of working for themselves one day and construction seemed the easiest way to do that.

What was your reason? Do you still feel the same today?

Whatever your initial reasons were, if you've been in construction for a good few years you may now be realising that it's a tough industry. How you imagined things were going to be when you left school may not be your reality day to day.

The construction industry is one of the first sectors to feel the pinch in a recession. I've felt the effects of two major recessions in my life and my father has faced many more. We are also starting to feel the effects of Brexit, which could trigger yet another recession.

Back in the '90s, mortgage interest rates went up to nearly 15%. The entire economy suffered, but the effects were felt for longer in the construction industry than in others. I remember worried conversations between my parents when my dad had run out of work for a sustained period – and my dad was never out of work, he was a grafter.

Things got so bad, I remember helping my mum deliver catalogues around the streets to supplement our income. At the time, being young, I thought it was quite fun but I can only imagine the pressure my parents must have been under. My dad, being the breadwinner, a bricklayer by trade, having his work completely dry up – how would they provide for the family? Having a family of my own now, I understand the immense stress this must have caused.

There was another big recession in 2008/09. It was unbelievable seeing big high street names going bust and disappearing one after another. At this point I was running a reasonably established construction company, but I clearly remember panicking when work started drying up. I'd just had my first child and had bought a new home that needed a lot of work. At this point I hadn't created the DEVELOP strategy and we were not prepared to cope with the downturn. Nevertheless, we tightened up and just about managed to ride it out.

There's never a good time for a recession to rear its ugly head. But if you are around long enough, you will experience one at some point. This is why it's even more important that your business is ahead of the rest of the pack, or it could be one of those that disappears.

Even if your company stays afloat, you may not be immune to the effects of others going bust around you. Carillion, one of the largest construction companies in the UK, finally collapsed in 2017. After a series of profit warnings and debts of over £1bn, it couldn't recover and finally went into liquidation. The problem didn't end there, though, as the fallout of that event affected thousands of smaller companies and subcontractors in their supply chain. Stories began to emerge of smaller businesses being owed hundreds of thousands. One owner had put debts of £25k on his personal credit card to try and keep his company afloat. It's heartbreaking to see small businesses forced into liquidation due to the actions of others, but this is the harsh reality of the industry.

Even if you don't have to cope with a large supplier you are working for going bust, there is the age-old problem of trying to get money out of them. Being large, powerful corporations, many insist on harsh payment terms of thirty to sixty days, or more. This exposure can cause a business owner great stress and creates cashflow problems that can stunt business growth.

On top of the above problems, the industry suffers from a huge skills shortage that only seems to be getting worse. How many young people do you know who are choosing construction when they leave school? Probably not many. Over the years it's become a real problem, as the next generation choose alternative industries.

This leaves the industry relying on migrant labour, but with Brexit causing many to leave the UK, it's not clear how the skills shortage will be met over the coming decade. As a result of the lack of skilled labour, wages are on the increase. Decent tradesman can now charge premium prices, but what profit does that leave the business owner?

Another issue facing the construction industry is its bad reputation among homeowners. With documentaries like *Cowboy Builders* portraying a poor stereotype, the general homeowner is wary and cautious about employing a company to work on their home. This leaves companies on the backfoot throughout the job, while the homeowner is convinced you are constantly trying to 'pull one over' on them.

After considering the above, it's no wonder that only 4% of construction business owners manage to break through the £1m turnover barrier. But is there a way of protecting your business from the wider economy and against bad payers? Is there a way of retaining and attracting the best talent without paying through the nose? Is there a way of scaling and keeping loyal clients happy?

Absolutely, there is. By applying the DEVELOP strategies presented throughout this book, you will be miles ahead of the competition. You can be one of the 4% that successfully smashes through the £1m barrier. First, though, you need to overcome some of the problems a small business owner will face.

Frustrations of a small business owner

Not only does a business owner have to face problems that plague the construction industry in general, they also have to face problems much closer to home. If these problems are not addressed, it will lead to a business owner that feels burnt out, unhappy and most likely struggling to make ends meet. What sort of problems can give a business owner the blues?

Through my coaching business, I have spoken to many business owners in construction and the number one problem they face is not having enough time. They feel run off their feet, moving from job to job, quote to quote, trying to keep everyone happy.

Many business owners have families or young children and wish they could have a bit more time at home. But when they are at home, they're constantly catching up on paperwork – invoicing, chasing up debt, sending out quotes, paying the suppliers, paying the staff. The list just goes on and on. Many feel like they are run ragged and juggling an ever-increasing number of balls. Do you feel like that? Maybe this is one of the main reasons why you haven't expanded the business, as you cannot fathom how you will find the time to do it.

The second problem that's high on everyone's list is not earning enough money. It seems to be an endless struggle to find the money to pay the suppliers at the end of each month, let alone the dreaded quarterly VAT bill. You find yourself using the next job's deposit to pay the bills of the last, and you never seem to catch up.

Then you have clients trying to 'knock' you or get out of a payment that you've rightfully earned. Subcontractors demanding higher rates of pay that squeeze your profits. You're constantly being undercut on your quotations and find yourself matching or beating the best quote, just to keep everyone working.

You take on all this risk of running a business, but for what reward? It certainly doesn't feel like a financial one. You have created no meaningful pension for yourself, wouldn't you just be better off going to work for a company? You start to take on more and more work to see if it makes a difference, but you don't seem to earn any more money. Wasn't it easier when you were on your own as a sole trader? Does this thinking sound familiar to you?

The third problem that stresses business owners is staff. You recognise that no one is going to know or love your business like you do, but can the staff not show a measure of care? Does everyone clock off immediately at 5.00pm, leaving you to hit deadlines on your own? Yet if you haven't paid their wages by 5.00pm, they'll certainly let you know about it.

When you do finally find a brilliant member of staff or a subcontractor, it's not long before they decide to part ways. All that time and effort invested into training them and fitting them into your business and they are gone and you have to start all over again. Have you experienced something like that?

The fourth common problem is the worry about running out of work. The bigger you expand, the quicker you run through your contracts. You can never seem to get far enough ahead to relieve the stress. You are constantly chasing sales and never seem to be in the position where you can just say no to that awkward customer you know you shouldn't work for.

These are just four of the many problems a small business owner faces. When you add to these the wider problems that plague the construction industry in general, you may be thinking, 'What's the point? I may as well give up now'.

Well, what if I told you that you could easily address all these issues? What if I told you that you could increase the amount of free time you have *and* earn more money than ever before? I can show you how to retain your best talent and help you fill up your order book so that you're only taking on the best work. You might wonder, what's the catch? The only condition is that you read and apply the principles laid out in the DEVELOP strategy in full. It's that simple.

Well actually, it's not simple. It's hard work and takes effort to get there, but the formula is simple. If you've come this far with your business and got through the startup phase, you're already used to hard work and effort. Now it's time to take it to the next level – this book is going to help you get there.

Is there a solution?

I've run my own construction business for many years, which you'll hear more about later. I hit a barrier once I reached £600–£700k turnover. The barrier wasn't just a psychological one, it felt physical. We were genuinely stuck and I didn't know in which direction to turn. I turned to learning, through books and coaches. It fascinates me that you can read a book in just a few hours, and gain the wisdom of someone's life experience, which can be fifty-plus years. I consumed book after book about how to scale a small business, business strategy, motivation techniques, and so on. I then tried to combine and apply the best strategies in my own construction company.

Without a doubt, you could put down this book and find hundreds of others out there that will add value to you, and I do encourage you to find and read some of them. You will find that most highly successful people are avid readers. Yet I realised that I could not find a single book written specifically for construction company owners on how to transform their business. It's as if we'd been completely forgotten about. Our industry is unique, it has its own challenges and there seemed to be no help out there, so I decided to write one myself.

I've taken everything I have learned from the hundreds of books I've read that covered every possible subject – from strategy, to goal-setting, mindset, and people management, you name it, I've probably read about and studied it.

More importantly, though, I wanted to bring my years of experience of actually applying this knowledge within my own business to the table. I've got a lot right, but I've also made a lot of mistakes along the way – and some big ones. I've been there, done it and got the T-shirt. I know that, without help, companies get stuck or, worse, crumble completely.

I want to see construction company owners succeed. I want to show you how to create more time for yourself, how to be paid what you are worth. I want to show you how to scale up without running out of cash. I can show you how to stand out from the rest and put yourself in line to win larger, more lucrative contracts. All of this combined will make your company more valuable and will set you up nicely for an exit sale one day. I believe I have the answers and the tools to get you there, so I've written this book to get you all of the above.

I'll show you how to successfully scale your business.

A viable answer: the DEVELOP system

As already mentioned, there is a solution. But to scale in the first place and then ensure you scale successfully you need to follow a process and strategy. I've tried and tested the DEVELOP strategy on my own business and with my coaching clients and I can tell you it works. Here's a brief summary of what DEVELOP stands for and what we will be considering in depth throughout this book:

- Detailed roadmap

- Exceptional service

- Visual branding

- End of month reports

- Loyal people

- Operating systems

- Profit and loss

Detailed roadmap

Here we will discover the importance of setting realistic targets and goals, and of knowing your final destination. We'll examine typical roadblocks along the way and how we can overcome them. This will be an invaluable tool in proving the strategy works, as you can go back and review how far you've come.

Exceptional service

The next phase of our journey helps to cement what it is you do that's better than anyone else. I'll help you identify your USP and how to communicate that to your clients.

Visual branding

Gone are the days of using the Yellow Pages to get your name out there. We've entered a new era of digital marketing and this section will show you how to ensure your brand comes across well and is being marketed correctly. We'll look at how we can harness the power of social media to increase leads, bring in sales and provide brand awareness.

End of month reports

What gets measured, gets managed. Here we discuss the importance of having an accurate up to date picture of everything your business is doing. As the owner, you should be able to see instantly the health of your business, and to spot trends and dangers in advance through data and reporting.

Loyal people

The key to growing fast and consistently is having the right people in place. How do you attract and retain the best people to work for you, and then keep them fiercely loyal and performing at their peak? This section will guide you through the right questions to ask at interview and how to keep your staff turnover rates low.

Operating systems

It's vital that you stay in complete control as you grow. You do this by having robust systems in place so your operations run smoothly. This is the only way to scale significantly. Here we'll analyse what things you may want to automate and how a systemised business will alleviate much stress.

Profit and loss

Let's focus on the first word here. We obviously want to be in profit, but it's shocking how many business owners cannot get their head around a profit and loss (P&L) report. Here, we examine why it's so important to be on top of this data, why certain figures are key to helping you grow, and how to fully understand a P&L report in detail.

Enjoying the journey

There's a lot of information to work through in this book. Depending on how far along you are in your business journey, you may already have some of these things in place, which is great. You should still endeavour to read through those chapters even if you feel you have it mastered, as you are bound to pick up a few helpful points. If you're starting from scratch and have none of this in place, that's OK too. You have a blank canvas to work from and this will help start you off in the right direction.

Before you start this journey, you need to be prepared to roll your sleeves up and get stuck in. It isn't going to be easy to put this all into place and it will take time. Some of my clients have been able to fast-track their success through coaching, but even then it takes longer than many hope. Stick with it and continue on the journey because the end rewards for getting this right will be worthwhile.

If you successfully apply all the DEVELOP principles you will have more time for yourself and less stress. You will make more money personally and greater profits for a healthy business. You will be building a great brand and reputation, which will increase the chances of a successful exit when the time arrives. Even though you will have scaled to turnover figures you had not thought possible before, you will feel in complete control and hopefully be having some fun along the way.

The rewards for getting this right are well worth the effort. Scaling up and getting it wrong will be your worst nightmare. Believe me, I've been there and felt the pain. Let this book help you make it successfully past the £1m barrier.

You're about to embark on an amazing and transformational business journey. Before you start any journey, you need a detailed roadmap. This is where the DEVELOP principles begin.

ACTION POINT CHECKLISTS

At the end of each section you will find a list of Action Points. Try to work through and implement these, ticking them off as you go.

2
Detailed Road Map

Know your destination

Imagine heading off on a long car journey that you've never travelled before. Your destination is hundreds of miles away, the roads are unfamiliar, maybe even a bit dangerous, and you just set off without setting up the sat nav or looking at a map. You know roughly what direction you're heading in, but you don't have an exact location and no definite idea of how to get there. Embarking on such a journey would seem a bit crazy, but that's what many business owners are doing day in, day out. They have started up a business, have a general idea of how much they want to earn or broadly what they want to achieve, but have no exact end goal in mind and no detailed plan of how to get there.

Have you thought about where you want to be in five years? Off the tools; owning a big new office; driving an expensive company car; working three days per week; mortgage paid off. These sound like great goals, and maybe you have some of your own. Or, do you? Sometimes you can get so caught up in the rat race of running a business and working hard that the years just tick by and you seem no closer to fulfilling your dreams. Why is that? Often, it's due to those dreams being simply that – dreams, rather than a concrete goal or destination.

You say you want things to change for the better, but have you got an actual plan or roadmap for what you are going to do to ensure those changes happen? If the answer is no, then it's just like daydreaming: a waste of time. Worse, it can be discouraging when you realise you haven't made it later on in life. This is why it's so important to know what your end goal and destination is. Not just a wishy-washy dream, but a real, concrete goal.

Goal-setting is such a powerful strategy; if you haven't tried it, you'll be amazed at the difference it makes. Why not sit down for a few moments and write down what your goals are, in business and also in life. These two things are intertwined, so it's important to write down personal aims too, not just your business goals. Think big, don't limit yourself. Putting your goals down on paper is a powerful thing. I was amazed the first time I did it.

I often write down five-year, one-year, six-month, three-month, and monthly goals. I call the five-year goal my 'destination goal' on my roadmap. Some people increase this to ten or twenty years, but things change so often in life, and we change as individuals. Five years is a better reflection of what we want within the current period of our life.

Stop for a moment and write down your five-year goal – perhaps even write it in the back of this book. Try to push your boundaries with this goal. It needs to be realistic to some degree, but make it huge. You may not be able to imagine how you will achieve it just yet, but don't let that stop you.

In his book *Built to Last*, Jim Collins analysed in detail the most successful companies that consistently delivered market-beating returns, and found that they were all visionaries. They had all set huge goals.[3] He referred to these goals as BHAG (pronounced bee-hag), which stands for Big Hairy Audacious Goals. The biggest companies in the world often started out with these kinds of goals. Set yourself a five-year BHAG, push your boundaries and your imagination and see what you come up with.

---

3   Collins, J and Porras, JI (2005) *Built to Last: Successful Habits of Visionary Companies* (new ed.). London: Random House Business.

'Aim at the sun, and you may not reach it; but your
arrow will fly higher than if aimed at an object on
a level with yourself.'
— J Hawes[4]

Once you've written down your goal, you need to
think about why you want that goal so much. How
will achieving that goal change your life? Try to visualise your life and imagine you've managed to achieve
it. How good do you feel? Try to link this goal with
significant others, if you can. If you have a partner or
kids, think about how they would be affected if you
managed to provide this life for them. Now visualise
the pain of not achieving that goal. How bad do you
feel?

It's not enough to do this just once. Now you know
what your five-year goal and destination is, you need
to think about it and visualise it on a daily basis. If you
can do that, it will start to become a burning desire, especially if it's linked to helping others you care about.

I was amazed when I tried this personally. I recently
looked back at some goals that I had written down
and I was stunned at what had been achieved. I wrote
down in detail how much money I would have in
savings, who I would have working for me in my
business, what turnover we would have, how many

---

4   Quoted in Mason, J (1993) *You're Born an Original – Don't Die a Copy.*
Altamonte Springs, FL: Insight International.

properties I would own, how many hours I would be working per week, and so on.

When I look back on it now, I can say that 75% of those goals have been achieved or surpassed. Yes, there are a few things on there that have changed and are no longer relevant, but that's life; things come out of the blue and we need to adapt. Annoyingly, there are also things on there that I haven't achieved yet and am still working on – like getting a six-pack beach body!

But it's incredible, almost scary, how close I got to achieving almost all my goals. I know that if I hadn't written them down and kept them in focus all this time, I would not have got close to achieving what I have in both business and my personal life. Make sure you set out on your journey with an end goal in mind. Have a fixed destination and then a clear plan for how you are going to get there. This is the first key to the DEVELOP strategy: have a detailed roadmap.

Now you have your destination, let's make a clear plan for how to get there.

Create your roadmap

One person who set his mind to a fixed destination or goal was Richard Williams, the father of Venus and Serena Williams. We often give the credit for being world class tennis stars to Venus and Serena themselves, but actually their mindset and drive came from their father. Venus was just five years old when Richard decided to take her to the tennis courts, and it wasn't long before Serena joined them. He didn't just take them for a fun game of tennis; from an early age, he was convinced they were going to become world class tennis players. He had a grand plan. Sure, they had natural ability, but so do thousands of other children. The overriding factor was the continual drive, goal-setting, determination and planning that Richard started when they were young girls.

In Richard Williams' book, *Black and White,* he lists his top ten rules for success. Number one is: 'Failing to plan is planning to fail'.

I wholeheartedly agree with the above, but find it shocking how often I speak to business owners who have no real plan in place. If they have set an end destination that's at least a start, but often they have no strategy or plan for how to reach that destination.

As I mentioned in the goal-setting chapter, I usually write down not just a five-year goal, but break this down into one-year, six-month, quarterly, and monthly goals. It just seems more palatable and achievable if you do it this way. It's also more actionable if you have bite-size goals to attack rather than one big goal that seems impossible to achieve. I'm always fascinated by how people manage to climb and conquer Mount Everest. With the summit sitting at over 29,000 feet it's a formidable mountain to conquer, with hundreds losing their lives attempting to do so. Do you think anyone would attempt to climb this mountain without a rock solid, detailed plan? It would be lunacy. Anyone who was serious about reaching the summit and staying alive in the process would be planning and preparing months, even years before they began their climb.

Running a business is no different. Hopefully by now you've set out your destination and I hope you've pushed the boundaries and given yourself a BHAG goal that seems challenging to reach. Now, you need to plan how you are going to reach your Everest.

If you were actually climbing Everest, you'd never be able to make it in one go. The mountain is too big, too daunting, and to do it safely requires that it be climbed in stages. It's generally broken down into six stages along the way, which makes the climb to the summit more achievable. First, you need to make the journey to Base Camp from Kathmandu. This alone can take a week and you'll have to climb to an altitude of over 17,000 feet just to reach Base Camp. There will have been lots of planning and preparation in getting you to this stage. Although it may not feel like a great achievement, you've started to lay the foundations from which to push on to the more challenging stages of climbing Everest.

From here, once you've settled, acclimatised and prepared your equipment and ropes, you're ready to push to Camp One, at nearly 20,000 feet. This journey is a challenge, as it involves traversing over a moving glacier of tumbled ice and crossing deep crevasses.

Once you've made it to Camp One, you're ready to trek to Camp Two, across the Western Cwm. This section of the climb is flatter and easier in some respects. However, extremes in temperature, from baking hot to ice cold, can make this part of the journey mentally tough to deal with. Importantly, though, from here climbers get to see the peak of Everest for the first time as they approach Camp Two.

The journey from Camp Two to Three is extremely dangerous and difficult. The steep ice wall of the Lhotse Face needs to be traversed and with a high risk of avalanches and falling ice rocks, there have been many deaths in this area. Once you've reached Camp Three the danger is still not over, as the camp is perched like an eagle's nest jutting right out of the wall. The views looking back from here are known to be stunning and this gives many climbers the mental push to keep going. They can see how far they have already come and this strengthens their resolve to push on to the South Col and Camp Four.

Camp Four is the highest camp on earth, sitting at 26,000 feet. It is also known as the Death Zone. From this point, the body struggles to survive unaided, as the oxygen levels are so low.

Most need to use supplementary oxygen from here on to make the next push to the summit. Although so close now, many climbers are forced to turn back here. It could be due to bad weather, or just complete exhaustion, but not everyone will make it to the summit from this point. Although the climbers have come so far, there is still another 3,000 feet to go. It is real strength of character and inner belief that pushes the strongest to keep climbing.

The summit

Finally, after navigating the South Summit and the treacherous Hillary Step, you edge ever closer to the true summit of Everest, the highest mountain on Earth. Then, you've made it. As you scan the horizon and the world below, you feel the satisfaction and achievement of knowing you have conquered Everest.

There are lots of lessons to be learned from the path to climbing Everest that also apply to your business goals. The first is that no one can reach the summit of Everest without being determined to set that as a goal. It may seem like a distant reality at first but, slowly and surely, your plans come together and you make things happen to start the climb.

The same is true for your business goals. We've already discussed setting a BHAG. Hopefully, a goal that may seem impossible to start with can become a reality. But you must set a determined goal or end destination if you want to achieve your dreams in business.

The second lesson is to ensure you build a good foundation before you start your climb. Just being at Base Camp may not seem like much, but often this is where a lot of the planning and preparation is carried out that will serve you well later on. In business, setting up a good foundation can seem boring and it may not feel like you are getting anywhere. But when you have planned, prepared and put good systems in place, these become invaluable as you scale up, and stop things from getting out of control when you start to grow faster.

The third lesson is that you need to make plans now for how you will reach your goal. You don't get to the top of Everest in one go. There are planned stops along the way where you regroup, take stock of what you've just achieved, build your strength and then push for the next camp. Business goals are no different. We've discussed setting not just a BHAG, but then breaking that down into one-year, six-month, quarterly, and monthly goals. You could go even further and break these down into weekly and daily goals if it helps. The important thing is to consistently take a few steps in the right direction each day, and you will get there in the end. Often, Everest climbers say that all they focused on was placing one foot in front of the other. When you set interim goals, the journey seems more achievable. If you want to lose weight and set the goal of dropping a stone, it's much easier to tackle that a week at a time by aiming to lose just one pound a week over fourteen weeks.

The fourth lesson is not to be afraid to ask for help. No one could climb Everest without the essential help of the Sherpas. The Sherpas are the world's best mountain climbers; they have been there and done it numerous times.

As you grow in business you are going to enter unknown territory and come across problems that you've never had to deal with before. How do you fire someone who isn't performing without risking a tribunal? How do you deal with a client who's reneging on a contract?

Don't be afraid to ask for help so you can tackle these challenges in the best way. I've continually sought help and gained advice from coaches, consultants and friends who have been there and done it before. This could end up saving you thousands of pounds, as making a serious mistake when you are a larger company can be costly. Ultimately, though, you need to be responsible for your own choices, so listen carefully, but only you will know what the best decision is for your company.

Another benefit of using coaches is that they can fast-track you to success. Just as the Sherpas know the quickest and safest route up Everest, coaches and consultants can often see past the day-to-day problems you are facing and work out a strategy to reach your goals faster.

The fifth lesson is to remember that the end goal isn't the only achievement. Each time you reach an interim goal, celebrate it. On Everest, climbers will look back at each camp they have reached and enjoy the views, letting it sink in what an achievement it is just to have got this far.

Sometimes we can be so caught up in chasing our dreams that we forget to stop every now and then and enjoy the journey. Stopping periodically and reviewing what you've done and how far you have come can be a real psychological boost to help you continue the journey.

It's great to have goals, as that pushes you to keep growing in life, but don't let the achievement of the goals define you. It's making progress each day that should be celebrated and enjoyed, not the end outcome.

> 'Take pride in how far you've come. Have faith in how far you can go. But don't forget to enjoy the journey.'
> — Michael Josephson[5]

---

5   Josephson, M (no date) 'Michael Josephson's What Will Matter'. https://whatwillmatter.com

The other thing to bear in mind is that goals can change. Life is forever presenting surprises and challenges, maybe a new baby arrives or there is a long-term illness in the family. Life doesn't take your goals into consideration, and sometimes you need to re-evaluate your priorities and perhaps set new goals. That's fine. As I've said, don't let achieving or not achieving the end goal define you; enjoy the journey.

On Everest, goals change when circumstances insist on it. Some climbers can be right up at Camp Four and then realise that bad weather is coming and they are not going to be able to make the summit. They then quickly have to change their goals. For some, their new goal is just to make it back down to Base Camp as safely as possible, and they may decide to tackle Everest another time in life. Even for those climbers who don't reach the summit, what an experience and journey they will have had. They will already have achieved much more than the average climber, and that too is something worth celebrating.

Follow the road, don't get distracted

Have you ever taken a long car journey that starts to get a bit boring, and found yourself staring out the window? What do you notice on the side of road? You'll see billboard after billboard of advertisements. What's their purpose? To distract you.

Take a McDonald's billboard. The aim is to get you thinking about nothing but a tasty Big Mac, and once you come across a McDonald's restaurant farther up the road there is no doubt you'll pull over and head in there if you've let yourself become distracted. You're no longer thinking about your destination; instead, you're devouring that Big Mac.

It's easy to get distracted on our business journey and there will be lots of things put in our way that can make us veer off course. Some of these distractions we can create ourselves. How so? One quality that most entrepreneurs have is creativity. This is a great quality to have, as they can come up with solutions that others may not see, but it can also present its own problems. Some have too much creativity and so are constantly coming up with new ideas and schemes, which can make it difficult to stick to one path.

One minute, you're chasing down one idea, the next you ditch it to follow the latest trend or the next get-rich-quick scheme. This can be triggered by boredom, or even stress. If you recognise this in yourself, it's important to control it, as it can be a severe weakness. While it's important to react quickly and make changes if needed, there needs to be a fine balance between coming up with new ideas and sticking to a path you've already set. There is nothing more frustrating for employees than when they are working hard on a project and it gets ditched to chase the next shiny new idea. It's also confusing for your clients. Continually changing products and services shows a lack of stability and can damage your reputation.

The aim is to become known as one of the best companies in your area for delivering a specific product or service. That takes a lot of time and consistent effort. Ideally, you will limit your service offering to just a few things at first and then put all your effort and focus into delivering an outstanding product. The next section of the DEVELOP strategy discusses this in detail. Only once you've mastered a specific service offering or product can you consider slowly expanding it to add others.

A great example is Pimlico Plumbers. In 2017 they generated revenue of over £35m,[6] offering services from electrics, to roofing, to carpentry. These days, they even sell branded jumpers and baseball caps. Originally, they were purely a plumbing and heating company, hence the name. Only once they had mastered offering an exceptional service in that area did they then decide to expand into other services. Their core offering is still plumbing and heating, and probably always will be.

This is a classic example of a sustained focus on building a quality reputation and brand for a specific product, before starting to add additional services to

6   Pimlico (2017) 'Press Release: Pimlico Plumbers continued expansion delivers record £35m sales!' www.pimlicoplumbers.com/media/news/pimlico-plumbers-continued-expansion-delivers-record-35m-sales

supplement revenue. The lesson: don't get distracted. Keep following the roadmap you have set.

Reaching your destination is not going to be straightforward. But if you keep your focus, you will get there. There will be challenges on the road to success. We could call these roadblocks. Only pure grit and determination will get you past these.

Let's see what the common roadblocks are, and how to overcome them.

Hitting a roadblock

If the economic climate is right and you are offering a great service, you could probably do quite well and expand without too much effort. But often things don't run so smoothly. Business can present one frustrating challenge after another. When things are going well, enjoy it, as it may only be a matter of time before something ugly rears its head. The key is not to get too disheartened when things start going wrong.

If you were in the middle of a long car journey and, after a few hundred miles, you found out they'd closed off the road ahead, what would you do? Would you turn around and give up on your journey? Or would you just sit there in the road until they removed the roadblock? Of course you wouldn't; that would be a complete waste of time and effort. Instead, you'd try to find a way around the obstacle and rejoin the road to your destination as quickly as possible.

The same will be true for your business. You can't just give up when obstacles appear. You also cannot stand still and hope that they will miraculously go away. You need to find your way around them as quickly as possible.

What are some of the challenges and roadblocks a company will face as it seeks to grow to £1m?

Cashflow

Cashflow problems are a huge obstacle and often get more problematic as you grow. This is highlighted as the first obstacle for good reason. Not only are cashflow problems extremely stressful for the business owner, they can sink a business even if it is profitable. It doesn't seem like that could be true, but it is. We've all heard the saying, 'revenue is vanity, profit is sanity, but *cash is king.*'

Imagine you own a business that is making good profits, but you are still waiting for the revenue to come in. Maybe it's a large contract and you don't get paid for sixty or ninety days, but you still have to pay your suppliers and staff. It may well be a profitable contract, but if it sucks up your cash and means you need to take on debt to fund your cashflow, you're going to see your profits quickly dwindle.

It amazes me how many business owners only focus on their profit and loss statements (P&L) and don't pay a blind bit of notice to cashflow. This is short-sighted as it's poor cashflow, not necessarily poor profit, that can send a business under very quickly. When the money runs out and banks won't lend any more, suppliers soon stop providing materials, subcontractors and employees will stop providing their services. Having thousands of pounds owed to you in profits will not help you in that situation. This problem will only get worse as you grow, unless crucial steps are put in place to manage it.

How do you get over this obstacle? The good news is, being in the construction industry it can be quite easy to manoeuvre cashflow to work in your favour.

Some simple things you can do that will make a huge difference are:

- Request to pay suppliers every sixty days.

- Pay subcontractors every month, or at least a week behind, not on a Friday at the end of the same week.

- Where appropriate, make it clear to subcontractors that they do not get paid until you do.

- Pay direct employees monthly not weekly.

- Insist on clients paying deposits for works that you keep on hold.

- Invoice clients regularly and promptly. If possible, insist on payment at the point of sale, or a maximum of seven days from invoice date.

- Give clients the option to pay by credit card.

- If clients have recurring transactions for identical amounts each month, set up a direct debit.

Other things you may need to consider (though these will affect profitability) are:

- Leasing rather than purchasing vehicles and equipment.

- Invoice financing: where you raise debt on invoices as soon as they are issued if your clients are slow payers. This means you receive a large percentage of the invoice immediately and the finance company takes over the debt. This is usually only suitable for commercial clients, not domestic, and can be costly if relied on too often.

- Offer discounts to clients if they pay early.

Ideally, you should implement the items in the first list as an immediate priority, as these will not affect profitability but will make a huge difference to cashflow. A secondary measure, which we discuss in greater detail in the section on end of month reporting, is to ensure you are provided with cashflow as well as P&L reports. Keep an eye on the trends and raise red flags if you see unusual movements in cashflow from month to month.

Although cashflow is a large obstacle in the road, it can be overcome. Ensure you maintain an awareness of it and try to see potential issues coming well in advance. Whatever you do, don't bury your head in the sand. Take some positive action to ease your situation; cashflow issues are not to be taken lightly.

Bad reviews

You've worked hard to build up your reputation and brand in your market. You've got some amazing reviews online and then, all of a sudden, someone posts something negative. There's nothing more painful than a bad review and, although you may have plenty of good ones, the bad one will stand out like a sore thumb. Sometimes it's unavoidable, as you'll never please every single client – some jobs will go wrong. The danger arises if you start noticing poor reviews on a frequent basis.

As you expand, the personal service you once offered will inevitably be affected. At first, your clients know you and only you, but as the business grows, you may become faceless. Your client only knows your company and feels no loyalty to you as an individual. Once the personal aspect has gone from the service offering, clients are less likely to put up with minor annoyances. You may have got away with these previously, as clients tend to overlook issues when dealing with an individual, but now you're a faceless company they will feel they have a right to, at best, have a moan if things go wrong, or, at worst, compensation or a scathing review.

It's important to recognise that this is the reality if you are going to scale up, so it's imperative you keep your personal brand at the head of the business. One way to do this is to create and publish plenty of online blogs and vlogs so clients still know who you are. Visit a client's project now and then, on a random basis. This means a lot to your client and shows that you take a personal interest.

Sam Walton, the owner of Walmart, was declared the richest man in America in 1985. He insisted on regularly visiting his stores and getting down to the storefront, promoting goods himself. He loved it; the business was his baby. More importantly, though, he was ensuring he didn't become a faceless company. People would see him, staff and customers, and he gave the impression that he genuinely cared about his business. He could have sat in a large office all day, but he ensured at least some of his time was spent on the shop floor.

Do the same with your business even as you expand, and note that it goes a long way. Doing this will ensure you're able to monitor the service you are giving to clients – you'll be able to see it first-hand. If you notice things going wrong, or the service becoming poor, you can act quickly before the reviews are posted.

The other thing to bear in mind is your reaction when a bad review appears. First, don't overreact in anger. Often, you'll want to reply immediately to defend yourself or 'have a go' back. But take your time and calm down before you respond, and then keep it professional. Apologise and acknowledge your client's feelings and let them know that you're looking into how to improve that area of the business. End your response positively, without making it look like you are dismissing the complaint. When potential clients see a response like this, they can sense you genuinely care, which can help with future sales.

Replying to a bad review

Here's a great example of a reply to a bad review:

'Dear [use first name to be more personal]. Thank you for taking the time to leave a review. I apologise on behalf of everyone here at [insert company name]. Please know that your situation was an exception. As you can see from our other reviews, we care deeply about our customers and strive to deliver an outstanding service. We can't fix the past but you have my personal commitment to improve the way our staff serves every customer. Until then, please accept my sincerest apologies on behalf of everyone on the team.'

Don't let the bad review knock you too much. Remember, it's just an obstacle in the road, one that you can easily get around. Learn from it, use it as an opportunity to improve and then keep travelling towards your destination.

Firefighting

Be under no illusions, your business will undoubtedly deliver problem after problem; it's all part of the journey. However, as the owner there is a danger that you get roped into dealing with and solving every problem. We call this firefighting. It can feel like an obstacle when you can't see a way of scaling while spending so much time firefighting.

While this may have been acceptable at the beginning, it will start to become unsustainable as you grow. If you end up spending all your time firefighting, your business will suffer, as no one will be paying attention to strategy and other important things that require your time. It's important to let others do the firefighting, so your time is spent more wisely. Learn the art of delegation as you start to expand and hire new staff. Delegation won't come easily if you're used to doing everything yourself, but you need to learn to start trusting capable people. If you notice your staff continually come to you to solve their problems, it may be that you haven't given them enough confidence to deal with things themselves.

Zappos, an online shoe retailer, is a multimillion-dollar company. There was no way the managers could cope with all the support calls they received at the help centre, so they put in place a policy of allowing their employees to offer up to $50 to solve a problem. Their employees have the complete freedom to use their discretion on whether or not to offer this amount if they receive a genuine complaint. This small step took a huge amount of pressure off line managers having to firefight and gave employees confidence to solve things themselves.

Could you do something similar with your employees? Alternatively, when a problem is posed to you, why not ask employees to suggest how to resolve it? Even if it's not the perfect answer, give them the dignity of implementing their suggestions when possible, as this will go a long way in improving their confidence.

Once you see that they can solve things themselves, let them run with it and ask them to only approach you with more serious issues. This will dramatically decrease the amount of time you have to spend firefighting and lets you concentrate on working *on* the business rather than *in* it.

Out of control

As you start to increase your staff numbers and workload, it won't take long before you feel completely out of control. No matter how many hours you spend at work, you can't cover all the bases. The danger is this might be more than just a feeling; you may actually be out of control.

Overcoming this obstacle requires putting the correct foundations and systems in place. This way, everyone knows what they are meant to be doing and you can have trust that your employees are doing what they should be. A good place to start is creating a company process handbook, in which everyone's job is described in detail, as well as every system that you use. It should be so detailed that anyone coming in on their first day should be able to pick up the handbook and be able to carry out their assigned task.

For example, what happens when you receive a complaint? Is the date, time and who is resolving the complaint logged somewhere? Who closes the complaint out, and is the resolution then recorded? This is a relatively simple system to document, but it puts you back in control. You know complaints are being handled correctly and all you need to do is receive a weekly or monthly summary.

Another thing that helps is having regular communication with your staff. Some recommend daily huddles with the entire team, just for five or ten minutes, so you have all the latest information to hand. It's also crucial to have in-depth weekly meetings with project managers or other senior staff to ensure your projects are running on time and to budget.

Also, at this stage of company growth your business should be small enough for you to regularly catch up with all staff (including your sub-contractors) one-on-one to see what issues they may be experiencing in the business. You'll be amazed at what you can pick up and you may start to notice trends; for instance, you may observe subcontractors complaining about materials being delayed. You can then investigate the supplier or buyer to see if the issue can be resolved and improve the project's speed and profitability.

Regular communication is crucial to feeling and staying in control. Don't rely on emails and reports alone; take the time to talk to your staff individually and as a group and retain that sense of control.

These are just some of the roadblocks you may find on your journey that can hinder progress or even bring growth to a complete standstill. There will be many more and some are addressed further in the book, like not getting enough sales or struggling to retain your best staff, and there will no doubt be other obstacles completely unique to you. The important thing to remember is that you can get around all of them with some thought. The key is recognising when they arise – or are about to – and then dealing with them quickly.

Don't allow roadblocks to stall your growth, push you too far off course, or cause you to give up completely. They are part and parcel of growing a business and every time you deal successfully with one roadblock you'll know exactly what to do next time.

If you find your growth stagnating, analyse if one of the above roadblocks is holding you back and then deal with it accordingly. Let nothing get in the way of reaching your goal.

ACTION POINT CHECKLIST

1. Write down your five-year goal – push your limits
2. Break down your goal into one-year, six-month, and three-month goals
3. Immediately implement the cashflow checklist
4. Respond tactfully to any bad reviews online
5. Implement a daily huddle with the team

3
Exceptional Service

Your number one priority

You've created your roadmap. You now have a clear path to what you want to achieve and interim goals to help get you there. It's time now to look at delivering results and turn those dreams into something tangible. One of the first things you need to focus on is your offer. What is the service or product you are offering to your clients, and, more importantly, why is it better than others? Are you able to articulate that? Can you pitch your product and explain why someone should use you in a confident and convincing way?

If you want to see significant and sustained growth then exceptional service must become a core value within your business. It must be the number one priority for you and your staff, and it needs to be constantly reaffirmed. We are focusing on this early on to highlight its importance. Without exceptional service, your company will be propped up by expensive marketing efforts, cheaper price points and new business only, which leaves you with low profitability. The easiest way to make profit is to sell again to existing clients and those to whom you have been recommended, but the only way you'll achieve this consistently is if you're offering a great service. But there is more to it than that. To offer something exceptional, it must be unique. You need to stand out from others – let's find out how to do that.

Stand out

Most service firms will claim that they offer a great product. What's going to make you different to the others? The reality is, if you have nothing unique to offer you will be competing solely on price – this is the worst position to be in. It may work in other industries, like discounted retailers (eg Walmart), who sell products cheap but in huge quantities, but it's not an effective strategy in the construction industry.

Competing on price may get you through the early days of a startup, when overheads are low, but as you start to expand you will require staff, offices, equipment, computers, etc. When overheads increase significantly you will find that your prices have to rise just to stay afloat. The problem is, your clients will not care about your overheads. When they are given a price for a service, if someone else is delivering the same product at a cheaper price then you can almost guarantee you've lost that sale.

It's imperative that you stand out, but that's easier said than done. Construction is a crowded industry and unless you're offering a unique, specialist product that the average Joe isn't, standing out will be a challenge. But you can still stand out, even if you do not have a unique product.

Let's take Apple as an example. They can sell a mobile phone for upwards of £1,000 when their rival Nokia can only charge £350 for their most expensive phone, which has many similar features. Even though Apple's product is triple the price, they will outsell Nokia time and time again and are hugely profitable. Why?

It's not that they have a unique product, as the Nokia phone is almost the same. Apple has developed a way to stand head and shoulders above the competition. They have managed to develop branding and a reputation that makes it cool to be seen with an Apple phone. They also offer an exceptional service in their stores, providing a unique experience that helps drive sales and inspire customer loyalty.

Your construction company is nothing like Apple, though, so why mention it? The point is, you don't have to be selling completely unique products to stand out from the crowd, and just because you are in a crowded marketplace, you still need to avoid being reliant on competing on price only. It is possible to stand out, but it involves finding your USP (unique selling proposition/point). What if you don't have a USP? We'd better find you one, and fast.

How to find your USP

It's not always easy to find your USP, but as we mentioned above it's essential to stop you competing on price, a position you do not want to be in. You'll notice that companies all around you struggle with USP, as they all seem to offer the same benefits. Some of the generic USPs you can find in the service industry include:

- 'Good quality and low prices'

- 'Affordable quality since 1990'

- 'Service with a smile'

- 'Satisfaction guaranteed'

- 'You've tried the rest, now try the best'

These are just taglines and certainly not unique, so don't deserve to be called USPs. Phrases like this are commonplace in the market and are not going to differentiate you in any way, shape or form. If you don't have a USP, how do you go about getting one? It needs to be good enough to differentiate you. You need to be able to deliver on it. You want to ensure it will make your clients choose you over the rest.

One of the first things needed is to understand who your client is, who you are selling to. What are their problems, fears and needs? You will attract the types of clients you focus on, so if you don't like your current crop of clients, maybe it's time to focus on selling to the ones you do want (provided you can deliver effectively to them). Going forward, design your marketing strategy to attract only your ideal clients.

Do the following as an exercise. First, start by writing down who your *ideal* client is. Be as detailed as you can. Create an avatar of that person. Ask questions like:

- What's their age?
- Where do they live?
- How much do they earn?
- Are they single or married?
- Do they have children?
- What are their interests?
- What magazines do they read?
- What Facebook groups will they visit?

Once you've worked out who that individual is, start thinking about how they think and feel:

- What are their wants?

- What are their needs?

- What are their worries?

- What problems do they have that need solving?

- What are they frustrated with in your industry?

Once you start building up this picture it can help you formulate what your USP needs to be to appeal to and reach this individual. Try to be as specific as you can and don't fall into the trap of trying to be all things to all people. You will have more success focusing on a specific or niche market. Next, think about what your company does or can do that might be different to your competitors. What are your strengths and company values? Are you faster than others? Do you offer better quality? Have you been established a long time?

Here are some great examples of USPs that might give you some ideas about your own:

- **Craftsman Tools:** 'If any Craftsman hand tool fails to provide complete satisfaction, return it for free repair or replacement. Period. The first Craftsman hand tool we sold back in 1927 is still under warranty today.'[7]

---

7 Swayne, W (2016) 'Unique Selling Proposition Formulation Guide with Examples (Updated For 2019)'. www.marketingresults.com.au/ unique-selling-proposition

This USP is based on being a trusted established company, it shows confidence in their quality and it signifies peace of mind for the client via a guarantee.

- **Dropbox:** 'Dropbox keeps your files safe, synced, and easy to share. Bring your photos, docs, and videos anywhere and never lose a file again.'[8]

  This USP talks directly to their clients' fears. No one wants to lose precious files, photos and memories. It also lets them know the service is convenient.

- **The AA (Automobile Association):** 'To our members, we're the fourth emergency service.'[9]

  This USP again talks to customers' fears. For someone vulnerable, it would be a nightmare for their car to break down on the side of a motorway. The AA reassures them that they will come to save them like a knight in shining armour.

Hopefully this will give you a few ideas on how to start generating your USP. Just to clarify, the five steps to finding yours are to:

1. Work out your ideal client and talk directly to them through your USP

2. Think of the challenges or worries they face

---

8 Swayne, W (2016) 'Unique Selling Proposition Formulation Guide'.
9 Lewis, D (2013) *The Brain Sell: When Science Meets Shopping.* London: Nicholas Brealey Publishing, p36.

63

3. Explain how you solve the problem

4. List your distinctive benefits

5. Make a promise

Even after working through the above steps, it can take some time to settle on something that fits. For assistance, why not ask previous clients what they thought was great about you? What were they worried about before they purchased your product or service? It's a great way of getting into the mind of your ideal client – just ask them directly.

Once you find your USP it will be liberating and give you direction and clarity on how to move forward. Now you need to let everyone know what your USP is. Let's find out how.

Communicate your USP

You've worked hard to hone your USP. Now it's time to start delivering this message to your clients. It's absolutely vital that it flows consistently throughout all your marketing. First, though, you need to enshrine it in your company culture. Hold a meeting with your staff and let them know what your new USP is and how important it is that you now deliver on that promise. Reinforce the message to your staff every week. Put the USP all over the walls of your office and as screensavers on your computers. Ensure the staff picking up the phones mention it, and that the sales team are discussing it every time they meet a client. It needs to become the core of your business, so as soon as someone asks your staff what you do, the USP should roll off their tongue. Once it's at the heart of the business, it will start becoming the thing you are known for.

Next, ensure it's added to all your marketing collateral – your brochures, flyers, estimates. It needs to be highly visible on your website. Put it at the bottom of your emails. Basically, it should be everywhere. Your client must come to see that you are better than those pricing against you. It's the only way for you to stop having to compete on price. You need to be paid what you are worth, and oftentimes it's just about ensuring that you are communicating that effectively to your client so that they don't even consider the company that doesn't have such an effective strategy.

It's important that the communication of your USP is consistent from beginning to end. It should be noted the first time someone sees your advert, the first time they visit your website. That same USP should be mentioned the first time they speak to you over the phone, it should be on all the emails they receive. It should be mentioned at the first sales appointment and on any brochure or estimate that is sent. You get the point. Once you have an effective USP, bang on about it, as this will be your key to greater sales wins.

The importance of delighting your clients

Winning sales is great and your USP will aid you massively in that. Now, it's time to deliver. If you've promised something as your USP, you need to follow through on it and provide an exceptional service for your client. If you can do this consistently, your growth will be fast and substantial.

I mentioned previously that the easiest way to make profit is to sell again to existing clients and those to whom you have been recommended. Once you have clients who are raving fans of yours, they will become ambassadors for your business. They will recommend you to their family and friends, and once you deliver a great service to them too they will repeat the process. Before long, you will have increased your fan base hugely, and the growth can be exponential.

It won't take long then for good reviews to go online, which cold clients (ones who weren't recommended) will read, putting you in a strong position to gain their business. This will be a dream for your sales staff, as with a reputation like this it will be easy for them to convert sales, even if you are a bit more expensive than others.

Another great tip to turn your clients into raving fans is to absolutely delight them in some way. Not just by delivering what you originally promised, but by going above and beyond that. Deliver beyond their expectations.

The highly successful shoe retailer, Zappos, does this all the time and has an almost cult-like following among its customers for its legendary customer support. Zappos' number one core value is to deliver a 'wow'.

The CEO, Tony Hsieh, has built the company on the principle of going above and beyond. This is often in small ways, like providing expedited shipping even if a customer opts for standard shipping. But they deliberately go much further than that, and Tony has empowered his staff to make judgement calls on how to delight and 'wow' customers. How about this great example:

Zaz Lamarr needed to return some shoes to Zappos but her mother had just passed away and, because she was still coping with the loss, she hadn't found the time to do it. When Zappos emailed her to ask about the status of the shoes, she replied explaining what had happened. Zappos took care of the shipping and had the courier pick up the shoes for her at no extra cost.

Zappos' customer care didn't stop there. Zaz writes:

'Yesterday, when I came home from town, a florist delivery man was just leaving. It was a

67

beautiful arrangement in a basket with white lilies and roses and carnations. Big and lush and fragrant. I opened the card, and it was from Zappos. I burst into tears. I'm a sucker for kindness, and if that isn't one of the nicest things I've ever had happen to me, I don't know what is.'[10]

Now, that is what you call going the extra mile. Customer loyalty is priceless and Zappos have clearly mastered how to give exceptional service. Think about ways you can do the same in your industry. Make it an obsession and part of your company DNA to offer exceptional service and you'll see staggering results.

Now that you offer a great service, it's time to ensure you are building a fantastic brand and getting the right message out into the world. Let's find out how with the next part of the DEVELOP system.

ACTION POINT CHECKLIST

1. Complete your ideal client avatar
2. List their wants, needs, fears
3. Formulate your USP to align with this
4. Add your USP to all social media channels and your website

---

10   Quoted in Bustos, L (2007) 'Good Customer Service Still the Best Word-of-mouth Marketing Strategy'. www.getelastic.com/good-customer-service-still-the-best-word-of-mouth-marketing-strategy

4
Visual Branding

Marketing has changed

Gone are the days of using the Yellow Pages to get your name out there. We've entered a new era of digital marketing. Never before has it been so easy to get your message in front of thousands of people in an instant; we are living in incredible times. We are in an age where customers make informed decisions about their purchases. They do this by researching a product or company thoroughly. They are looking for the experts in the industry. They want to consume information, and quickly.

Think about your own buying habits. You no doubt do the same thing when you want to buy a product. You search online, compare prices, then read reviews.

You research the company you think you want to buy from some more. You then develop trust and, boom, you make a purchase.

Trust is key to the whole transaction. Your clients must feel like they can trust you even before they make that first appointment. Once clients have decided that they trust your company, they will want to buy, or book an appointment, quickly and easily. These are all important factors to bear in mind when designing websites and getting your message across to potential leads.

As we've mentioned, it's easy now to get your message in front of thousands of people in an instant, but unfortunately so can all your competitors. The marketplace has become more crowded than ever and this can cause confusion for your potential clients. Who do they choose? Who should they call first? More than ever, it's vital to ensure the whole brand image is correct if you want to stand out among the crowd.

This section will show you how to ensure your brand comes across as first choice through a consistent message, and how to market your brand correctly. We'll look at how we can harness the power of social media to increase leads, bring in sales and create brand awareness. We'll also touch on other cheap, traditional methods that still increase the leads that come through your door. First, though, let's look at the brand itself.

Your brand

What is a brand, and does your company have one?

This is the definition Wikipedia gives:

> 'A brand is a name, term, design, symbol, or other feature that distinguishes an organisation or product from its rivals in the eyes of the customer. Brands are used in business, marketing, and advertising.'[11]

The purpose of your brand is to distinguish your business from others. But it's more than just a fancy logo. A strong brand should be reflected in your USP, your customer service style, your message, your staff uniforms, your business cards – everything.

It's identified by the colours and fonts you use, and especially the imagery. For example, if your target market is families, you would use warm and/or bright colours to reflect trust and happiness. The imagery on your website and blogs would show families and children or pets.

You can pay a specialist company to draw up some brand guidelines that will identify all the colours, fonts and imagery that should be used across your website, copy and social media channels. The ultimate aim is that when people see any of your

---

11   https://en.wikipedia.org/wiki/Brand

marketing collateral, they automatically associate it with your company.

In the previous section about developing a USP, we discussed how it's important to tie emotion in to branding. If you are offering a service rather than a product, it's less tangible so you need to demonstrate perceived value through your branding. People need to realise that buying from you will solve the problem they face.

This is a key point, so I'll repeat it again: *people buy from you to solve a problem.*

This is important to remember and will help distinguish your message from others. For example, imagine your specialty was emergency call-outs for electrical services. The client could do a Google search and find thousands of electricians, but the one that stands out will be the one that focuses on the client's problem and the solution that they offer. When the client sees your advert or landing page, they see messages like, 'Has your power gone off as you're about to cook a family meal? Don't fret, we'll get you up and running within the hour and you'll be back at the dinner table.' That sort of thing.

Rather than focusing on your company being emergency electricians, you have focused on the problem your client is experiencing and the fact that you provide the best solution. The company with this type of ad is the company that will get the call above others.

Another way of tying emotion to your branding is by ensuring your personality runs through it. People buy from people, especially in the service industry. Think of Richard Branson and Jamie Oliver, their brands and companies are intertwined with their personalities, and because people like and trust them they then buy into their services, airline, restaurants and books.

Let's see how we can start building up a strong brand for your business.

Social profile

Although Facebook has over two billion users, I know plenty of people who detest it. Not just Facebook, they detest social media all together. Whatever your personal feelings are, you need to get over yourself. Social media is one of the most powerful ways of creating an online brand; if you don't use it, you are putting your business at a huge disadvantage. This is where your clients will be hanging out socially, consuming information in their private time or at work, and this is where much of their research is done before they purchase a product or service. You need to be in that space to have a chance of getting in front of your clients. If you're not there, your competitors certainly will be.

What social media platform should you focus on? That will depend on what you're offering and who you are targeting. With my construction company we targeted architects and other professionals through LinkedIn. LinkedIn is generally viewed as more professional, so it makes sense to use this for your architects, surveyors or whoever in your sector has a professional type of work profile. However, to target our ideal clients, which for us was family homeowners, we used Facebook and Instagram. We used Facebook for advertising and sharing interesting blogs or vlogs to try and generate engagement, as well as before and after photos, often accompanied by case studies and/or testimonials. Instagram and Pinterest are primarily visual platforms, so we used these to showcase our finished products, refurbishments, extensions, kitchens and so on.

We mentioned in the last chapter how successful companies headed by the likes of Richard Branson and Jamie Oliver have been at generating a brand around their personalities. These personalities are prolific on social media and people learn to like and trust them as individuals, which encourages them to buy into their brand and the products they sell.

Vlogs are a great way to get your personality across. People get to see who is running things, which increases trust. Remember, people buy into people more than products, especially in the service industry. Try to get your personality out there by creating videos and personal blogs – you'll be amazed at the leads it can generate.

Another platform to try is Twitter. Twitter is text-based, so although you can attach pictures people have to actually click the link to see them. Often, short phrases and sentences reminding people of what challenges or customer problems you are solving can be enough to attract interest.

With all the platforms mentioned above you need followers to see your content. Resist the temptation to pay companies for a quick boost in followers, as these schemes are often worthless. They promise a thousand followers within a week, but these won't be relevant to you and you won't get many leads.

Unfortunately, slow and steady wins the race when trying to gain followers, so just persist in following relevant people in your industry in the hope that they follow you back. If you take an active role by commenting, liking and retweeting, or sharing their posts, you'll find that they do the same for you as a courtesy. It doesn't take too long to build up a decent and, most importantly, relevant following.

The point is, you need to set yourself up on the main social media platforms and use them to their full advantage by getting your personality across. Remember, you represent your company's core values, so get out there and show people who you are.

Harness free marketing

Where most people fall down with social media is struggling to generate content. This can be a challenge at first, especially if you want to post something every day. The good news is, you can repeat a lot of your content and pictures, but you still need to get organised and prepare at least some content to get you through a month.

One thing worth doing is getting a thirty-day content calendar together. Sit down for a few hours and write content for a whole thirty days (sometimes just a few sentences) for one of your social media platforms. It's quite easy to then use software like Hootsuite to automatically post that content across all your social media channels.

Once you've got a month's worth together, try to be more specific with what you post to each channel, bearing in mind the comments in the last chapter. Your message on LinkedIn targeting professionals will likely be different to the message on Facebook targeting homeowners. Their problems will be different so your message needs to adapt accordingly.

You should also work hard to build up a portfolio of pictures that you can use and, if necessary, get some stock pictures to include in blogs and articles. There are lots of companies out there providing free or cheap stock pictures for the construction industry. It's much better to use your own if you can, though, as you can often tell when an image is stock.

Remember to use your USP as content. Write articles about what your clients' problems or fears are and how your service solves or alleviates them. As we said, this talks to your potential clients on an emotional level and can be very powerful.

File away all your reviews and testimonials and use these as content. Reviews are crucial, as we all use them to make purchase decisions. Whether it's eBay or Amazon, we are conditioned to look at reviews before we buy. It gives you peace of mind when you see a company has four- or five-star reviews, and you begin to trust them. If they have no reviews, or very few, you'll already be suspicious.

Make sure you get your clients to post reviews across social media, any trade body websites you belong to, and of course on Google. This is so important but it amazes me how many companies produce great work and don't follow through on getting reviews from clients. It is a must. Ensure you prioritise this if nothing else.

Finally, follow some of your competitors and see if you can get some ideas from them. Don't copy them, as you want to stand out as different, but you might get some good ideas. If not, at least you'll see where they are going wrong.

The beauty in all of the above is that it's free. Social media is *free marketing*. It does take time, but it's absolutely essential in today's world. People will expect you to be in this space and if a client sees that you have followers, post regular content and have good reviews, you will have already eased their concerns and selling to them will prove much easier. But the true power of social media goes even further than this – this is where it starts to cost money.

Paid digital advertising

We've already seen how much can be accomplished with free social media channels. Depending on how many leads you need to generate each month, you may need to start thinking about paid advertising on these channels.

Paid advertising on social media can put you in front of thousands of your ideal clients, even if they don't follow you. You can generate 'lookalikes' based on your client avatar and target only those people living in a certain locality. It's a powerful, targeted form of marketing and not much else can rival it.

Imagine putting a £5 note into a vending machine and it spews out £20. It would be the best vending machine in the world. If you master paid advertising, that is exactly what it can be like. You put money into advertising, and it should give you an increased return.

What you don't want is to put £5 in and get nothing out, or less than £5. That's when paid advertising isn't working and you need to make changes fast.

The purpose of this section is not to give you a step by step guide to using paid advertising, as there are specialists out there who can set up campaigns bespoke to your needs. This section is intended simply to show you what can be achieved and why paid advertising should not be overlooked.

Facebook, Instagram, LinkedIn and Google Ads let you choose exactly who you want to target. You can target by sex, age, where they live, what they do for work, keywords they search for, how much they earn, if they are married, have kids, etc. The list goes on and on and means you can target specific people if that's what is required.

For some companies, paid advertising is their biggest source of lead generation. One of my clients, an electrical contractor, wanted to increase his earnings. His main service was emergency call-outs, charging an hourly rate. Often, these call-outs would only be three or four hours and, although highly profitable, he needed lots of leads each day to keep his workers busy. We first analysed his profit and loss in detail to see what cuts could be made. We realised he was running a tight ship, but his workers were not at full capacity, they had plenty of unfilled hours in the day. We then looked at how much work he generated from paid advertising – it was over 80%. As we'd been tracking how much he'd been spending on paid adverts, we knew exactly what the return on investment was. He was spending £15 for every lead he generated (in this example, a phone call or email received). On average, he was converting 25% of his leads, meaning it cost him £60 to win a single job. The average job value was £270. He was making a gross profit of £135 on average per job, which meant that after the £60 spent on advertising, he had £75 left over to pay overheads.

It was clear how powerful paid advertising was for him. All he needed to do to increase his income was to increase his advertising spend on Google Ads. This would max out his workers and increase his earnings without having any effect on his fixed overheads. A no-brainer. But he was only able to make this decision because he understood his numbers.

We'll look at this in more detail in the section on profit and loss, but for now the lesson is: if you are going to use paid advertising, you have to analyse the numbers. Learn how much you are spending to get a lead, how many leads on average you convert, and how much profit this generates. That way, you can turn the tap of paid advertising on and off as required and know exactly what returns you'll get on average. This sort of analysis and confidence in figures doesn't come overnight. Paid advertising can be frustrating, as some campaigns work and some don't. Often, much trial and error is needed to finetune it.

Be persistent and hire a great digital marketing expert who specialises in paid advertising and you could see great returns from this strategy. Just be sure to set a budget and keep monitoring it. It's not uncommon for newbies to let a budget slide and spend hundreds of pounds on ads within a short space of time, with no results.

Certain types of paid ads may not be the answer. Sometimes, certain media channels just will not work at all for your product and you need to turn off the paid adverts. For our company, we knew Facebook ads worked, but Google Ads were becoming too expensive for our lead generation so we killed it off. Once you find something that works, stick with it and don't be afraid to increase the spending budget in line with increased growth.

Paid advertising is also a great way of moving people into your funnel and onto your landing pages, where you can start tracking them with cookies for re-marketing. Cookies are great. Once a cookie is placed on the browser of someone who has visited your website or clicked on a Facebook post, it will follow them all around the internet; you can re-market back to that client again and again. For example, they may be reading an online news website and then, all of a sudden, your advert pops up in the corner of the page. The beauty is it will happen again and again for a very low cost. You can also re-market advertise on Facebook itself, so you keep popping up on their feed.

e probably experienced it yourself. You go on a te to buy a tent, then all of a sudden you see that ~~~, any selling tents all over the internet. That's the power of cookies and re-marketing.

Another strategy to keep in mind is SEO (search engine optimisation). This helps you to be organically found on Google. The aim is that you appear near the top of the list when someone types in a keyword related to the service you offer. For example, if someone needs an emergency plumber they may type 'plumber, London, same day' into Google, or one of many other variations of those terms. If you have optimised your site to show up strongly on Google for those keywords and any other variation, you will appear higher up the list of search results.

An organic Google search is an extremely important way for cold leads to find you and it's important that you rank on the first page of Google. If you're not, then you may as well be on the last page – your clients are not going to find you:

'The best place to hide a dead body is page two of Google.'[12]

You'll need to find and pay for an SEO specialist who can help you climb the Google rankings and, although

---

12 Pollitt, C (2017) 'The Best Place to Hide a Dead Body Is Page Two of Google'. www.huffpost.com/entry/the-best-place-to-hide-a_b_5168714

this is a free form of advertising (you're not paying per click), you will have to pay for SEO on an ongoing basis, so I generally consider this a marketing and advertising expense. The beauty of SEO is that once you are ranked highly, it's relatively easy and cheap to stay there. Once you get there, all the clicks you get from then on have already been paid for by the previous SEO work. Google loves newness and ranks websites higher if they produce new and original content, so ensure you are uploading videos and blogs that relate to your keywords. This is a great way to rank higher for free.

Collateral branding

Not to be dismissed are the old-school forms of branding. It's not all about going digital. Having company uniforms, branded hardhats or hi-vis tops for all your workers gives a professional impression. One of my clients insists on his workers having clean overalls, which is a challenge in the construction industry and requires paying for regular replacements, but it does make his company stand out from others. Remember, your brand and USP is represented by you, your staff and your sub-contractors, so try to get everyone to buy into it and be proud to wear your uniform and present a favourable image of your company.

Other ways of getting your brand out there are having things like sign-written vans, all the same colour and style if possible. When we first started out we had two identical vans sign-written and we had clients tell us they saw us everywhere; they thought we were a much bigger firm because they saw our 'fleet of vans', even though we only had two.

If possible, ensure billboard signs are put up outside your jobs if you will be there for a while. These are cheap to buy, but again show local residents that you are in the area when they walk or drive by. If you're working in an area, put flyers through the doors of the local streets. It's a cheap way of generating interest. If you have offices, these also need to have high quality signwriting and brand logos. Spend a bit more on this than on your other signs, as this is where clients will visit you and needs to reflect the highest standard of professionalism.

There are other forms of branding you could try, if they fit with your brand promise. One client of mine owns a general building company and his USP is based around serving his local community. If anyone local needs a builder, he is the first person who springs to mind and has saturated his local market. He decided he wanted to give back to the community and sponsor the local football team. This proved to be a great brand strategy, as it meant every time the team played and all the local residents watched, his brand logo was on the front of their shirts. This created loyalty and an emotional connection with the local residents who supported the football club, and they would recommend him to all their friends and relatives. It was a great way of getting his brand out there while doing some good for the local community and it fit perfectly with his USP.

Other basic things you need as branding collateral are high quality brochures and business cards. Don't underestimate the power of sending out a beautifully coloured glossy brochure. These are the small, inexpensive things that can make a psychological difference when a client is about to make a purchase. The key is to do whatever it takes to give yourself the edge over your competition.

We have gone through a lot of information in the last two sections. Ensure you've grasped the importance of it and refer back to it regularly. Underline and highlight the bits that you want to focus on first. Don't be disheartened if you do not have much of it in place yet. It's a good thing if you don't, as your business has a greater chance of making a fantastic transformation. You will find that many construction business owners aren't doing half of this and so, once you've implemented the advice in this section, you will already be miles ahead of the competition. It takes time to implement these things, so first pick one section or task and focus on seeing it through; the next week, pick another. One by one you'll eventually get everything in place. It then becomes like a snowball gathering pace and you'll find that your sales naturally start increasing without too much effort.

ACTION POINT CHECKLIST

1. Create a brand guideline document
2. Register for an account on the relevant social media platforms – Facebook is generally most important
3. Plan thirty days' worth of social media content
4. Find an SEO and possibly a paid advertising specialist
5. Get branded clothing for your staff and your vans sign-written
6. Get a quality brochure printed

5
End Of Month Reports

What gets measured gets managed

Hopefully, at this stage you've seen the value and wisdom in fully implementing the first three parts of the DEVELOP strategy. Once you do, I guarantee you'll start seeing results and growth fast. This is great and what you wanted, otherwise why would you have picked up this book? However, the speed at which you grow can start to cause problems if you are not measuring things correctly.

As you grow quickly you may start to feel out of control. Work is coming in fast, but can you cope with the capacity? You are taking on new staff, but are they performing effectively? You've invested money in advertising but are not sure which channel is delivering the best ROI. You are invoicing more money than ever before, but are you profitable?

Ask yourself these questions; if you don't know the answers, you will become stressed. Now you've grown so fast, with so much on your plate at any one time, how can you cope with the added work coming in and keep on top of it all?

The answer is: good reporting. Receiving regular reports – which is why we call this strategy 'end of month' reporting – will be crucial for you to retain your sanity and continue to grow at a fast pace. There is a saying that I'm a big believer in:

'What gets measured gets managed.'[13]
— Peter Drucker

Let that sink in for a moment. If you are measuring something by way of regular reports, you can then manage that problem or, in the case of a positive thing, continue doing it.

If you're not measuring things, you have no clue what's working and what isn't. You will be running the business based on your gut and intuition, which may work for a while, but not when you get to £1m. Be aware, though, that it is possible to go over the top with reporting. If you're a perfectionist it can be

---

13 Drucker, P (1954) *The Practice of Management*. New York: Harper & Row.

easy to fall into the trap of measuring everything, even the small details. This wastes a lot of time, and your focus can then be diverted to fixing small things that have no significant effect on growth. The key is to measure the *right* things consistently. Throughout this section we will review why reports are so valuable and what exactly you should be measuring to help your growth.

The value of reports

Imagine knowing the answer to these questions at the click of a button:

- Who is your best salesperson?

- What is your most profitable product?

- How much profit will you make this month?

- What is your best advertising channel?

- How do your customers feel about your service?

- What are you doing well?

- What problem needs to be solved immediately?

If you asked yourself those questions now, would you honestly know the answers? You may have an idea based on intuition, but could you back that up with statistics so you *know* you are right?

When you grow rapidly and your attention is diverted, your intuition can become distorted. You thought Bill was the best salesman, but you haven't realised that his performance over the last three months has been shocking. He has a problem in his personal life that you knew nothing about. You thought your customers loved your service, what you hadn't realised is that they can't stand one of your subcontractors and he never gets good reviews.

Can you see the problem? As you grow you can naturally lose touch with different parts of your company, but it's absolutely crucial at this phase that you know exactly what is going on. Your finger needs to stay on the pulse at all times, so consistent reporting is vital. Reporting will give you all the answers to the above questions. Think of the power that gives you over your competitors. If you know exactly what social media channel is delivering the best results, you know where to allocate your advertising budget. If you know someone is underperforming, you can nip the problem in the bud early, before it starts affecting profits. If you know how much money you will make this month, you can forecast whether you need to cut back for lean times, or plough ahead with investment.

Having these answers gives you great power. This is why all the big companies are obsessed with gathering data. The more data they collect, the quicker they can react when they spot trends. You can do exactly the same on a smaller scale.

I've emphasised end of month reporting in this section. When you grow bigger you may find you want daily or weekly reports, and there is nothing wrong with this. For now, though, as you approach £1m and are just starting to implement the strategies, focus on monthly reports. You'll find it easier to stick with, it's not too much of a burden for employees, and it's still regular enough to spot trends and dangers. Not too much can get out of control in four weeks.

The key is to be consistent and start creating an archive of data that you can look back on and analyse. When you receive these reports, ensure you block out some time to analyse them properly. In my own business, I receive a report at the beginning of each month showing me last month's results. I spend about fifteen to thirty minutes looking over them and highlighting the good and bad, then I hold separate meetings with each department – sales, marketing, operations and finance – to discuss the reports in detail. It's vitally important that you share the information with your employees and help them interpret the data too. That way, they can also be alert to problems and advise you quicker. It also holds them accountable when they can see that everyone can review performances (especially sales staff).

These monthly meetings have proved extremely valuable and give us all an hour each month to reflect on what has gone well, and then to focus on what went wrong and the steps required to stop that happening again. Employees can also come out with great suggestions and new ideas in these meetings – listen to them, you'll be amazed at the gems you'll pick up.

When you keep doing this month on month, before long you will have a finely tuned machine. Not only that, your personal stress levels will drop dramatically as nothing will take you by surprise and you'll feel in control.

Let's look at what should be measured and included in these reports.

How to measure marketing

We'll start with learning how to measure the lifeblood of a company: marketing. Without marketing, you have no leads; without leads no sales; no sales, no profit.

How effective is your current marketing strategy? Do you have more leads coming in than you can handle? Are they quality leads that your sales team find easy to convert? If your answer is no to any of those questions, you need to review your strategy. Something is not working.

If you've fully implemented exceptional service and visual branding then you should have noticed leads increasing naturally, and sales conversion should also be up. But where are your leads coming from? What lead source is the most effective? You need to find this out, so you know where to find more.

92

This is why reporting is so vital; you need to know the answers to these questions and to quantify your leads. That way, if you see a dip in lead numbers, you'll know exactly why and what steps need to be taken to resolve it.

Lead source report

Have a look at the simple chart below that we use in my company (numbers altered for confidentiality).

Inbound

These are the enquiries that come into your business. Every time you receive a new lead from a telephone call, email, social media enquiry, or completed website form, it should be tracked on your CRM system (see the section on operating systems, which discusses this in detail). Don't use spreadsheets for this, as they are not advanced enough and take too much time to create. CRM systems will track that enquiry all the way through the sale process, so when you win a sale you know exactly what lead source it came from.

It's vital that the staff who answer your phones or respond to emails are trained to *always* ask: 'How did you hear about us?' Make sure you also do the same on your web form enquiries. Have a drop-down menu with multiple possible answers. Over time, this will paint a clear picture that will prove invaluable.

Lead Source Report

Lead Source	January	February	March	April	May	June	July	August	September	October	November	December	Total
Council Work	13	12	10	14	8	7	13	6	3	3	1	2	92
Recommendations	7	4	7	5	6	3	6	8	5	12	14	11	88
Google Organic	7	7	3	2	8	7	9	6	10	14	11	3	87
Facebook Organic	1	2	3	7	4	3	4	3	2	3	7	6	45
Google AdWords		2		3		5	4	4	3	6	2	4	33
Not Stated/Unknown	2		4	1	2	3	1	7	2	6	3	2	33
Facebook Ads		1		1	1		2	3	8	4	5	3	28
Signage	2	3		1	1		4	3	3	6		4	27
Which?	1	3	1		1	2	1	3	1		2	1	16
Other	2	2		1	1		3	1		2			12
LinkedIn		1				2			2		1	3	9
Federation of Master Builders		1			1	1	1		1		2	1	8
Flyers								3	1	1	2	1	8
Check A Trade	1				1			1		1			4
Employee Referral				2						1	1		4
Instagram								1			2	1	4
Total	36	38	28	37	34	33	48	49	41	59	53	42	498

It was clear from our charts that one of our biggest lead sources was recommendations. This is what we would expect, as our goal has always been to deliver exceptional service. But imagine if we noticed over time that this lead source had gradually declined. This would be an indicator of a wider issue that needed to be investigated. If you didn't have this info, how would you know your customer service was declining? Knowing what our biggest lead source is helps us plan loyalty schemes and recommend-a-friend campaigns to harness this powerful source of new business.

Another point we noticed from our chart was that our council (local authority) leads were dropping significantly. This was a cause for concern, so efforts were made to reach out to our contacts there to see if we had upset them or done something wrong. We were told that public sector funding had been dramatically cut to meet government targets and would last for the entire financial year. Although not good news for us initially, this was vital information, and we could plan a strategy to take on different work and not be so reliant on this lead source.

Can you see, then, how powerful and valuable this simple lead source chart is? It can help you make informed decisions and analyse your strengths and weaknesses, as well as raising red flags that need further investigation every now and then.

Social media

You also need to measure how effective your social media is. A lot of time can be spent – and wasted – on social media. Just because you're busy and active on it, doesn't mean it's working as an effective marketing strategy. Fortunately, Facebook, YouTube and the like provide easy access to reporting. These reports can be as detailed as you need, but keep it simple, as you are only after information on a few things. Are people looking at your posts, sharing them, engaging with you, liking your pages? Are followers increasing? Ultimately, your lead source report will also show you how effective your social media strategy is, but the platform reports do help drill down into it a bit further when needed.

ROI

Another vital report to see each month is your return on investment. Most of your marketing channels will incur expense and it's important that you track what each channel is costing you each month. This can be straightforward with things like AdWords, but a bit trickier with others. For us, even though recommendations are generally a free lead source, we still add a figure to this chart each month as we spend out regularly on client gifts and sometimes recommend-a-friend vouchers. Each month's accounts provide a combined figure for these items and we add that into the chart (see the ROI report opposite).

ROI Report

Lead Source	Marketing Spend	Quotes	Cost Per Quote	Won	Undecided	% Q to W	Job Value Average	Job Value Total Won	ROI
Google Organic	£15,115	87	£173.74	19	1	22%	£37,027	£703,507	46.54
Google AdWords	£13,075	33	£396.21	2		6%	£24,487	£48,973	3.75
Facebook Ads	£6,351	45	£141.13	6		13%	£20,939	£125,632	19.78
Recommendations	£4,250	88	£48.30	26	1	30%	£43,214	£1,123,560	264.37
Instagram	£1,500	4	£375.00			0%	0%	0%	0.00
LinkedIn	£1,350	9	£150.00			0%	0%	0%	0.00
Facebook Organic	£1,280	45	£28.44	9	1	20%	£41,003	£369,025	288.30
Signage	£725	27	£26.85	5		19%	£56,110	£280,550	386.97
Flyers	£675	8	£84.38	1		13%	£35,750	£35,750	52.96

97

Once you have input your costs, your CRM system should make it easy to track which lead source generated which sale. For us, this is one of the most valuable reports because it tells us exactly where we should be allocating our marketing spend. We were able to see instantly that it is quite expensive to gain a lead – and therefore a job – through AdWords, so we cut back on this. We are now testing new ads to refine the campaign, or we'll drop it altogether. On the other hand, we know that our signage delivers great ROI, so we ensure all our jobs have banners and signs erected. The sales we generate with our signage far outweigh the initial outlay.

Once you've run this report for six to twelve months, you'll start to build up a clear picture of what's working and what's not, and can divert your budget accordingly. Don't be afraid to discontinue investing in a channel if it's not paying off. Once you have accurate ROI reports you can see clearly where your leads are coming from, but how successful are your sales team in converting these leads?

We'll find out how to measure that in the next chapter.

How to measure sales

The larger you grow, the more the pressure to keep up with sales intensifies. If sales dry up, you're on a quick path to negative cashflow and going out of business.

Your overheads are higher than ever before and you need the sales just to stay afloat.

By applying all the principles we've discussed, eventually you'll be in the enviable position of having a full order book and turning work away. Until then, you need to measure how your sales team are performing and keep a close eye on what can be improved.

Look at the chart below to see some of the sales metrics that can be measured.

First, you need to be able to distinguish not just the sales in general but how each individual salesperson is performing. This is especially important if you are linking performance to commission or bonuses. In the chart below, we track in each quarter how many appointments have been visited, how many quotes sent, and the value of the combined quotes. We can also see the win rate, which helps when analysing trends.

We go even further than this. In an effort to constantly improve, we also measure the time it takes from visiting an appointment to when the quote is received. When this figure is too high, we know the salesperson is either overloaded with work, or is not prioritising sending out quotes. We know from experience that the longer a quote takes to be sent, the less chance we have of winning the sale, so it's important we monitor this.

Sales Analysis

Potential Type	Leads	Appointments	% Lead to Appointment	L to A days	Quotes	A to Q days	Amount Quoted	Chased	% Quote to Chase	Q to C days	Won	Undecided	% Quote to Win	Lead to Win days	Amount Average	Amount Total
Direct	373	261	70%	7	215	5	£10,202,152	201	93%	7	52	3	24%	27	£35,617	£1,852,063
Tender	125	85	68%	10	72	7	£8,156,252	65	90%	10	16		22%	41	£52,183	£834,934
Total	498	346	69%	8.5	287	6	£18,358,404	266	92%	8.5	68	3	23%	34	£43,900	£2,686,997

Another important thing to constantly measure is your pipeline. A pipeline segments each phase of the sales process so you can see at a glance the progress of a client or many clients. This can be found in any CRM system and will show exactly where people are in the sales funnel; the lower down the funnel they are, the closer you are to landing the sale. The pipeline is helpful because if you see a lot of clients stuck in a particular part of the funnel, you can make a special effort to move them to the next stage. Our pipeline is configured to show us how many leads we have, how many have had an appointment, or a quote, how many have been chased up, how many are in negotiation or review (this is close to being a sale), and how many have been won. If you see a bottleneck in your pipeline, eg lots of people stuck in the quote stage, you know that you need the sales team to prioritise chasing them up for a decision or trying to move them towards a negotiation.

The pipeline is also a great way of forecasting future sales. By combining the sales chart with the pipeline, you can measure the win rate and the average time taken from sending a quotation to closing a sale. In the example given, it took an average of fifty-two days (L to A column) to close the sale, and the win rate was 23%. This information is fantastic for forecasting because if there is £1m sitting in the pipeline, the company knows that within the next fifty-two days, they should close approx. £230k of sales.

When the pipeline is monitored closely you can react as needed. If you notice the pipeline is looking empty you know you need to focus on leads coming in and quotes being sent. The other good thing about a pipeline is it breaks down the sales process into manageable chunks. Rather than panicking if sales are looking slow, you can focus on where the bottleneck is and concentrate on that one part of the sales funnel.

How to measure operations

Once you have your marketing and sales under control, it's time to consider how effectively your operations are running. As you grow, it's easy to lose control of operations; this is where a lot of internal waste can occur, eating into your precious profits. Operations will be responsible for delivering the service or product once the sales team have won the work. The first thing you need to be able to measure is how much work the operations team are managing at any point. This can be done with simple spreadsheets showing what jobs are running and what stage they are at. For complex and long projects, it may be helpful to use Gantt charts to monitor progress and timelines.

It's also important to know your invoicing forecast for the future months, which your operations team will be responsible for delivering. You could again use a spreadsheet to track current projects for the month and then note down weekly how much you expect to invoice per week per project. This will give you an end of month forecast of whether you'll hit your target.

Depending on your service and product, your spreadsheets may need to be different, and more complex, but the important point is you must develop an internal system that tracks how well operations are performing and if they are delivering enough of your service.

When you have a good system in place you should easily be able to generate a forecast report for the next month and use this to see if you're going to meet your invoice and revenue targets. If you see a low revenue figure forecast, you know that you either need more sales to bring in more work fast, or, if you have a full order book, you need to bring jobs forward and start more work.

You should also run operations reports each month to see how profitable your completed *individual* jobs have been. This means tracking the profitability of each job. See the section on operating systems for further details on this. When you run this report, you get a general overview of which jobs are profitable and which are not. If some jobs are less profitable than others, this report lets you delve deeper into why. Were they priced poorly by sales? Did the team overspend? You can react accordingly. This is vital information that can save you a small fortune every month; all these small improvements add up.

David Brailsford was knighted for his services to British cycling. He transformed the sport and the teams he managed won many gold medals and competitions. He pioneered the strategy of *marginal gains,* where you break down large processes into minute details. David theorised that if you continually focused on a 1% improvement in different processes, over time, this would add up to a huge improvement. He concentrated on the small things, like ensuring riders had the right pillows and mattresses to get a good night's sleep. That may seem like it would make a minor difference, but when you add all those 1% improvements together, collectively it transformed British cycling and allowed the team to dominate the sport under his leadership.

Use the marginal gains strategy when you analyse your reports. Don't spend all your time analysing to the point that it becomes unproductive, but if you can see easy ways of making small improvements to some of your feedback data, put those into action and you'll be surprised at how all the 1% improvements will transform your business further down the line.

How to measure client care

We've already highlighted the importance of exceptional service, but the bigger you grow the easier it is to let your standards drop. To maintain a high standard, performance must be monitored.

One of the best ways to do this is by simply asking your clients how you did each time you've completed some work; this can be done via a feedback form. Ask them which employee performed the best and get them to give you a score. Don't be afraid to ask if there is anything to improve. The answers to these questions are like gold dust; you'll learn of things that you may not even have realised were happening. These could be things your clients are telling their friends, which could result in a sale or a lost opportunity. Each month, these forms can be compiled; if there are lots, get the team to filter out the most important ones for you to review – the good, the bad and the ugly.

To keep track of a general score, use the average of your ratings. For example, if you ask the question, 'How would you rate our overall performance?' (between one and ten), take the average score to monitor how exceptional your service really is. Have some fun with it and put the current score somewhere visible in the office and make it your aim each month to beat the last month's score. If you beat a target, take the team out to celebrate or get some pizzas in. This is a great way of getting the team customer focused and maintaining exceptional service.

When you do receive poor reports, try not to be disheartened. It will happen; you can't please everyone. Use it as an opportunity to learn and change. Don't be so focused on the other areas of your business that you lose touch with your clients. Receiving these regular reports is a great way of keeping your finger on the pulse.

We've only briefly covered reports in this section, as each report needs to be tailored to your business. The important lesson to learn is that, as you grow, you must stay in control, even though you can't be involved in every aspect of the business at all times. The beauty of reports is that you get a snapshot of how healthy the business is looking. Although they are just snapshots, they should provide enough detail to raise red flags when something is going against the norm. Ensure you take the time to set up templates for these reports; these will pay dividends. More importantly, once you start receiving them, make sure you take some time out at least once per month to review them carefully.

ACTION POINT CHECKLIST

1. Set up a lead source report via your CRM or MS Excel
2. Look at social media reports monthly
3. Set up ROI reports on MS Excel
4. Look at your pipeline via your CRM
5. If you have sales staff, set up a sales performance chart
6. Ensure all projects can be analysed for profitability, and review each month
7. Set up a client care report

6
Loyal People

Get the right people on the bus

One of the big barriers to growth is hiring the wrong staff. When you grow at a rapid pace and struggle to keep up with the workload, you can seem desperate to get anyone at all on board, even if they are not the right fit. I've done this many times throughout my business journey and, when I look back, it's a huge regret. So much time and money are wasted training someone up if they were never the right person in the first place. If you start having doubts about someone, your gut instinct is probably right – maybe it's time for them to go.

Your business isn't a charity, and you cannot carry people. Although it can feel ruthless, if someone isn't working out you will be doing yourself and them a favour to part ways and move on. It would be much easier, though, if you didn't put yourself in that position in the first place. Who enjoys firing people? It's an awful position to be in. How much better would it be to get the hire right in the first instance?

The challenge doesn't stop there. What about when you have found exactly the right person? They are fantastic, better than you could have hoped for – now you start to panic that they may leave you. They are a hugely valuable member of staff now, how would you cope if they left?

This section is designed as a guide to both attracting and retaining the best staff. Paying attention to the next chapters *could* save you thousands of pounds and months of pain and frustration. I stress the *could* because, despite your best efforts, some may slip through the net; you only know 100% if someone is the right fit once they start work and you can monitor them over a few months. Some have a gift for presenting themselves in an amazing way and breezing through an interview. It's only further down the line, when the cracks start to appear, that you realise they are not the right fit. That's OK, I'll show you how to deal with those situations.

Let's find out now how you can protect yourself and your business as you grow, and how to find loyal people.

The cost of a bad hire

The first thing to understand is why it's so important that the recruitment process is successful. You may think, 'I'll just sack them if they don't work out and hire a replacement'. Well, yes, you could, but you don't want to be carrying people if they're not right for your business. Letting people come and go from the business can be extremely damaging. Why?

First, it can damage staff morale. People generally don't like change. If a member of your staff has got used to working with someone closely, maybe even becoming good friends with them, and then, all of a sudden, they are out of the door, how do you think that will make them feel? The staff member who stays won't be thinking about what's best for the business, they will be focusing on how it has affected them emotionally. They've just lost a good friend. This could make them resentful of the business, and you as its leader.

Additionally, if you have a high turnover of staff, this could make some within the company anxious. 'Am I going to be next?' they may ask. Staff worrying like this will damage morale and their performance will be affected.

What's the answer? Should you try to retain poor staff as long as possible, in the hope that they might improve? No, certainly not. If you know someone isn't working out, you've addressed the issue with them and provided training and they still haven't improved sufficiently, you need to take some advice from an HR consultant and let them go without delay. Allowing someone who is underperforming to stay on can damage the morale of the existing staff. When they are working hard, beavering away at their jobs and the person working next to them is getting away with murder, this will be extremely frustrating for them.

Even though it's you paying the wages, they will start to think, 'Why am I putting in all this effort, when he/she clearly isn't?' The attitude and work habits of a bad employee can gradually infect the entire staff. Are you starting to see how damaging it can be when the wrong person is brought, and kept, on board?

It's not only damaging for morale, it's extremely bad news for your profits. You may think working out how much a bad hire costs a business is straightforward: John was paid £2,500 per month and was kept on for three months = £7,500. In fact, it works out to be much more than that.

First, you'll need to pay for an ad or a recruitment consultant to find that member of staff for you. For a mid-level employee like John, this might cost £2,500 in recruitment fees. Then, as the business owner you will take a day to review all the CVs and select three for an interview. Next come the telephone interviews, then the formal interviews, which will take up another day of your time. References then need to be checked and a job offer made. You have a new employee – hooray! So far, it's cost you over £3,000 to make the hire.

Next comes the onboarding. You need to show your new employee the ropes, how your systems work, how you do things. There may be an element of training needed to get them up to scratch. It can take anywhere between two and four weeks before a new employee is fully up to speed. That's another £2,500 spent, without much productivity to show for it. One month in, and the new employee has cost you £5,500.

They start getting on with the work in earnest and you expect great things, but it soon becomes evident that they are not cut out for the task. Now it's costing you in productivity. Only you will know how best to measure this for your business but it could be thousands each month. If you sack the hire in month three, they've already cost you £10,500, and that's without factoring in the productivity losses. I learned this the hard way in my own business when we were growing rapidly. Although I've now got a fantastic team around me, who I would re-hire in a heartbeat, I've previously had bad hires who have lost me contracts worth hundreds of thousands, stolen money from me, and damaged company vehicles, among other things. I even had an employee who was absolutely amazing at interview but turned up on the first day drunk as a sack – and then was arrested by the police for attempting to drive home. As you might have guessed, they were fired immediately. You can see that I've certainly experienced the pain of a bad hire.

Getting it wrong can have a huge cost, far more than the employee's wages. The lesson: take your time and recruit carefully. Don't take on a risky hire just to fill a seat when you are growing quickly and can't keep up with the workload.

Attract and retain the best

We know now that we need to avoid bad hires like the plague, so how do you attract the *right* people to come and work for your business? You only want A-players – ideally, you want to employ people who are more skilled than you in certain areas; this way, you get a well-rounded mix of talent throughout your organisation. How do you attract people like this? Why would they want to come and work for you?

This is where we revert back to visual branding. In that section we discussed how to market effectively, communicate your USP, and get ahead of the competition. Marketing isn't only useful for winning clients; you can also use it to help you hire.

Think about it. If you go for an interview, what's the first thing you do before you turn up? You'll check out the website, read reviews of the company, look at their social media pages and so on. If this is non-existent or shabby, you'll immediately form a negative opinion of the company. This greatly hinders the company's chances of hiring you, or anyone else, as an A-player. On the other hand, if you browse around the net and find a strong social media page with a large following, great reviews, and a solid website highlighting the USP, you immediately begin to trust that the company is run well and is going places. This is the sort of thing that will help attract the A-players and get them to interview.

Company culture

What is company culture, and why is it so important to have it written down? Your company culture is what defines who you are as an organisation. It's the DNA of your company. It's the internal values that all your staff believe in and strive to work towards.

We looked at the company Zappos in the section on exceptional service, as they are world-renowned for delivering an amazing customer experience. The reason they can do this consistently is because this is a value that runs through their company DNA and is part of their culture. Their values are listed on their website:[14]

1. Deliver WOW through service

2. Embrace and drive change

---

14 www.zappos.com/core-values

3. Create fun and a little weirdness

4. Be adventurous, creative, and open-minded

5. Pursue growth and learning

6. Build open and honest relationships with communication

7. Build a positive team and family spirit

8. Do more with less

9. Be passionate and determined

10. Be humble

You'll notice that the number one value is customer service. It's drummed into all the staff as the top priority, which is why they are so successful in this area. You'll also notice that, in addition to number one, numbers three, six, eight and nine are also closely linked to how the company delivers amazing customer service. These values are available for all to see on their website; this is why Zappos is able to attract A-players, and anyone who wants to work at the organisation knows they will be working to these values. Zappos has a huge advantage over other companies when interviewing, as people *want* to work for them.

Try creating your own company culture. Think about what values are important to you, and how your organisation can be summed up. Once you've decided on what you want your culture to be, ensure everyone in your organisation knows about it. Write it down and put it up in the office and, even better, add it to your website. Doing this will greatly assist you in attracting new hires and, most importantly, the right kind of hires. Not only that, you'll see a positive effect on your existing staff as they all start to rally round and work towards a common goal.

Retain the best

Let's presume you've managed to hire an A-player. They've bought into your company culture, they've been working for you for a good few months, and you can see they are working wonders for your business. Though things are going great, you start to panic, thinking, 'What if they decide to leave? I'm so reliant on this person, I couldn't cope.' This is a common fear once you start hiring great people and things are going well, but that kind of thinking is wrong for two reasons.

First, you should never become so reliant on one person that losing them would significantly damage the business. Ensure that others know how to do elements of the role, so that if that person did leave or get knocked down by a bus (you never know) you could carry on without it destroying the business.

Second, why would they want to leave? You need to create an environment that encourages people to stay because they love their job. A-players generally want a few things to be satisfied where they are:

117

- Given praise and recognition

- Able to work with other A-players

- Able to grow

- Rewarded for their efforts

This is the sort of environment that needs to be created to keep the best people. Some of these things are relatively simple to do, like giving praise and recognition, but when you're busy and growing fast it can be easy to forget to take the time to thank someone for a job well done. There is nothing worse than feeling unappreciated. Ensure you have a huddle with the team at least weekly, and let people know publicly when they have done a great job. Everyone loves a bit of genuine praise and recognition.

Point two is something Steve Jobs noticed when he formed his A-player team that created the Apple Mac. The best employees get frustrated working with people who are lousy at their job, so this needs to be managed carefully. Even so, you won't be able to get an entire organisation made up of the absolute best; you always get one or two who quietly get on with their job but are not exactly setting the world on fire. A-players may find it frustrating working with people like this. It's not always possible, but where you can, get them working alongside other A-players. If you have no one else, then on occasion you should work directly with them on a project, this can help keep their spirits high.

Point three is important as A-players are never standing still and feel a constant need to grow and improve their abilities, or to see that they are directly involved in the business growing – if you're reading this book, that shouldn't be a problem. One way to help them grow is through a training plan that's reviewed every six months to a year. When you have your staff appraisals, ensure that training is discussed and ask the staff directly what they feel they need or would like training in. Investing in the growth of your staff is money well spent and will pay dividends, so ensure you have some kind of training planned for all your staff, but especially your A-players.

Point four is the tricky one. When you discuss rewarding someone, a pay rise is what immediately comes to mind. But as you grow, and with the challenges you will face with increased overheads, etc, a pay rise isn't always a viable option. You need to make sure that rewards are varied and not always in monetary form. There are lots of ways you can reward your staff for a job well done. It could be as simple as getting a pizza and/or some beers in the office on a Friday afternoon if a weekly target is reached, or letting staff leave an hour or two early. Maybe tickets to a concert or event if a particular employee has performed well.

If you have an A-player who is vital to the business and is helping you grow it significantly, the above may not be enough; they may want a stake in the business. If this is the case and they deserve it, then don't panic at this. It can be a good thing – if they are sharing in the profits then it's in their interests to work harder and help you grow. However, don't be giving away shares willy-nilly. You've taken on all the risk and worked long and hard hours to get your business off the ground and sometimes people expect to get a share of the business while taking a regular salary, working nine to five with no risk. If you are thinking of giving shares away just to retain an A-player, I would suggest trying to offer them a profit share first. That way, you keep 100% ownership of the business but still reward the employee for their efforts.

If that's not enough and you feel you need to part with actual shares and dilute your ownership, how about suggesting an option agreement? This is where, at the end of the year, if certain targets are met the employee has an option to purchase a stake in the business. For example, let's imagine John the A-player has a sales target of £500k for the year. You offer John a £10k bonus if he hits that target; or, he can choose to use the £10k he would have received to buy an equivalent stake in the business. If the business was valued at £500k, he would get a 2% stake by forgoing his £10k bonus.

Options can be a powerful incentive if used well, as it can keep the A-players motivated to perform and also gives them a small stake in the business, which ties them to you and minimises the risk of them leaving. Note: before you arrange option agreements, ensure you take legal advice and have them drafted correctly to protect you and enable you to take ownership back if the employee leaves or is fired.

The above is a headache that may be worth having if you've managed to get an A-player on board. But going back one step, how do we find these A-players in the first place? With all the CVs you get sent when hiring, how can you pick one out? Read on for some great tips in the next chapter.

Resumes and interviews

Hiring new staff can be time-consuming, painful and frustrating. But it's a necessary pain to get the right person on board. We've already looked at the huge costs involved if you get it wrong, but there are huge benefits if you manage to land an A-player. So, how can you get it right?

Being completely honest, after interviewing and subsequently hiring and firing many people, I can tell you there isn't an exact science behind it. I've brought people in who have had amazing CVs, ticked all the boxes, and gave a great interview, but once they started working were a disaster. There is no substitute for seeing how people perform in the workplace, that's the true test, but the cases of mistaken hires slipping through the net are rare if you put some robust procedures in place before you make the job offer. This starts with how to find your ideal candidate.

Where do you start? Some ask around among friends, family and other work colleagues. This is a start and you may get lucky, but often it doesn't yield results. Friends will recommend people they like and get on with. That doesn't mean they are a good fit for your company culture. However, if an A-player recommends someone they have previously worked with, this may be worth pursuing. Remember what we said earlier: A-players like to work with other A-players.

Where else can you look apart from a narrow circle of family and friends? Well, why not harness that great social media presence you've now built up? Facebook can be an extremely good platform for posting job availability and posts can be shared by others to give you greater outreach. Look to post in local construction-related Facebook community groups, as this doesn't cost anything. In addition, you could even boost your post with paid Facebook advertising, which can specifically and accurately target your target demographic, skillset, interests and area. Failing that, if you have no time or desire to hunt around, you could approach specialist recruitment agents. There are some agencies that let you post paid adverts on their internet boards. This can be useful if they have a high reach of candidates on subscription, and it doesn't cost too much.

If you want to take a complete backseat in the entire process, then you can offer the position out to a construction recruitment consultant to fill. They have years of experience in finding people specifically for your sector and can give you guidance on the right salary and other advice. If you have a good consultant they should be able to screen out anyone you don't want to see, so you are not wasting your time viewing endless CVs and interviewing the wrong kinds of people. They will also sell your company to the candidate, making them more likely to accept an offer. A specialist recruitment consultant like this will cost you more, but it may be worthwhile in the long run if it lands you the right candidate.

Whether you choose to use a consultant or find a candidate by yourself, you will have to read through a number of CVs. This is a boring task, but it's vital you go through these in detail, as a CV can contain clues about the character of the person you may be about to hire. One of the key things to look out for is gaps in employment dates. If there are gaps, it might be worth asking why in the interview, as some candidates may be deliberately missing out positions they have had where things didn't work out well.

Another important thing to look for is how many previous jobs they have had, and how frequently they tend to move around. If you notice the person moves to a different company every year or so, then it's more than likely they'll do the same with you. Do you really want to be hiring and then training someone who is probably only going to stick around for a year?

Also look out for how they portray themselves in their CV. Are they claiming a lot of credit and boasting amazing achievements? This could be an indicator that someone isn't a team player and is only out for themselves.

Yet a CV only gives away small clues about the person, and more often than not most people get professional CVs written, or they are heavily edited by recruitment agents, which means it can be difficult to work out what's genuine or not. The true test comes when you conduct an interview. I personally prefer a phone interview prior to the face to face. A five- to ten-minute call gives me a good indication of who I am dealing with. Are they personable? Can they hold a conversation? Are they interesting? It's also a good chance for me to write copious notes, which I can then refer back to in the main interview to see if everything still lines up.

Once the CVs have been reviewed and candidates whittled down via phone interviews, you are then ready for the formal face to face interviews. This can be just as nerve-racking for you as it is the candidate, especially if you really want them on board. Take your time and let the candidate do most of the talking; try to keep the atmosphere relaxed and informal, you want them to open up and be honest. Don't be afraid to ask them to expand on their answers if they haven't been clear enough. You want to ensure all your doubts are dispelled; this is a big commitment for you both.

Once you have got all the technical questions answered and you are satisfied they have the capability to fulfil the role, it's then time to understand the psychology of the candidate. Try asking them questions like:

- If we were sitting here a year from now reviewing your performance, what would make it a successful year for us both?
- When have you been most satisfied in your life?
- Who is your role model, and why?
- What things do you not like to do?
- What is your biggest talent?
- What is your biggest weakness?
- What decisions do you find easy to make?
- What decisions do you find it hard to make?
- What's your most significant and proudest accomplishment in a previous company?

These types of questions, or a variation on them, can prove vital in understanding what makes someone tick. They could also reveal some major flaws. For example, if you asked someone what their biggest weakness was, and they said 'working in a team', you would need to think carefully about whether they would fit with your company culture and dynamics.

125

Once you've got through the interviews, it is absolutely essential that you get and check references. If someone cannot provide any references, or makes excuses, alarm bells should be ringing. Try to call the references rather than email, because you want their gut reaction, not a pre-prepared, carefully thought through statement.

Once you've read the CVs, carried out both phone and face to face interviews, and checked out the references, what next? You are not quite ready to hire. First, I suggest you offer the person a trial. A trial period is the true test of whether a person is compatible with your company, and should ideally be around three months. This is a great way of ensuring that a candidate is suitable before you make a long-term commitment. This is enough time for them to get to grips with the role and long enough for you to truly get to know them as a person. Within this period you should find out if they are full of hot air or are delivering on what they promised in the interview.

If the candidate is not keen on a trial and you don't want to risk losing them, I suggest that you have a three- to six-month termination clause built into their contract, so that if things don't seem to be working out you can let them go immediately. If it's not working out you want to be able to cut that person out as quickly and cleanly as possible.

Invest in your people

You've finally found the right candidate, you've got them onboard and things are going well. It's important now that this person grows as your company does. How is that achieved? Well, you need to invest in your people. You want them to grow and develop so that they can perform at their absolute best in their position. Some companies hold back on training for fear the person may leave and they would have wasted valuable time and money. The reality is, the odds of the person leaving dramatically increase if you don't bother helping them grow, as they will quickly lose interest. As we outlined in Section 6.2, it's more costly to replace someone than it is to spend on development and training.

We mentioned in the last chapter the importance of having regular appraisals and discussing with your staff how they would like to grow. Rather than just telling your staff what you want them to improve on, try to get them to buy into it too. What would they like to work on to help them advance their career, or increase success within the company? As long as it aligns with your goals, try to let them run with their idea so it feels like it's coming from them. This also holds them more accountable – after all, they suggested it.

You don't have to invest fortunes in training courses, as many of these can be done online, but you do need to give your staff time to complete them and then let them have a go at putting their new skills into practice. Sure, they'll make a few mistakes to begin with, but before long they'll have added another skill to their skillset and be an even more valuable member of staff. Most importantly, this keeps them interested in their job and the company, as they can see that they are personally growing through their work.

Apprentices

I'm a big believer in hiring apprentices and have had many over the years. Although apprentices can be extremely frustrating to work with at the beginning, as it seems they are useless at everything, it doesn't take long before they start finding their feet.

Most apprentices will be stepping into the workplace for the first time and will be completely 'green' to how things work and the way they should conduct themselves. Rather than getting frustrated, view them like a piece of clay. They are your responsibility to mould and adjust. In the end, if you spend enough time on them, you can create a work of art. You can mould them to work in the exact way you want and expect, as they will not have had the chance to develop bad habits with previous companies. Apprentices are also loyal. They usually have to stick with you throughout their college or university courses, which is a great way of retaining them for a few years. Even after that, I've found that, on the whole, they stay with the company a lot longer than other staff.

One of my best decisions was hiring an apprentice architect. I saw a gap in our company where we needed a design team, but I couldn't afford to go out and hire a full-time architect at that point. I also knew it would take a couple of years before this side of the business grew into a substantial revenue earner, as we hadn't marketed design services to any of our clients yet.

My apprentice came on board, enrolled in a one day a week course, and within six months was sketching plans that we could use. Granted, they were basic at first and needed much input and oversight, but within two years they were of a very high standard. We could start to market this side of the business aggressively, and had already started to build up a market for it over the previous months. This was a fantastic return on investment and I ended up with a loyal and valuable member of the team who I could grow another section of the business around.

Invest in apprentices and their training and you will see a great return on investment in the years to come. Their wages generally stay low during the training period, which makes up for the amount of time you or other members of staff spend training them. Once they are fully qualified you will have a valuable member of staff that will be working in the exact way you've trained them to and have come to expect.

In summary, you've now found the right candidate, you've managed to convince them to work for you and you know how to keep hold of them and train them for future growth. Once you've got a team of these people in place you'll be setting the foundations to finally be able to step away from the day-to-day firefighting and have the free time to go and play a round of golf, or whatever else takes your fancy. Actually, no golf just yet, we still have a bit more work to do to get this company running like a well-oiled machine. Next up, operating systems.

ACTION POINT CHECKLIST

1. Write down your ideal company culture
2. Follow the guidelines for reviewing CVs and interview questions
3. Ensure you have a training plan for your staff, especially A-players

---

7
Operating Systems

Embrace your systems

One of the biggest objections I come across from the construction owners I work with is that they are not tech-savvy. They prefer to be more hands-on and work with pen and paper rather than spreadsheets. This is not true in all cases, as many embrace technology and see the obvious benefits, but far too often there is an automatic rejection and an immediate barrier is put up.

If this is true in your case, you need to get over this limiting belief immediately. Embracing technology, especially putting systems in place, is absolutely essential for the successful growth of your company. If you are serious about scaling and ensuring your company runs like a well-oiled machine, it's time to learn to become tech-savvy. I know people in their seventies comfortably using iPads and the like, as they've pushed away their limiting beliefs and embraced a new challenge. It's time for you to do the same, as you will need to implement technological operating systems in your business.

Operating systems are not purely about technology. What is an operating system? We are not talking about Microsoft Windows or Mac iOS here. Here we are focusing on how you operate at work, on the methods and systems you put in place that can be repeated again and again for a specific task. It's the way you do what you do.

When you are a one-man band, or an owner-worker, you will often have these systems in your own head. For example, when quoting for work you may have booked an appointment in your diary, visited the client, typed the estimate and then sent it out. A week later you remember you haven't followed it up so you give them a call or drop them an email. This is a system of working, it's just all in your own head. You may not realise it yet, but you will have a way of operating or a system of work for almost every task you carry out: estimating, invoicing, paying bills, carrying out the work, etc. Whether these operating systems are effective or not is another matter.

One important question to ask yourself is: if I had a bad accident and was laid up in bed for a few months, could a new hire come in and immediately understand the way I do things? If you answer that honestly, it's probably a no – so you can start to see the problem and understand why it's so important to systemise everything you do.

One of the best examples of a company who systemise everything they do is McDonald's. You'll notice the same system every time you walk into one of their restaurants anywhere around the world:

'[Greets customer] May I take your order, please?'
'Is there anything else, or will that be all?'
'Let me repeat that.'
'That's [total price], thank you.'

This simple four-step process is one that every employee who takes orders has to follow. It cuts down on mistakes, increases the order value, and speeds up the delivery. That is just one small system out of hundreds that McDonald's have perfected. It's this obsession with systemisation that has led them to be worth over $100bn.[15]

The importance of operating systems in your business is vital as you start to grow. The danger is that many

---

15   Smashing Lists (2017) '10 Most Valuable Companies 2017'. www.smashinglists.com/10-most-valuable-companies

owners are so busy working and expanding that they don't have time to think about analysing and documenting their systems. A word of warning: if you try to expand your business without putting systems in place, you will be in for a painful ride. You'll be stressed, overworked and exhausted. The whole purpose of growing is to give you more time and less stress. This can only be achieved if you have excellent systems in place. Let's find out why.

Why you'll come to love your systems

One of my clients, John, was growing his facilities management company rapidly. He had more work than ever before but was starting to lose money hand over fist. He couldn't understand why or how, as he knew his jobs were running at a good profit. After looking at the cash he had in the bank and the debt he was owed from invoicing, it took only a few moments to realise that someone was stealing from him. He had a rogue employee. John was so busy focusing on growth and getting the contracts completed that he had put too much trust in others and hadn't developed robust operating systems. This rogue employee had worked out that he could invoice for jobs that he hadn't actually completed, receive his wages for carrying out the work and then go back into the computer system and delete the invoice so that the client wouldn't be chased for the money. He knew it would only be a matter of time before he was caught, but he got away with it for nearly six months. Not only that, the systems in place for invoicing and tracking work were so weak that there was no way of proving what he had done.

Once the penny dropped, John was fuming – but he was mostly angry at himself for being so naïve. When he was growing fast and cash was coming in left, right and centre, all was well. But now someone had exploited him, and he had lost thousands of pounds with little hope of recovering any of it. Having a good operating system in place would have prevented this; if the rogue employee had tried to steal, it would have been noticed within a week rather than six months.

In my own business I saw the wisdom of having strong systems early on. At one point, I had over thirty subcontractors out on different sites all on a daily wage. It used to frustrate me each morning that we had to ring around every single subcontractor to see if they had turned up on time. It was such an easy system for the subcontractor to manipulate; they'd just not answer their phone or call back later saying it was on silent, and I would have no way of knowing whether I was being played or not. This caused no end of stress and I became distrustful.

So I put a simple operating system in place. Each employee had to log in when they arrived on the site and when they left. The login on their mobile was GPS-enabled so they couldn't do it while lying in bed. This was a simple system that saved me about thirty minutes each morning that I'd previously spent calling everyone. It paid for itself within a month. Less stress for me, giving me more control and more time to focus on more important things. Now, I'm not saying that this system wasn't also open to manipulation. It was, and if you get a rogue employee who is determined to cheat the system then you will suffer a momentary loss. What the system will do is reduce how long it takes to work out who these people are.

As we've said, systems are crucial as you start to expand. They don't always need to be complicated and involve software. Sometimes a simple Word document or spreadsheet/flowchart is all you need to define a process. The important thing is actually defining it. The beauty of an operating system is that you can onboard a new employee and, after some training, they should be following a documented system that enables them to perform a task perfectly and exactly the same way every single time.

Charlie Mullins of Pimlico Plumbing (turnover of £43m in 2018[16]) calls his operating system the Pimlico Bible, which sets out precisely how all engineers should work, dress and conduct themselves. Nothing is left to chance. Although this may sound controlling, it's how he has been able to expand so efficiently and with huge profitability.

---

16   O'Dwyer, M (2019) 'Pimlico Plumbers Boss Charlie Mullins Takes Home £4.9m in Dividends'. www.cityam.com/pimlico-plumbers-boss-charlie-mullins-takes-home-49m

Think of a name for your new 'bible' and let's now look at the fundamental things you need to be developing systems for.

Fundamentals first

The fundamental systems you need to have in place can be broken down into three main areas:

1. Operations
2. Sales and marketing
3. Finance/accounting

Of course, there are other areas that need systems, like HR and IT, but the above are probably the most important to focus on for now.

Operations

Here we need to create systems to track whether our operations are running smoothly and consistently. You can use simple spreadsheets to do this, or cheap off-the-shelf software. The important thing is that you have something in place to track the following for each project:

- Job description and category
- Original cost

- Extra costs requested by the client

- Running cost of labour

- Description of the work subcontractors/workers are assigned

- Running cost of materials

- Materials having a unique order number

- Length of project – predicted and actual

- Overall profitability

The above may sound basic but I notice that almost all of my new clients are missing some or most of these fundamentals. I'll ask them the question: what is your most profitable category of work? They will stare at me blankly, not having a clue. But this is one of the most important questions you should be asking yourself. If you know what service category generates you the most profit you should be spending all of your time trying to win that type of work. Conversely, what's your least profitable category of work? Is it time to ditch that offering if it's not bringing in a decent profit? These questions can only be answered accurately if you have the relevant data available, which you collect by tracking each project.

When you're preparing a tender or pitch for a new sale, you should know exactly what sort of profit margin you are going to have before you even start the project. By tracking all projects consistently you'll end up with valuable data that can tell you instantly what the average cost of labour and materials should be, how long the project should take, and what profit you will likely earn. Not only that, the above system helps with tracking your suppliers. Are they overcharging on certain items? Are you being billed for stock that you haven't received? When you assign unique order numbers to each project and every order that is made, it's easy to reconcile this when the supplier invoice arrives. If you receive a bill without an order number, you can reject it or investigate further what it relates to rather than blindly paying it and assuming someone must have ordered it.

Sales and marketing

We briefly discussed the benefits of a CRM (customer relationship management) system in Section 5.3. A CRM system will keep track of the data for every person who has ever contacted you; all your interactions, phone calls and emails that you have with that person will be stored and tracked. Every time you speak to a client (potential or existing), you can learn something new and potentially that could be of value. A CRM system will store that information. If a sales employee dealing with a client leaves the company, anyone can pick the sale back up and continue to nurture the client, as all the information is stored.

There are lots of companies that provide off-the-shelf CRM systems, and they are not difficult to use. The current market leaders are Salesforce, but there are many out there to choose from. They will also offer lots of add-on products that may be useful, like marketing and accounting, but for now we'll just focus on the standard models.

Here is a brief summary of what a CRM system can do for you:

- Stores all customer data
- Notes how a client originally found you (useful for analysing marketing)
- Stores all interactions
- Defines the sales process
- Books appointments
- Provides reminders to follow up on sales calls/ appointments
- Analyses opportunities and forecasts future sales
- Provides reports and dashboards

This is only scratching the surface, but as you can see, having all this data to hand and a systemised process for tracking sales is extremely valuable. If you haven't got one yet, sign up to some software right now as without a doubt you will be missing out on sales.

Not only do you need a process for tracking sales, you should also have one for simple things like taking a sales call. Provide your receptionists with a sales script and flow chart for calls so they can qualify leads efficiently and have a variety of answers and scenarios prepared.

Accounting

It goes without saying that you need a robust system in place for accounting; this goes for a person with £100k turnover let alone someone who is trying to break the £1m barrier. Time and time again I've had business owners tell me how much money they think they are earning, only to be shocked at the end of the year when a huge tax bill or VAT bill catches them completely off guard and messes up their cashflow.

There is no need for this; with all the software available now, you should be able to see a snapshot of the health of your business and liabilities owed at any time. We'll discuss this more in the next section on how to analyse profit and loss reports. Fortunately, there is an abundance of cheap software out there that can track your invoices and accounts. One I've used for many years is Xero. It's completely cloud-based, which means you can create invoices, see what bills you owe, and view reports on the go wherever you are in the world.

It's not enough, though, just to have decent accounting software. You need a written system of how it should be used. Asking yourself these questions can help you write a clear system that anyone in your company can follow:

- When will I invoice for a project stage?

- How will I mark off that I have invoiced a project? (You would be surprised how many jobs get done for free because this gets forgotten)

- What payment terms will be given to clients?

- When will we chase overdue invoices?

- What is the procedure for chasing debt? When is it escalated to legal letters?

- When will suppliers be paid?

- How do we reconcile supplier order numbers to ensure we have received the correct goods?

This is not an exhaustive list, but by working through these questions and formulating your own answers, you should get a decent accounting system in place.

Even with all the systems discussed in this section in place, you will still notice mistakes creeping in, which can be extremely frustrating. Use these mistakes as opportunities to re-analyse and improve the systems and eventually you'll have something watertight.

Advanced systems – worth the investment?

We've looked at some of the basic systems needed, but as you start to grow and put these systems in place, you'll realise how valuable and successful they have become. It can almost become an addiction as you start to look at more ways you can improve efficiency. As your business grows bigger, you'll soon notice that the off-the-shelf software has limitations. Sometimes they just don't do quite what you want them to, and specific features needed for your industry may be missing. It's tempting in this scenario to look at custom-building a system specifically designed for you. In principle this is a great idea, but you need to be aware of what you are embarking on in terms of both time and cost.

I have successfully designed and built (with the aid of a brilliant software developer) a fantastic operating system that tracks every job, every order and where every worker is. No invoice or extra for the client is ever missed and I have accurate data that enables me to analyse what job types are most profitable, meaning I can forecast where I should focus my efforts. I've linked it to my accounting software (Xero) and to my contract software (Docusign) for increased speed and efficiency. This system is fantastic and completely bespoke to me, but it did not come cheap. Over the years I have spent about £30k on the system and hundreds of hours designing, developing and testing it. However, when I look at the off-the-shelf software that is available now, most seem to do exactly the same thing. This software wasn't around for me at the time, which is why I went bespoke, but with a bit of searching around and undertaking a few trials, you can usually find something that fits the bill. This will obviously save you a huge amount of time and money.

Although this operating system was a success, I've also had a big failure with developing a custom-made app. I spent almost three years and nearly £15k designing and developing it. The first place I went wrong was when I picked a programmer who promised the world but couldn't deliver. A second developer then came along who tore the first one apart and started almost from scratch. He left before the project was completed and I was left with a half-built app that had been tinkered with by two developers, and which was pretty useless. Very frustrating. It started out as a great idea but, on reflection, it diverted time and resources that could have been spent developing the business in other areas.

As I've mentioned, failure isn't all bad; you learn lessons and move on, wiser for it. As Henry Ford said, 'Failure is simply the opportunity to begin again, this time more intelligently.' With that quote in mind, if I was to begin again I would have doubled my initial budget and used a respected company that could have delivered the app first time around.

In summary, I do think there is a place for bespoke software, but if you embark on this task, know that you are in for a long and expensive ride. Often, you can find software with similar features already out there at a fraction of the cost. For those features the off-the-shelf software doesn't have, you can normally think of a workaround, so think carefully before you commit. Whatever you decide, whether you go bespoke or not, ensure you have some operating systems in place as this will transform the speed and ease of your growth. It will also give you time to step away from the business and ease your stress levels, as you can be confident things are running exactly as you want and expect them to be.

ACTION POINT CHECKLIST

Develop your company bible and write out (or record a video with) step by step instructions for your core tasks in:

1. Operations
2. Sales and marketing
3. Finance/accounting

8
Profit and Loss

Learn to love your numbers

This may have been a chapter you were tempted to skip. Branding, marketing and so on are so much more fun than discussing a profit and loss (P&L) report. Although this chapter comes last, it's by no means the least important. According to the Small Business Association, over 50% of businesses fail within the first five years. Some manage to get through the early hard years, but then fail as they start to grow. A good understanding of the profit and loss report would greatly reduce the likelihood of failure. Not only that, if you want to grow past £1m turnover, you have to know this stuff, it's absolutely crucial to success. Don't rely on a quarterly or biannual meeting with your accountant. You need to know where you are every single month. Three to six months is too long a period if you're bleeding money and you could well be about to fail without even knowing it.

When you understand your P&L you can sense when danger is on its way. You'll see if sales are starting to slow, when the cost of products is increasing and your margins are being squeezed. You'll fully understand what your overheads are and how much you need to make each month before you make a penny in profit. You'll know how much tax to set aside and what you can draw in dividends/salary. During a growth phase you will see your cashflow at its tightest. You may start feeling like you are making no money and there is hardly any spare cash in the bank – but you could still be profitable. Your P&L will show you this and give you a sanity check in those difficult times; understanding it gives you reassurance and helps you make informed decisions.

Business owners trying to grow without fully understanding their P&L are like blindfolded captains of a ship that is heading for the rocks. If you don't understand your P&L you are blind to whether your business is navigating well or about to be sunk by a rock. When you hit that rock, it will be sudden and unexpected; not being prepared, you will not survive.

It's not a coincidence that some of the world's richest people love their numbers. Warren Buffet, who was worth $87bn in 2018,[17] is numbers-obsessed. As an investor, he spends all day reading financial reports and pouring over the numbers. His understanding of these reports has helped him invest in the right companies over the last fifty years and propelled the growth of his fortune. John D Rockefeller is argued to be the richest man who ever lived. As an oil magnate he was worth $1.2bn in 1918 – the equivalent of $340bn in 2018.[18] Rockefeller was an accountant and bookkeeper when he started out; he loved numbers. He kept a strict accounting of his finances in ledgers. Even when he was ridiculously wealthy he still poured over the ledgers himself, correcting the smallest errors that would save cents or dollars.

There is a lesson to be learned here from some of the richest men in history: learn to love your numbers. Even if you absolutely detest numbers I urge you to spend a good amount of time re-reading this chapter until you fully understand how to interpret your P&L. It's not difficult once you know the basics, but it's surprising how many business owners will never take the time to do this.

---

17 Loudenback, T (2018) '24 Mind-blowing Facts About Warren Buffett and His $87 Billion Fortune. www.businessinsider.com/facts-about-warren-buffett-2016-12?r=US&IR=T
18 Lord, B (2018) 'America 2018: More Gilded Than America 1918'. www.counterpunch.org/2018/09/28/america-2018-more-gilded-than-america-1918

What is a P&L?

What does a P&L report look like, and how can you interpret it? It's an important question, as it's not enough to look only at the figure shown at the bottom of the report. Although the profit figure is a summary of the whole report, you still need to fully understand each section to be enable to pull the right levers as and when needed; to tighten up or spend on expansion.

In this section, we will analyse a typical P&L report. Although the format may vary slightly to the one you or your accountant produces, you'll see the relationship with the figures and sections you have in your own. Take some time to have a good look at the example P&L report here, we'll refer back to this throughout the chapter.

You'll notice the report is split into these main categories:

1. Turnover

2. Cost of sales

3. Gross profit

4. Administrative costs

5. Operating profit

Profit and Loss

Turnover	March
Interest Income	1.81
Sales	177,847.90
Sales - Architecture	10,300.00
Total Turnover	**188,149.71**

Cost of Sales	
Architecture & Consulting (CoS)	16,503.13
CIS Labour Expense	74,490.84
CIS Materials Purchased	17,318.31
Council planning fees (CoS)	310.83
Equipment hire	2,327.33
Materials	12,533.88
Subcontractors No CIS	12,546.00
Total Cost of Sales	**136,030.32**

Gross Profit	52,119.39	28%

Administrative Costs	
Advertising & Marketing	3,044.89
Amortisation	250.00
Audit & Accountancy fees	530.00
Bank Fees	12.73
Cleaning	122.90
Depreciation Expense	72.93
Directors Renumeration	7,500.00

(Continued)

Profit and Loss *(Continued)*

Employers National Insurance	2,265.93
Estimating - QS	1,055.00
Goodwill	500.00
Insurance	1,940.49
Light, Power, Heating	424.63
Motor Vehicle - Fuel	829.65
Motor Vehicle - Parking	44.11
Motor Vehicle Expenses	140.00
Motor Vehicle Insurance	183.06
Motor Vehicle Lease	125.03
Payroll costs	45.00
Pension	97.14
Postage, courier	16.80
Printing, stationery and office equipment	43.47
Rent and storage	1,720.85
Software	1,057.69
Staff - IT support	1,425.00
Staff - Marketing	725.00
Staff - Salaries PAYE (gross)	14,715.80
Staff welfare and office supplies	43.47
Subsistence	13.09
Telephone - mobiles	131.91
Telephone - office line & broadband	299.71
Travel - director & staff	544.65
Website	250.70
Total Administrative Costs	**40,171.63**
Operating Profit Before Tax	**11,947.76** 6%

Turnover

This is simply the total of the invoices you generate per month, the amount of work you can bill for. In this example, the business (a design and build construction company) has two types of chargeable service he is tracking under the same company, so the turnover is split into 'sales' (main building company) and 'sales – architecture' (secondary design and architecture business). This could be good to do if you have multiple products or services and you want to keep an eye on what each is generating. For example, if you have a plumbing business but also an electrical division, you may want to separate those out for better analysis. Also under this section is interest earned on money in the bank. Usually not of note, but any income generated needs to be included in this section.

Cost of sales

This section should include all the costs associated with providing the service(s) or product(s) directly. It will not include overhead costs, which we will cover shortly. Using this construction company report as an example, you'll note it is split into further categories:

1. Architecture costs: the fees paid to architects and other related professional services.

2. CIS labour: CIS is a UK tax in construction. This labour category is the cost of subcontractor labouring services.

153

3. CIS materials: the cost of subcontractor materials purchases.

(The above could be lumped together under the category of 'subcontractor costs', but splitting them up lets you see if further profits can be gained by removing the material purchases from the subcontractors. They will be making a mark-up on these material costs, so you need to weigh up if it's worth taking these costs on yourself. It's often a choice between hassle/practicalities and extra profit.)

4. Council planning fees: local authority fees related to the architecture service.

5. Equipment hire: cost of hiring in plant to perform certain services.

6. Materials: purchase of materials related to carrying out a job.

7. Subcontractors no CIS: again, this could be lumped together with subcontractor costs, but in this case it specifically relates to specialist subcontractors who are exempt from CIS tax.

The above combined give you the total cost of sales.

Gross profit

Once we know the total cost of sales, we can work out the gross profit. This isn't the total profit that you're left with in your back pocket, you still need to deduct overheads. Gross profit is the difference between invoiced revenue minus direct costs. Gross profit is a vital figure to keep track of and can also be expressed as a percentage. You'll note that the gross profit in this example is about 28% (£52k of £188k). This figure can be used to set targets, which we will look at in further detail in the next section.

Administrative costs

Once you know your gross profit, you can look at your overheads or administrative costs. In our example case, we are left with £52k per month to play with. Out of this we must pay a multitude of overhead costs, which eat away at that figure until we're left with our total profit before tax, or operating profit. The aim is to keep your regular monthly overheads as low as possible to stop it eating up your overall profit.

The overhead costs should be pretty self-explanatory but below are some of the less common ones that you may not be as familiar with:

1. Amortisation: this is commonly used to show the regular monthly decrease in the value of an intangible asset. For example, it may refer to a bank loan that is decreasing by a set amount each month.

2. Depreciation: this refers to tangible assets decreasing in value, like a truck or van.

3. Employees national insurance: a UK tax due to be paid by employers.

4. Goodwill purchase: this covers the regular cost of a payment made when purchasing a company for a higher cost than its assets. The example we have used is paying for the brand name (the goodwill) purchase of a company it had previously bought out.

Operating profit

Simply put, the operating profit is what remains after the total overhead and administrative costs are deducted from the gross profit. This isn't quite what's left for you to go spending, though – we can't forget the dreaded taxes. Tax rates vary from country to country, so I've deliberately left that out, but the tax deduction should always be included in your P&L to see exactly what you are left with in your back pocket at the end of the month.

Now you should understand your own P&L report. If you haven't got one yet, use one like this example to start tracking your figures – without it, you are running your business completely blind. The real power of a P&L comes not just from understanding it, but having the ability to interpret the figures and then set targets. Once you start doing this, significant changes can start to occur within your business.

Set growth targets

Now you understand the P&L, it's time to use it to maximum effect. Don't let the report become something you only look back on month by month. If you do this, you are like a driver on the lookout for hazards, but only looking in your rear-view mirror. Looking back is great for understanding how and why things have happened, but the real success comes when you use it to look ahead and affect future events.

The first thing you want to do is set some realistic targets. You can do this as soon as you have gathered three to six months' figures, as by that point you can generally take a reliable average of trends. Some of the key figures you want to be setting targets for are:

- Sales revenue/turnover

- Gross profit percentage

- Operating profit percentage

Sales revenue

It's good to set a regular monthly target for your sales team, and this can generally be reviewed quarterly depending on the speed of your growth. Often, this number is derived from a figure you need to hit to cover overheads, but this isn't ideal. The target needs to be realistic and may be different for each sales person you employ. It may not need to be a monetary figure at all; it could be more motivating to set a target for the number of jobs you want your sales team to win each month.

Whatever you decide the metric should be, ensure you track this like a dog with a bone. If you want to smash through the £1m turnover barrier and beyond, you must set sales goals every single month and ensure everyone knows what they are.

Gross profit percentage

This is one of the most important figures to track, because without good markup and profit, your turnover will be pure vanity. You'll end up a busy fool if you do not have a decent gross profit (GP) figure. In my companies, I've always aimed for around 30% GP. In your service industry it may well be higher, especially if you do lots of small jobs, or reactive call-out work.

This figure is a good one to track because the higher you can get it, the easier it makes things for your sales team. For example, in our sample P&L the company had a GP of 28%, working out at £52k. This was on a sales turnover of £188k. If they could have increased the GP to 33% (a 5% increase) they would only have needed to generate about £160k per month. That would certainly take some pressure off the sales team. Or, you could keep the pressure on; if you achieved £190k sales with 33% GP, you would have nearly £10k per month extra GP. That's £120k per year, for the same volume of sales, by increasing gross profit by just 5%. That is the power of improving gross profit even slightly, and it can make a big difference further down the road.

How do you improve GP? Either by increasing your sales prices, or by cutting the cost of delivering the product (ie getting cheaper suppliers or materials). Or, a combination of both. Could you realistically increase your prices to get an extra 2.5% profit, and drive down the cost of your suppliers by 2.5%? I'm sure most could, and that simple strategy could make you tens of thousands of additional profit each year.

Operating profit

This is not the easiest figure to manipulate, as often your overheads will be fixed – although we will look into how we can decrease them in a later section. However, it's still good to set some targets for this metric. You don't want this percentage to be too low otherwise you won't have a buffer for when times get difficult. You also have to consider the winter months, which in construction generally mean a downturn. If you have low OP throughout the year, one month where you lose money could wipe out the entire year's profit gains. You'll notice in our example P&L that the company had an OP of 6.4% (£12k /£188k)

In the book *Scaling Up*, Verne Harnish gives some valuable metrics to track the health of your Operating Profit:

- At 5% pre-tax profit, your business is in the danger zone.

- At 10%, the business is doing well but has untapped potential.

- At 15%, your business is very healthy.

- Anything above 15% indicates you should earn it while you can, until the market works out you are onto something good and the competition shows up.[19]

Ensure you set yourself a realistic but robust OP target, as this is the money you will potentially have access to at the end of the year – to spend on yourself, re-invest in the company, or buy out other businesses. Achieving an OP of 15% or more may seem impossible right now, but it can be achieved when you apply the DEVELOP strategy. As you are growing, you will need to invest money through additional overheads, even if you are not yet at 15% OP. Can you afford to make a new hire or take out that new lease on the office? This is what we will look at next when we learn how to set budgets.

---

19   Harnish, V (2014) *Scaling Up*. San Diego, CA: Gazelles Inc.

Setting a budget

Now you've got this far through the book, I'm sure you can visualise and get excited about the rapid growth of your company. What can be scary, though, is not controlling that growth from a financial perspective. If you don't control your growth and keep a firm tab on the figures, you could grow yourself broke even if you are profitable. Let me repeat that: you can grow yourself broke *even if you are in profit*.

It's not uncommon for high-growth companies to simply run out of cash as they focus purely on profits rather than cashflow and budgets. We are not going to discuss cashflow analysis in detail here, but it can be done by keeping a simple spreadsheet of your monthly outgoings in cash (by date) and your expected income (by date), spanning three months. This should ideally show whether you are in positive or negative cashflow and help you take action accordingly, eg by calling in payments faster, or agreeing longer creditor payment terms.

Before you worry about the above, the first step is to ensure you are growing profitably to start with. If you're not growing profitably, you won't be able to sustain the losses for long at all and will eventually go bust. The key to growing profitably is to set a budget P&L. What's that? A budget P&L is simply a realistic and ideal P&L report that you think you can sustain each month. If you are in a growth phase, the figures may change each month as you set higher revenue targets. If you have a seasonal business, it may be worth plotting an entire year's budgeted P&L so you can set aside profits for the leaner months.

Whatever phase your business is currently in, a budget P&L will help greatly as you plan to grow. It can tell you instantly if you can afford to push up your overheads and, if you can't, how much you need to increase your sales revenue by to enable that to happen. For instance, in our example P&L you will notice the company had an OP of about 6%. They wanted to maintain at least 5% OP as they grew and would not let it drop below this (remember, a figure lower than this and the company is in the danger zone). They also wanted to grow and take on another salesperson but could not yet afford it. An additional salesperson would have added £5k per month to the wages overhead, reducing OP to £7k – only 3%. The only way they could afford a new salesperson was by either cutting other overheads, which in this instance was not possible, as they were mostly fixed, or increasing sales revenue. But how would they do this with the sales team already stretched? They would have to either:

- Increase their prices; or,

- Save money on the materials from their suppliers; or,

- A combination of both.

By adjusting their budget manipulating the above levers, they could increase their OP each month by an extra £5k, which would give them the budget needed for the extra salesperson. Once they had the extra sales person, this would enable another growth spurt and budgets can be readjusted again.

Sticking to a budget is not easy; no one likes it. Maybe you've had to do it with your personal finances to save for a holiday or a new car. It's a pain and it often results in some sacrifice on your part. Your business is no different, but the consequences are more severe. A lack of a budget in this instance can mean complete failure in many cases. In terms of sacrifice, you may have to hold off on buying that new Apple Mac until you've got sufficient profit. That new spacious office may need to wait until your margins improve.

Business can be a slog at times, especially when going through growth phases, but setting and sticking to a budget will remove a tremendous amount of stress and pressure. You will know exactly what your outgoings are each month and what your sales targets should be. Don't delay, create your P&L templates, set a budget and stick to it.

Waste not, want not

The bigger your business becomes, the more waste you produce. It can't be avoided. Staff will over-order supplies or get orders wrong. Subcontractors will waste materials. It's extremely frustrating as, when you were a one-person outfit, you were in complete control.

Waste cannot be avoided, but it can be controlled. The P&L can help with this. Periodically, maybe every quarter, sit down with your accountant and have a good look at your overheads. Not just at the high-level figures, drill down into each transaction under the main headings. Ask yourself, do I really need that direct debit coming out each month? Sometimes you can find that you're still paying for an old mobile telephone contract or insurance product that you no longer need.

Can you get on a better tariff? Get someone to shop around for your IT software solutions. Can you move to a different package for broadband, or software for your Cloud storage?

Can you bring services in-house? You may be paying for a consultant or marketing expert. Are they still delivering value, or do you have a team member who could take this on in-house without being too stretched?

Have you asked for a discount? When was the last time you looked at your lease or rent? Why not ask for a reduction, as a loyal customer? What about your suppliers, could you agree fresh terms?

Can you buy in bulk? Are there certain items or materials you purchase a lot of throughout the year? You may be able to negotiate a better rate if you bought in bulk. Although, also ask, what's your inventory? Although sometimes it's worth buying in bulk, keep a close eye on your inventory – this can ruin a company's cashflow. You don't want your money tied up in long-term assets. Try to order only what you need and keep your inventory as low as practically possible if cashflow is tight.

Are all staff members still performing? Some of the biggest waste can be produced through staff not performing. Analyse this, and if a staff member is not performing like they used to, get to the bottom of the issue quickly and, if needed, let them go. Loyalty to staff who don't deserve it or who are not pulling their weight can bleed you dry. Sometimes you need to be ruthless and cut the waste.

Keeping your business lean will greatly help in an economic downturn, as your margins might shrink and it may not be possible to increase your prices. At times, the only way to maintain your OP is by cutting your overheads, and although it's difficult, you'll be surprised what you can find to cut when you need to.

Save during the good times

You may have heard the Biblical story or watched the theatre production of *Joseph*. In the story, Joseph had a dream that there would be seven years of plenty followed by seven years of famine. Today's economy goes through similar cycles of booms and recessions (although the recessions hopefully won't last seven years). In Joseph's story, he was put in charge of storing up supplies for seven years to prepare for the famine. When the famine arrived, everyone went to Joseph to buy grain and he greatly expanded the pharaoh's wealth.

The same principle should be applied in your business. You will go through periods when things are flying; you will be making great profits and it will seem as if it's never going to end. But trust me, it will.

At some point, whether it's triggered by a recession, or a new competitor entering the market, you will suffer a lean period. It can be tempting to spend profits on dividends or a new company car, but it's so important that when you have those great periods, you set some money aside to prepare for the lean times. It's true that when things are going well you do need to reward yourself in some way, otherwise what's the point of it all? But be mindful when rewarding that you need to keep something aside. Don't withdraw all of your profit, leaving yourself exposed.

Going back to the *Joseph* story, you'll note that when the famine came, Joseph was the only one who had stored up grain, so he became the go-to person and created huge wealth even in the famine. The same can be true for you in a recession. If you future-proof yourself during the good times, you will see companies left, right and centre falling at the wayside and you may be one of the few companies in your niche still standing when the recession passes. While everyone else is cutting their marketing costs and slashing staff, you will be there to pick up the pieces. At that point, if you play it right, you could greatly increase your market share and poach some good talent from other companies. The only way you can do that is if you have a buffer built up before the hard times hit. Once you've done this, if you've still got plenty of profit left over, why not go and buy yourself that new car. You've put in the hard work, you deserve it.

ACTION POINT CHECKLIST

1. Ensure you have online accounting software, such as Xero
2. Set up (or get your accountant to set up) P&L subheadings
3. Ensure you fully understand them all
4. Create your budget P&L
5. Set your growth target
6. Review every month
7. Analyse your overheads and cut back where possible

Conclusion

If you've managed to get to the end of this book, you deserve huge congratulations. You clearly have a thirst for knowledge and the mindset to run a growth business. I'm sure you've found numerous ways in which you can go out and 'smash it' with your business. The future will look exciting for you now and I'm confident that if you apply the principles found here you will easily break through the £1m barrier, and will have built a fantastic foundation to take it way beyond that. Be sure to go through the action point summaries at the end of each chapter and implement them. You now have the knowledge, but that's meaningless without positive action to go with it.

If you've gone through the DEVELOP principles and realised you still need some help implementing some of them, don't worry. Some of us thrive on our own, whereas others work better in a group or with a coach. Ensure you follow me on Facebook for weekly tips and updates: www.facebook.com/developcoach/

Bill Gates famously said in the opening words to a TED talk, 'Everyone needs a coach'.[20] I've had consultants and coaches throughout my business life, and the payoff has always been huge. It's saved me from making awful mistakes, and sometimes it's just nice to have someone to bounce ideas off and give a different perspective. A coach can often see things that you can't, or they might have worked with another company who has experienced something you haven't. They can be brutally honest when your employees and friends won't.

Different coaches will help with different phases. Some are best for start-ups, whereas a coach like myself is more suited to established businesses looking to grow. Other coaches have the skillset to help you transition into a large organisation. Whatever phase you are currently in, consider using a coach to keep you accountable and take you to that next level. You will experience faster growth with a coach than without one. Even if you decide to go on this journey alone, I wish you all the best for the future. By applying the DEVELOP principles you will stand out

---

20 Gates, B (2013) 'Teachers Need Real Feedback' [TED talk]. www.ted.com/talks/bill_gates_teachers_need_real_feedback?language=en

from the rest, and that will give you a tremendous advantage. I hope you achieve the life you deserve, with less stress, more time for yourself and your family, and greater financial rewards. Go out there and build your future!

The Author

Greg Wilkes is a business owner and entrepreneur. He has over 20 years' experience running construction companies from the ground up. He has successfully created multiple businesses that have achieved over £1m turnover using his DEVELOP principles.

Greg is willing to share the DEVELOP principles to enable other business owners to grow their companies profitably. His valuable experience and success within the construction industry makes this honest and informative book a must-read for anyone aiming to run a successful construction company.

Greg now works as a coach and consultant assisting business owners who wish to fast-track their results or require assistance putting the systems in place to run an effective and profitable company.

Find Greg online at:

⊕ www.developcoaching.co.uk

🔲 www.facebook.com/developcoach

Printed in Great Britain
by Amazon

25771568R00106